SEA OF
OKHOTSK

S I B E R I A

LAKE
BAIKAL

TRANS- SIBERIAN RAILROAD

msk

MANCHURIA

Irkutsk

Harbin

Vladivostok

1950, 1952, 1953,1954, 1957, 1959, 1961 & 1964

Ulan Bator

Mukden

SEA OF
JAPAN

1954

1960

MONGOLIA

Peking

KOREA

Tokyo
JAPAN

Kyoto

Tientsin

1919

C U H I N A
NKING

Paoan

Yenan

Nanking

Shanghai

Wuhan

Shao-
hsing

EAST
CHINA SEA

1963-64

THE
GREAT
GRASSLANDS

TIBET

Changsha

1920

1961

GREAT SNOW MT.
TATU RIVER CROSSING

Chungking

Juichin

TAIWAN

Tsunyi

THE LONG MARCH
1934-35

PACIFIC OCEAN

Lhasa

Canton

New Delhi

Kathmandu
NEPAL

1954 & 1955

1954,1956
& 1960

Hong Kong

Calcutta

1920

INDIA

BURMA

Hanoi
VIETNAM

1960

1960

LAOS

1920

PHILIPPINE IS.

pay

BAY OF
BENGAL

Rangoon

THAILAND
Bangkok

Madras

1920

Saigon

SOUTH
CHINA SEA

1920

A Y S I A

1955

OCEAN

Colombo

1920

M

Singapore

BORNEO

INDONESIA

Bandung
JAVA

CHOU

CHOU

AN INFORMAL BIOGRAPHY OF
CHINA'S LEGENDARY CHOU EN-LAI

John McCook Roots

1978
DOUBLEDAY & COMPANY, INC., GARDEN CITY, NEW YORK

Grateful acknowledgment is made for permission to include excerpts from the following copyrighted publications:

From *China and the West* by Roger Garaudy. Reprinted by permission of Humanities Press, Atlantic Highlands, New Jersey.

From *Chou En-lai* by Kai-yu Hsu. Copyright © 1968 by Kai-yu Hsu. Reprinted by permission of Doubleday & Company, Inc.

From *The Great Road* by Agnes Smedley. Copyright © 1956 by the Estate of Agnes Smedley. Reprinted by permission of Monthly Review Press.

From *Prisoners of Liberation* by Allyn & Adele Rickett. Copyright © 1957, 1963 by Allyn & Adele Rickett. Reprinted by permission of Doubleday & Company, Inc., and Joan Daves.

From *You Can Get There from Here* by Shirley MacLaine. Copyright © 1975 by Shirley MacLaine. Reprinted by permission of W. W. Norton & Company, Inc.

PHOTO CREDITS

Courtesy of Hsin-Hua 1, 2
Wide World Photos 3, 4, 5, 10, 13, 14, 15, 16, 17, 23, 27
Helen Snow, Magnum 6
Richard Hadden Photo 8, 9, 28
United Press International 11, 12, 20, 21, 22
Pictorial Parade 18
Eastfoto 19

Library of Congress Cataloging in Publication Data
Roots, John McCook.
Chou: An Informal Biography
of China's Legendary Chou En-lai.
Bibliography.
Includes index.
1. Chou, En-lai, 1898–1976.
  2. Prime ministers—China—Biography.
DS778.C593R66   951.05′092′4 [B]

ISBN: 0-385-03804-6
Library of Congress Catalog Card Number: 74-2758
Copyright © 1978 by John McCook Roots
All Rights Reserved
Printed in the United States of America
First Edition

To the memory of my father
LOGAN HERBERT ROOTS

ACKNOWLEDGMENTS

First I must express my appreciation for being one of the earliest American correspondents permitted to return to China for a fresh look at the land of my birth. Those weeks, which included a memorable visit with the late Premier, were a key element in the preparation of this book.

My sister, Frances Roots Hadden, has given invaluable help in documenting certain sections of this book. Her many years in China, where she was born, her personal knowledge of the country, her long friendship with Chou En-lai, Chu Teh, Huang Hua and their wives, together with our family's lifelong ties with most of China's twentieth-century leadership, have made possible unique contributions to several key chapters.

Former Canadian Ambassador Chester Ronning, an intimate of Chou En-lai and also born in China, read the manuscript and counseled perseverance when difficulties multiplied. To his daughter Audrey Topping, brilliant photographer of modern China, as to my photographer brother-in-law Richard Hadden, I owe a special word of thanks. I am particularly grateful to veteran China expert O. Edmund Clubb, Professor Emeritus of Columbia University, who examined the manuscript with his usual scholarly care and made extensive suggestions. I also owe a debt to Professor Ross Terrill of Harvard, who checked the whole in the light of his own frequent visits to the People's Republic and his wide connections there.

Invaluable in the China field is that rare combination—the scholar of mixed Chinese and Western background. Three such have been of assistance in different ways: Professor Paul Lin of McGill University in Montreal, Dr. Han Suyin of Paris, and especially Professor Hsu Kai-yu of San Francisco State College, whose research on Chou En-lai, until recently virtually the only authoritative material existing outside Asia, was generously placed at my disposal.

I wish to express my thanks for the longtime encouragement which, until his death, I invariably received from my old Harvard teacher, Dr. Arthur M. Schlesinger, Sr. In the China field I am also grateful to Dr. John K. Fairbank, Professor James C. Thomson, Jr. and Dr. Edwin A. Reischauer, all of Harvard, Professor Lucien W. Pye of Massachusetts Institute of Technology, Dr. A. Doak Barnett of the Brookings Institution, and Dr. Allen W. Whiting of the University of Michigan.

Dr. Ralph Mortensen, a friend from Hankow days, has shed important light on an obscure period in Chou's life; writers Lois Wheeler Snow and Helen Foster Snow (Nym Wales) have provided valuable insights; and the late Edgar Snow, long the pioneer and dean of all China reporters, generously shared with me at his Lake Geneva home in Switzerland, highlights of his own unrivaled experiences.

My editors, Tom Hyman and, earlier, Tom Congdon (now editor-in-chief of E. P. Dutton), have provided encouragement as well as expertise, while Ken McCormick, veteran senior editor at Doubleday, did much to cheer me on the way. My agents Paul R. Reynolds and the late Malcolm Reiss contributed valuable advice during the early stages of the writing.

Warm gratitude goes to my friend Mary Reynolds, who has given freely of her time, energy and talents, and likewise to Polly Bloch for unremitting and painstaking care in the research, editing and transcribing of the manuscript. I also wish to thank Ola Cook and June Blair, who, with others, have shared much of the burden of the secretarial work.

Other friends, old and new, who provided vital encouragement and support, have my sincere gratitude.

Full responsibility for all evaluations and conclusions is, of course, mine alone.

CONTENTS

PREFACE

Though the relationship between my family and Chou En-lai was for nearly forty years one of warm friendship, this is a strictly unauthorized biography. More than any national leaders in history, more than the leaders of other Communist states, including even the Russians, the publicity-shy men who run the People's Republic of China are opposed, on philosophic grounds, to talking about themselves. Their concept and attitude was well expressed by Chou's wife of fifty years, Madame Teng Ying-ch'ao, in a remark to the noted author Han Suyin in 1956. "She compared the people of China," writes Dr. Han, "to a great ocean, and the leaders (such as herself) to the white froth on the wavetops, born of them, carried by them, forever renascent, but nonexistent without the ocean."

It is not easy for Westerners, and especially for Americans, to understand the Communist aversion to any emphasis on individual accomplishment. In our capitalistic society, as a matter of actual practice, personal success, gain and status are considered worthy goals. Our entire political system, as well as the gigantic sports, entertainment and information industries, is operated on the "star" system. City, state and federal officials generally campaign on the basis of their own merits and charm. The "image," as Marshall McLuhan would point out, is indeed the message. Our candidates actively seek, and with rare exceptions covet, public office and public acclaim. And increasingly we utilize every device of the most massive and sophisticated advertising apparatus on earth to sell the voters on our individual personalities, achievements and views.

The Chinese attitude is the exact opposite. The "passion for anonymity," which was President Franklin D. Roosevelt's chief requirement for his White House aides, has been a general characteristic of China's Communist leadership from the beginning. It is true that Edgar Snow in 1936 managed to persuade Mao Tse-tung to relate his early life story during several night sessions in Mao's Yenan cave, and that the American writer Agnes Smedley similarly succeeded in that same period with Marshal Chu Teh, the famous founder of the Red Army. But these were exceptions. In those far-off days following the Long March, the Party was still a small and virtually unknown band of guerrilla fighters, incessantly harassed by General Chiang Kai-shek's well-armed and vastly superior government forces. They were holed up in an obscure corner of China's remote Northwest and, until Snow penetrated the Kuomintang[1] blockade, were inaccessible to the outside world. They felt an urgency—long since outdated—to make their story known, and this need overrode their habitual reticence.

Even so, Snow has described his extreme difficulty in convincing Mao that details of his personal life were of consequence to anyone. "It is the Party that matters," China's top revolutionary kept insisting. "The individual is unimportant." So ingrained was this belief that only after repeated prodding was Mao induced to reconstruct a narrative of his younger years. For the period after 1921, when he, Chou and others had founded the Party, it took

[1] Kuomintang (KMT), National People's Party. Originally founded by Dr. Sun Yat-sen in 1905. Its philosophy was expressed by Sun as the "Three Principles of the People" (San-Min Chu-i), roughly translated as Nationalism, Democracy and the People's Livelihood. This was the earliest attempt to express a political philosophy for the new regime which in 1911 was to take the place of the Manchu dynasty, and later continued as the formal philosophy of Chiang Kai-shek's Nationalist government. Even the later Communist regime has never repudiated the "Three Principles," and Sun Yat-sen's widow remains a vice-president of the People's Republic.

all Snow's ingenuity to dig out any details whatever regarding Mao the man, and prevent the emerging biographical account from lapsing into the relatively dull chronology of a movement.

In retrospect, it is fortunate for the world that Snow was persistent, and that Mao was sufficiently open-minded to lay aside his personal distaste for autobiography and co-operate. As everyone knows, Snow's *Red Star Over China*, published in 1938, became an international best-seller and still remains, even for Chinese, the one indispensable source on the founder and leader of the People's Republic, and the cause he served.

Of Red China's original "Big Three"—Chairman Mao Tsetung, Marshal Chu Teh and Premier Chou En-lai—only Chou never consented to give a first-person account of his revolutionary career. Though granting occasional interviews to Snow and others on matters of policy, he never went into any detail regarding his personal life, and resolutely rebuffed earlier efforts of the American journalist Jack Belden to obtain his life story. As recently as the autumn of 1972, the author's sister,[2] an old friend of the Premier and his wife from the 1938 United Front days in Hankow, received a courteous but firm negative when she told him of my wish to attempt a biography.

There is no reason whatever to doubt Chou's sincerity in all this. Modest by nature, as well as by reason of his lifelong Communist faith, the Premier also faced an extremely sensitive situation with respect to Chairman Mao Tse-tung, who was the unquestioned idol of the country, and whose thinking provided the universal guidelines for national policy. Chou, although Mao's oldest and closest colleague, had, since 1935, deliberately subordinated himself and clearly felt reluctant to consent to anything that might appear in any way to dilute Mao's preeminence. Moreover, the crises connected with former President Liu Shao-ch'i, and with the late Defense Minister Marshal Lin

[2] Frances Roots Hadden and her husband, Richard Hadden, are the duo-piano team who made international headlines when they were invited by Premier Chou En-lai to give the first concert of Western music in China since the Cultural Revolution, and who became the first American artists to perform in the People's Republic. They have generally been credited with paving the way for the visit to China of Eugene Ormandy and the Philadelphia Orchestra thirteen months later. At this writing, the Haddens and the Philadelphia Orchestra still are the only American artists to have played there.

Piao, who had been Mao's designated heir, naturally heightened the delicacy of Chou's position.

Nevertheless, while respecting the late Premier's sensibilities, no advocate of Chinese-American understanding can disregard three weighty considerations. First is the fact, previously mentioned, that in consequence of the traditional American preoccupation with personalities—i.e. the "star" system—the U.S. public far more readily absorbs news and views if presented in terms of individuals rather than of abstractions. Second is the fact that Chou En-lai himself played, on the Chinese side, the most visible part in the heyday of the Washington-Peking courtship. During those years, because of his public role, his was the name and face most familiar to American newspaper and television audiences, and popular interest in him was as intense as information about him was meager. Third, there is the unique character of Chou's revolutionary experience—an experience in top Party posts longer and richer than that of any other Communist, past or present, not excepting Mao, Lenin or Stalin.

It has seemed to me, therefore, clearly in the interest of our two countries that an up-dated biographical portrait of this remarkable man, based on both currently available and previously unpublished material, be offered to the public.

In the New York *Times* of January 8, 1977, appeared this evaluation by Fox Butterfield in Hong Kong:

"Since his death last January 8, [1976,] Chou En-lai has emerged as the real folk hero of China, and has triumphed over his longtime antagonists and tormentors, the 'leftist' group around Chiang Ching, the widow of Mao Tse-tung.

"Chou's ambitious program to modernize China by the turn of the century has now become state policy, and his disciples have assumed power in Peking. . . . Mao remains too valued a source of authority for China's new leaders to cast aside. But in hindsight it now appears that for most Chinese Mao had become more a deity or an abstract mythic figure than a man, while Chou was a revered and sympathetic leader to turn to in time of trouble.

"It was Chou that Chinese parents wrote to when they worried whether their Red Guard children had coats against the cold of Peking's winter, and Chou whom harassed artists and writers asked for help when they were persecuted by the leftists.

"From all accounts, Chou's death last year drew more spontaneous grief from the Chinese than Mao's passing nine months
later.

"A million people lined the streets when Chou's body was
taken to be cremated, and, according to some witnesses, at one
point a large group tried to prevent the vehicle carrying his body
from moving, thinking the cremation was a trick of Miss Chiang
and her cohorts. It was allowed to pass only when Chou's widow,
Teng Ying-ch'ao, herself a respected veteran revolutionary, came
forward to explain it was Chou's own wish. . . .

"The first scenes showing the demonstrations can be seen in
a new documentary film of Chou's life, entitled: 'Eternal Glory
to Esteemed and Beloved Prime Minister Chou En-lai,' which
had its premiere in Peking today. . . .

"Part of Chou's appeal was that he seemed to embody all the
virtues the Chinese admire and used to associate with a Confucian gentleman. He was intelligent, kind, gracious and modest,
shrewd without being scheming, ambitious and forceful without
being overbearing. He was also a good diplomat and conciliator,
ready to repair the damage done by Mao's more apocalyptic
style.

"Peking's new leaders, most of whom were his followers, have
not been slow to hold Chou up as a new model of Communist
rectitude. . . ."

Of necessity, a life of Chou is also a history, however partial,
of the Chinese Communist revolution. All revolutions have their
cost in human lives and suffering; this revolution—from the
Kuomintang's decimation of the early Communist Party leadership in 1927 through the liquidations of Nationalists and others
in 1949 and later years—was no exception. Casualty figures ranging from hundreds of thousands to twenty million and more are
bandied about. Mao himself publicly acknowledged that there
were some eight hundred thousand deaths during the early
months of the new regime; Chou frequently referred to the cas-
ualties of the revolution, and deplored them. American families
who, like my own, lost the flower of a generation in our Civil
War, will realize that these pages make no attempt to weigh cas-
ualties, but confine themselves to the underlying issues, events,
and personalities.

If this volume serves in any degree to bring to life for Americans and others one of the giant personalities of our era, it cannot fail also to dispel many widespread myths about his country, thus deepening our understanding of the revolutionary cause he personified for half a century, and its implications for our common future.

New Year's Day 1977

CHOU

To expect a change in human nature may be an act of faith, but to expect a change in human society without it is an act of lunacy.

—Lord Eustace Percy.

CHAPTER 1

BITTER HERITAGE: THE CHINA OF
CHOU'S YOUTH

Communist China's chief delegate to the Geneva Conference on Vietnam had arrived early that Cold War morning in July 1954. Entering the ornate Grande Salle Lounge of the Palais des Nations, he began studying the murals when he heard another delegate enter and, wheeling sharply, instantly recognized his government's arch-antagonist, the United States Secretary of State, John Foster Dulles.

The trim Mao-jacketed Chinese statesman had noted Dulles' earlier curt retort to an inquiring reporter's question as to whether the two men planned to meet privately: "Only if our automobiles collide!" Nevertheless, hesitating only an instant, he stepped forward, crippled right hand outstretched to the American, his normally alert but imperturbable face wreathed in smiles. Dulles drew himself up, frowned, shook his head, thrust his hands firmly behind him, turned his back and strode from the room.

Until the Kissinger handshake at a Peking lakeside villa in midsummer of 1971, that traumatic encounter in Switzerland seventeen years before was the last meeting between any emissary of the United States of America and Chou En-lai—from 1949 until his death on January 8, 1976, Premier of the People's Republic of China and her voice to the world.

Edgar Snow, to whom Chou told the story in 1960, told me that even then, six years afterward, the Chinese statesman winced as he recalled the scene.

On the eve of Washington's birthday, 1972, with one hundred million Americans, and millions more around the world, glued to their television screens, this same Chou En-lai, in the most spectacular foreign-policy reversal of our time, welcomed Dulles' former Cabinet associate Richard Nixon, then President of the United States, to the capital of the long-forbidden China mainland, and the Premier's own life story and life style at once assumed a special importance for every American.

Chou's record is one of superlatives. Since the death of North Vietnam's President Ho Chi Minh, he was by far the most sophisticated of world Communism's elite. Neither Lenin, Stalin, Khrushchev—nor, of course, the peripatetic Soviet leader Leonid Brezhnev—can match Chou's half century in high Party posts. He had been an international figure longer even than Mao. His survival, furthermore, through sixty years of revolutionary turmoil—including no less than five civil wars, two world wars, twelve years of Japanese invasion, twenty years' hostility by the United States and ten by Russia—marked him as surely the most durable statesman of our era and, quite possibly, the most resilient top political figure of all time.

Perhaps the most vivid example of this resilience was his emergence from the near chaos of the Cultural Revolution with his authority not only intact but enhanced. Before 1965, the dour intellectual, President Liu Shao-chi, with his popular pamphlets on Communism and his control of the Party apparatus, was generally regarded as Chairman Mao's successor and senior to Chou. Early that year Mao, already incubating his revolutionary assault on the Communist bureaucracy, decided that Liu could not be persuaded to co-operate, and would have to go. The clash of wills and principles produced a leadership interregnum through 1966–68, with radical extremists in the ascendancy. When Mao regained control, he formally designated Marshal Lin Piao as heir-apparent. But for the basic task of reordering the country's foreign and domestic affairs, he turned to the veteran Chou En-lai.

By January 1975, at the time of the key Party Congress which formalized the elimination of Marshal Lin, it was clear that whatever place any younger leader might achieve over the long term, for the immediate future Premier Chou, ailing though he was, fully shared with Chairman Mao the leading role in the nation.

During the two decades (1949–1970) of an almost total absence of hard news between Peking and Washington, myths regarding China's leaders had flourished in inverse proportion to the scanty facts available—and vice versa. Everyone recalls, for instance, how Mao for years had been variously reported as dead, mad, ailing or deposed. Even today, with a senior Washington diplomat in permanent residence in Peking, the state of health of China's leaders poses for Westerners what Henry Kissinger would label a prime "element of conjecture."

Chou En-lai came out of it all somewhat better, for the simple reason that he often traveled abroad and could be seen. But in those bitter Cold War years he was ever the man of mystery, and the Western press had blossomed with headlines: "Red China's Gentleman Hatchet Man," "The Elastic Bolshevik," "The Rubber Communist," and, during his Cairo visit, inevitably, "The Chinese Sphinx." Meanwhile dark rumors from his Shanghai underground days, and unverifiable but horrendous figures regarding the cost of the revolution in human lives, combined to create in many Western minds an image ruthless, devious, and at times sinister.

Now, with access to the mainland in process of normalization, a juster insight is possible into the qualities of this remarkable man who, with Mao, personified the new China and the multifaceted revolution which gave it birth.

Among the many intangible results of the Nixon visit to Peking was a tacit decision by both sides to lay aside the mutual atrocity charges and imputations of bad faith and evil motive current during the previous two decades. Included in this decision on the American side was a radically revised White House estimate of Chou himself as being, within the context of his own lifelong philosophy, an extremely able and farsighted statesman. This view contrasts sharply with that long held by most Americans. So if the present restrained and somewhat equivocal relationship between the two countries is to achieve anything approaching permanent friendship, and the quarter-century's venomous feud between the oldest and most populous nation on earth and the richest and strongest is to be finally ended, then a major reassessment of the man, his country and his cause is mandatory.

Moreover, Americans are increasingly realizing today that every thoughtful citizen should acquire at least an elementary knowledge of the history, particularly the recent history, of the Chinese people.

President Charles de Gaulle, when France decided in 1964 to recognize the People's Republic of China, gave a crowded press conference three reasons why he had defied the United States and other Western nations in taking the step. "First," he explained, "China is very old. Second, China is very large. Third, China has been very abused."

Officials of the United States State Department, still operating within the Dulles Cold War straitjacket, took violent exception to de Gaulle's decision. But they were unable to fault his facts. Of his three reasons, it is the third that concerns us here. For it was the spectacular and protracted abuse of China by foreign powers, as well as by her own rulers, that played the decisive role, following the First World War, in propelling young patriots like Chou En-lai and Mao Tse-tung into the Communist Party.

An unforgettable experience of my China childhood will serve to introduce this third point.

It was a sunny winter morning of the pre-World War I era in the great Yangtze River port of Hankow, six hundred miles inland from Shanghai and the sea. Riding at anchor in midstream were warships of the international Yangtze patrol—American, British, French, German, Japanese—with the high-turreted U.S.S. *Helena* bravely flying the Stars and Stripes.

Along a gleaming white sidewalk in the British Concession—one of the immaculately landscaped foreign enclaves imposed on China by the "Unequal Treaties"[1] of the previous century—I was trying out my prize Christmas present—a pair of roller

---

[1] Unequal Treaties: China, following her defeat in the Opium War of 1840–42, and another in 1860, was forced to pay an indemnity to the victorious Western powers, to forfeit the area later to become Hong Kong, to open certain ports to foreign sovereignty and trade and to keep import duties to 5 per cent and under. For fuller details see succeeding pages.

skates. The muddy main road alongside was filled from curb to curb with a mass of enormous bobbing cotton bales, under each of which was hidden an emaciated Chinese coolie earning his daily pittance from the English tycoon Liddell's "godown" (warehouse) nearby. But I was happy and alone on my sidewalk, where coolies were not allowed.

Suddenly I heard someone whistling behind me and a Western businessman strode by, complete with bowler, spats and a flower in his buttonhole, merrily twirling a cane.

At that moment one of the coolies, staggering under his burden, stumbled and fell half across the curbside gutter, his head and shoulders involuntarily violating the white man's right of way.

Instinctively I started forward to help. But the white man was ahead of me, belabored the coolie with his cane till the blood ran, and walked on, whistling. Horrified and choking with outrage and frustration, I promptly lost my balance, hit my head a resounding thump on the concrete and ran home weeping to tell my mother.

That was my first exposure to what the Chinese call their "Century of Humiliation" at the hands of the West—a traumatic national ordeal whose legacy of bitterness and steely resolve still casts its shadow today over the recent tragedies of Vietnam, Cambodia and Laos, and the dwindling remnants of the entire American military connection in Asia.

Since the U.S. experience in Vietnam—not to mention Korea and Japan—suggests that Americans still have little conception of how Asians, and particularly Chinese, regard these abuses perpetrated by the white race on the ancient peoples of the East, a brief historical summary is in order.

China today may be compared to a long-submerged volcano whose fiery cone has recently erupted from the ocean. Only a small part shows above the surface. The rest is sunk deep in thirty-five centuries of history—the longest continuous national and cultural existence of any country on earth.

It is almost as if some nation of the West were to combine in a single unbroken historical tradition the legends of Greek mythology, the pyramids of the Pharaohs, the conquests of Alexander, the moral philosophy of Plato, the authority of the Papacy, the creative energy of the Renaissance, the Oxford-Cambridge academic tradition, the dynamics of the Russian Revolution and the world's discovery of the bomb.

China is a land of superlatives. Her people number almost a quarter (some eight hundred million) of the human race. Until recent years, the population growth alone in any fifteen-year period approximated the total population of the United States. By the year 2000, every third person in the world may be Chinese.

China is vast. Only the Soviet Union and Canada are vaster. She possesses two of the six longest rivers (the Yangtze and the Yellow), the greatest mountain peaks (fourteen of the twenty-two highest, including Everest) and the longest land frontier (ninety-three hundred miles) in the world. The famous Yangtze Gorges rival the Grand Canyon in grandeur. Climate ranges with infinite variety from Manchuria's subarctic winters and Turkestan's windblown steppes to the tropical jungles of Hainan in the Tonkin Gulf.

One hundred million Chinese live in cities and towns, many with fast-growing industries. The teeming seaport metropolis of Shanghai (eleven million people), surpasses New York and Tokyo as the world's largest, and the ancient city of Peking (eight million) is the repository of a magnificent concentration of classical Chinese art and architecture. Other well-known commercial centers are Tientsin, Shenyang (Mukden) and Harbin in the north, Nanking, Wuhan and Chungking along the Yangtze, and the southern port of Canton, ancestral home of the revolutionary hero Sun Yat-sen and of most of the twenty million overseas Chinese.

China's borders are hotly disputed. In the view of most Chinese, Nationalists as well as Communists, they ought by right to include sizable portions of Siberia, Mongolia, Soviet Central Asia, India and Southeast Asia—all at one time under her suzerainty. Along the current Soviet-Chinese frontier some one hundred and fifty incidents were reported during one recent year alone.

Long before Chou En-lai and Mao Tse-tung, the Chinese were accustomed to the principle of absolute government. Long before Chou and Mao, they had been trained to believe there was only one correct doctrine, and that power belonged to whoever best understood and applied it.

Heading the elaborate, centuries-old pyramid of China's government was an emperor counseled by wise men. The sage Confucius (551–479 B.C.), originator of this system of rule by scholars, was a thinker whose ideas may have affected more human beings than those of any other philosopher in history. Confucius was primarily interested in how people might live together in harmony. He conceived of the state as a family, with the emperor as father setting an example to his subjects, the children. His advice to monarchs was: "If the ruler is virtuous the people will be virtuous also."

For over three thousand years, until the late-thirteenth-century arrival of Marco Polo,[2] the Chinese Empire had lived out its life virtually unknown to the outside world and unaffected by it. Even when the great Venetian explorer returned to Europe with his tales of wonder, he was generally disbelieved, and was in fact haled before the Inquisition for bearing false witness.

Then, beginning in the sixteenth century, the Portuguese, followed at intervals by the Dutch, Spanish, English and French, established trading posts along the coasts of South China, Japan and the Philippines. But for three hundred years they were successfully contained and kept at arm's length by the Imperial Court at Peking.

Not until the Napoleonic Era, from which England emerged as the mightiest power on earth, did any foreign nation feel herself strong enough to force the issue. After Waterloo, in 1815, England felt able to act, and throughout the next quarter century sought a plausible pretext.

By then long in control of India, the British found cultivation of the poppy there to be commercially profitable, and for many years carried on a contraband export trade in opium along the South China Coast. U.S. traders selling Persian opium were second in this commerce. The Peking government, understandably concerned by its people's growing demand for the drug and its consequent menace to Chinese society, moved early in 1839 to impound and destroy twenty thousand chests of opium at Canton. Seeing in this the desired pretext, British warships went into action, silenced the forts defending the city, sank the primitive

2 Known as the "young bachelor," Marco Polo was about seventeen years old when he set out for the Far East, learning Chinese and not returning to his native Venice till twenty-four years later.

armed junks sent against them, and eventually forced China to submit.

This English victory in what has become known to history as the "Opium War" (1840–42), began what every Chinese to this day refers to as China's "Century of Humiliation" at the hands of the West. Hong Kong in the South was seized, and Weihaiwei in the North, and the proud but helpless Peking government was forced to open selected "Treaty Ports" to Western trade. Thus China's isolation, eventually doomed under any circumstances, was in fact ended by an incident so morally indefensible that it has become a byword for infamy to every Chinese schoolchild and a treasure trove for Communist propagandists around the globe.

Other European powers eventually followed Britain into Asia.[3] France took Indo-China (Vietnam, Laos, Cambodia); Germany annexed Tsingtao, port of Shantung, the province where Confucius was born; Japan, Korea and Taiwan. Russia seized Vladivostok, the Soviet Far East and Soviet Central Asia, penetrated deeper into Manchuria, and turned hungry eyes on Mongolia.

The devastating T'ai-p'ing (Great Peace) Rebellion[4] in mid-century, China's first popular protest against these foreign depredations, was eventually suppressed with the help of Britain's famous General "Chinese" Gordon.[5] Its leader, Hung Hsiu-ch'uan, "characterized himself as the younger brother of Jesus and for-

[3] The catalogue of foreign territorial concessions in China was long, and comprised almost every conceivable shade of legal status—from the most tenuous leasehold to outright annexation. All, of course, were equally hateful to Chou and his contemporaries. To them, naturally, what mattered was that foreign occupation of Chinese soil existed at all. In their view, the United States was no exception, for though she did not formally sign the "Unequal Treaties," she claimed and received all rights accorded nationals of the signatory states. I myself was born of American parents in the British Concession at Hankow, and my first sight of the American flag was of the one flying over the U.S.S. *Helena*, anchored in the Yangtze River six hundred miles inland from the sea.

[4] For further details see Jen Yu-wen, *The Taiping Revolutionary Movement;* Edgar Snow, *Red China Today—The Other Side of the River*, pp. 63–65; and John K. Fairbank, *The United States and China*, pp. 159–66.

[5] Ironically, General Charles Gordon, a regular British Army officer and a devout Christian, played a prominent leadership role in the final suppression of the pseudo-Christian-oriented T'ai-p'ing Rebellion (1851–64). Gordon later died defending Britain's imperial interests at Khartoum, in Africa's Sudan. He has been regarded as a hero by the British, if not by either the Chinese or Sudanese.

mulated a revolutionary ideology that was a Chinese version of Protestant Christianity."[6] He came close to success, and failed only after fourteen years (1851–64) of civil war and at a cost of forty million lives. Historically, the T'ai-p'ing Rebellion (now renamed the "T'ai-p'ing Revolution" by Peking), was in many ways a forerunner of the better-known Boxer Rebellion at the turn of the century. Hung was much admired by Chou and China's later Communist leaders because of his radical social reforms such as the redistribution of land, the abolition of slavery and the sale of women and children, the outlawing of footbinding, prostitution, arranged marriages, polygamy, and the importation of opium. These reforms, and participation by the Army in agriculture and industry, foreshadowed many of the reforms reinstituted a century later under the People's Republic.

In 1900 during the Boxer Rebellion an international army relieved the besieged Legation Quarter of Peking, turning it into a final foreign "concession." As the twentieth century began, China was hardly more than a geographical expression. Foreign warships patrolled her rivers, harbors and coastal waters. White men were not answerable in any Chinese court. Signs in a Shanghai park read: "Chinese and dogs not admitted."

The hated foreigner was of course only half the story. China's bitter colonialist yoke was more than matched by the oppressions of her own feudalistic government and society.

Every year, in the China of my youth, five to ten million people would die from preventable causes—flood, famine, disease, civil war. The infant mortality rate ran at a staggering two hundred per thousand live births. The nationwide TB rate was estimated at 6 per cent.

During my Shanghai school days, the police of the International Settlement, on winter nights, would often collect in garbage vans a couple of hundred nameless corpses off the streets. In the cities beggars were everywhere and the filth and stench indescribable. No national illiteracy figures could be verified, but all agreed they were astronomical, running well over 95 per cent.

Some knowledge of the scenes and atmosphere of treaty-port China is essential if Westerners are to understand how completely all Chinese in the People's Republic have repudiated

[6] O. Edmund Clubb, *20th Century China*, p. 13.

their colonialist past when white men dominated their country. Chou En-lai knew colonialist Shanghai well during his underground years there. Neale Hunter, an Australian who taught at the Foreign Languages Institute in Shanghai from 1965 to 1967, paints a vivid picture of the racecourse, which I well remember from my school days:

"The physical center of colonial Shanghai was the British racecourse. This spacious oval of green grass acted as a lung in the middle of the grimy metropolis . . . The Communists, with a touch of irony, had converted one of the grandstands into a public library. I would sit and read in the former clubrooms, where Englishmen had presumably discussed the White Man's Burden over gin and tonic. Outside the windows the tiers of seats were still there, and I would picture great crowds assembled for the 'sport of kings,' or perhaps a more select audience for the cricket that was played on the oval circumscribed by the track.

"That was how Shanghai was: the master race, center stage, playing a game which it alone understood; and the 'natives' unable to advance beyond the magic circle of the race track, where they were offered the tantalizing but remote specter of wealth. . . .

"Life for the Chinese in old Shanghai cannot have been much fun. The Communists, swept into power by an army of paupers, certainly failed to appreciate the sporting mentality of Western business. With the zeal of angels, they set about suppressing opium, prostitution, child labor, gangsters. . . .

"The racecourse came in for special treatment, a sign that the Communists were not unaware of its symbolic importance. It was summarily ripped up and made into a 'People's Square,' with a circular park to replace the old track, and the members' grandstand became Shanghai's public library."[7]

While the men of the old China, including the youthful Chou En-lai, wore the Manchu-imposed queue or pigtail,[8] women were little better than slaves of their men. Millions of them—my own beloved nurse or "amah" included—had their feet bound[9] in

[7] Neale Hunter in *China and Ourselves*, edited by Bruce Douglass and Ross Terrill, pp. 174–75.

[8] A queue or pigtail, from the hair of the crown—all the rest of the head being shaved—was enforced by the Manchus.

[9] Footbinding: a centuries-long practice throughout China resulting from the traditional admiration for women with small ("lily") feet. Families with

infancy and walked on the stumps the rest of their lives. Ask a Chinese father how many children he had, and he would likely reply by giving the number of sons. Girls did not count.

Marriages were generally arranged by the parents, and the first sight a young man had of his bride, or she of him, was on their wedding day. One of the rare facts in common between Chiang Kai-shek and Mao Tse-tung is that both had their first brides picked by their families. For some years the Chiang marriage survived, producing his son and heir, the present Premier Chiang Ching-kuo on Taiwan. In 1921 he divorced Ching-kuo's mother and six years later allied himself with the glamorous Soong Mei-ling. Mao was more forthright; following the wedding he drew aside his bride's veil, took one look, and fled!

Thus the China of Chou's youth, in both domestic and foreign affairs, was long overripe for revolution. The first stirrings came on October 10, 1911[10] when a bomb exploded prematurely near our Hankow home, triggering the revolt of the Wuchang garrison against Manchu rule. I can still dimly recall being led as a toddler by my mother to the Hankow "bund," or riverfront, watching the flashes of the rebel guns on the Wuchang shore a mile away bombarding the Imperial arsenal on the Hankow side, and having her explain the time lag between flash and report. It was my earliest lesson in the speed of sound.

The 1911 "revolution," however, was one chiefly in name. True, Manchu[11] rule was abolished, a republic proclaimed, footbinding outlawed, and queues cut off by barbers who set up shop on city streets. Chou lost his at age thirteen. But though China's best minds sought ways to restore some measure of national power and dignity, nothing seemed to succeed—neither

---

daughters from age four or five customarily subjected their children to the excruciatingly painful breaking of the foot's main arch and bending under of the toes to produce the tiny pointed shape. Peasant women were an exception, as they worked the land and could not afford crippling their feet to half the normal size. Thus footbinding was just one of many ways in which class distinctions were further deepened and women were kept subjugated. (See Margery Wolf and Roxane Witke, *Women in Chinese Society*.)

[10] Thereafter known as "Double-Ten," tenth day of the tenth month, when over four thousand years of Empire ceased, and China's first Republic was born.

[11] Manchu: a people from Manchuria who conquered China in 1644 and founded the Ch'ing, or Manchu, dynasty which ruled until the Revolution of 1911.

the short-lived Republic, nor the rival warlords who succeeded
it, nor the later Versailles Treaty on which many had pinned
their hopes. By 1920, China's George Washington, Dr. Sun Yat-
sen, was declaring bitterly that "the Chinese people are just a
rope of sand—the poorest and weakest nation on earth. Foreign
powers are the carving knives and the dish; we are the fish and
the meat."

CHAPTER II

THE MAKING OF A COMMUNIST

Into this colonialist China of bitterness and despair, Chou En-lai was born in 1898[1] in Huai-an in Kiangsu Province, about two hundred miles northwest of Shanghai. Like most Chinese of his generation, though, he always claimed as his ancestral home the town of his forebears, Shao-hsing in Chekiang, the same seacoast province where Chiang Kai-shek had been born a dozen years before. Here in the old "Hundred-year Hall" stood the tablets of his ancestors, and for years Chou continued the custom of visiting to pay his respects, even in the years when, as leader of the Communist underground, he risked his life to do so.

Chou's father, youngest of seven brothers in a proud but impecunious mandarin[2] family, which Chou himself had described

[1] The exact date of Chou's birth remains obscure. An edict adopted during the Communist takeover in 1949 stressed a policy of de-emphasizing all strictly personal aspects of relations with and among the leadership: "No presents to each other; no streets named after individuals; no birthday celebrations."

[2] Mandarin: a term used to describe a family of privilege under the Chinese Empire, which traditionally from generation to generation contributed at least one civil-servant scholar, chosen by examination, to the state. The color and shape of the large round button that adorned the hat of a high official gave its name to the mandarin orange, sold in today's food markets.

as "feudalistic," was gentle and charming, but something of a
drifter, with a love of ease and the famous Shao-hsing rice wine.
His mother, a sensitive and kind-hearted woman to whom Chou
was always devoted, was a gifted artist and connoisseur of classical Chinese literature. The families of both parents were constantly torn between nostalgia for China's receding past and
perplexity over a rapidly changing world wholly beyond their
comprehension.

Chou's mother died when he was nine, the father married
again, and the son, as often happened in those days, was
adopted by the most successful of his uncles—a former provincial
governor and leading Shanghai citizen who had no son of his
own. At age ten, Chou was moved again, this time by another
uncle, a police commissioner, who took him to Mukden, industrial metropolis of Manchuria, where for several years the boy
attended the missionary-sponsored Sheng-ching elementary
school. In time, En-lai came to regard this uncle as his father,
and the uncle's strong-willed wife, for whom he developed a
deep affection, as his foster mother. Later she bore a son of her
own, Chou En-chu, and insisted, over family objections, on arranging for foreign missionaries to instruct both youngsters in
the much-coveted Western learning, including the English language.

The genius for dealing with people so evident in Chou's diplomacy throughout his long life, was developed during these
formative years. Apparently, he alone had known how to handle
his foster mother's tantrums, waiting smilingly until she calmed
down and then quietly offering a solution acceptable to all parties. It seems, too, that his keen interest in people's family relationships—a notable element in his handling of foreign visitors to
the People's Republic[3]—sprang from his own experience during
these same early days.

Addressing a student audience in Chungking in 1941 during
the Japanese war, Chou interjected a sentimental note: "As for
me, the grave of my mother, to whom I owe everything that I

[3] China-born Ambassador Chester Ronning, last pre-World War II Canadian envoy to Nanking, has told me of the extraordinary lengths to which
Chou went to arrange for his (Ronning's) visit in 1971 to his mother's
grave deep in the interior of Hupeh Province—an experience duplicated by
my sister Frances when the Premier similarly planned her return to the
Central China mountain resort of Lu Shan, where our mother is buried.

am and hope to be, is in Japanese-occupied Chekiang. How I
wish I could go back there once to clear the weeds on her grave
—the least a prodigal son who has given his life to revolution and
to his country could do for his mother."[4]

Several years later, during the postwar Marshall mission, Chou
touched on the same emotion-packed theme at a Chungking reception during one of his frequent visits from Yenan. "It has
been thirty-eight years," he recalled with a catch in his voice,
"since I last saw my old home. The poplars in front of my mother's
grave must have grown very tall by now."[5]

Following his school years in Manchuria, during which he first
learned something of Western thinkers like Darwin, Mill and
Rousseau, as well as eagerly absorbing the best of China's ancient patriotic literature, young Chou, at age fourteen, conceived
a burning desire to continue his education in the United States.
The 1911 Sun Yat-sen Revolution had discredited the country's
age-old tradition of grounding her governing elite in the Chinese
classics, and the United States had just offered her share of
China's Boxer indemnity reparations[6] for the purpose of training
young Chinese in America. To Chou this seemed a monumental
stroke of luck and he eagerly applied, only to be rejected because of the oversupply of candidates from his native east
Yangtze River area.

Deeply disappointed by this failure to reach America, regarded by China's students at that point in history as something
of a promised land, young Chou took what seemed the most attractive alternative. Despite opposition from his uncles, he
enrolled in 1913, at the age of fifteen, in the newly established
and American mission-supported Nankai Middle School in
Tientsin.

[4] Hsu Kai-yu, *Chou En-lai: China's Gray Eminence*, p. 8.

[5] Ibid., p. 156. Biographical data, except when otherwise documented,
may for the most part be verified in this carefully researched book by Professor Hsu.

[6] Boxer indemnity reparations: China's Boxer indemnity reparations of
$330,000,000 were imposed by the Western powers following the so-called
Boxer Rebellion—a popular uprising (June 20–August 14, 1900) directed
mainly against foreigners and Chinese Christians, with widespread loss of
life. The United States renounced claim to her share of the indemnity, stating that she would prefer to use these funds for the education of selected
young Chinese in the United States. For further details, see Kenneth Scott
Latourette, *A Short History of the Far East*.

The next four years were among the most fulfilling and formative of Chou's life. Outstandingly brilliant in social studies and
languages, he was allowed to skip a year and join the fourth
class. Often he would complete a composition assignment in half
the required time. This proficiency won him the admiration of
the school principal, Chang Po-lin, one of pre-Communist
China's foremost educators, who encouraged the boy to gain
financial independence from his family by making him his student assistant. Thus began an intimate association that endured,
despite their later differences in political philosophy, throughout
China's civil-war period and into the early years of Communist
rule.

Chou's years at Nankai, between the ages of fifteen and nineteen, covered the turbulent World War I era of Chinese politics.
Sun Yat-sen's Republic had dissolved into chaos, with reactionary holdovers from the Manchu regime first attempting to restore the monarchy under Yuan Shih-kai, then joining with rival
warlords in competing for personal power and wealth, and
finally yielding to some of Japan's humiliating "Twenty-one Demands"[7] on the stricken country's territorial and political integrity. Yuan's death in 1916 began the notorious warlord[8] era.

Encouraged by Principal Chang, young Chou's immediate reaction to all this was to form a lively student association known
as "Respect Work Enjoy Group Life." He began to contribute to
the association's journal, assailing the nation's venal leadership
and stressing the need for unity, patriotism, resistance to foreign
aggression, and economic and social progress.

[7] Twenty-one Demands: five groups of demands (twenty-one in all) presented in January 1915, and designed to gain for Japan virtual control over
all China. The United States protested these demands, China resisted most
of them, finally acquiescing only in some of those affecting Shantung and
Manchuria.

[8] Warlord: a Chinese military commander exercising independent military
and civil power in a specific region of the country, whether in nominal
allegiance to the national government or in defiance of it. The warlords
varied widely as to character and ability: for instance two that I personally
interviewed were General Yen Hsi-san, the so-called "model governor" of
Shansi province, and the considerably less model General Wu Pei-fu,
scandal-ridden commander in Central China. The declared objective of the
1926 "Northern Expedition" under Chiang and the Chou-Borodin coalition,
described in the next chapter, was to eliminate the warlords and unite
China. For further facts, see Lucien Bianco, *Origins of the Chinese Revolution 1915–1949*, pp. 22–27.

For a teen-age schoolboy, Chou's whole Nankai career was an incredible *tour de force*—a clear indication of the shape of things to come. By the age of sixteen, he was organizing student demonstrations, protesting traitors on the home front and aggressors from abroad. When a school play, *One Dollar*, needed a heroine to portray a victim of the evils of money, Chou took the part, and the wild applause of the youthful audience turned his thoughts more and more toward the saving of his country and the key role of young China in that task.

Long after Chou assumed national leadership, his sentimental devotion to Nankai remained firm and deep. Often he would confide to his intimates that he planned someday to do a series of biographical sketches of his schoolmates. Even when traveling incognito and in mortal peril from the Kuomintang police, he would risk arrest by telephoning some former Nankai friend, student or teacher. From the caves of Yenan he sent a message by Edgar Snow to Principal Chang, and on becoming Premier after the Communist takeover, intervened to protect his old head-master—who always kept his distance from the Party—from harassment by overeager zealots of the nation's new regime.

Graduating from Nankai at the top of his class in the year of the Russian Revolution, the nineteen-year-old Chou En-lai decided to continue his studies in Japan—at the university of Kyoto. It proved a momentous decision, for it was at Kyoto University, where he settled into lodging with a Nankai friend and the latter's young wife, that the future Premier of the People's Republic first encountered Marxism and began furiously to ponder China's past. Reduced by lack of funds to a meatless subsistence diet, Chou read daily in *The Social Studies Journal*, edited by a Kyoto University professor just returned from Russia, while the taunts of his Japanese acquaintances at China's decadence and impotence spurred him on. Chou realized his country was undergoing a unique historical experience: facing within the span of a single decade the onslaught of five major revolutions—political, industrial, cultural, religious, social—that the West had hardly succeeded in absorbing over a period of four centuries. He was drawn to Lenin's writings mainly because they alone appeared to offer a doctrine and a dedication potent enough to cope with these combined revolutions, and simultaneously with

the depredations of Japan and the colonialist powers of the
West.

One memorable evening in Kyoto at the house of his Nankai
friend, these pent-up thoughts burst out as young Chou, down-
ing glass after glass of wine, exclaimed passionately: "You cannot salvage China with strong leadership alone. You must have
strong followers to support the leadership. You have to start with
a complete re-education of the younger generation—and the
older generation, if that's possible—of the students, the workers,
even the peasants. You must have them all with you before you
can push a revolution to success. And without a revolution,
China cannot be saved."

Unimpressed, Chou En-lai's friend grabbed the bottle and,
smashing it on the floor, shouted: "You are not going to save
China if you hang on to that stuff."

Meanwhile events at home were hurtling to a climax. The
Paris Peace Conference, despite the fact that China had fought
the war on the Allied side, had just awarded defeated Germany's
colonial rights in Shantung to Japan. Furious, several thousand
Peking students took to the streets in protest, burned down the
home of one Cabinet minister and beat up another. To them,
these men were traitors who had sold their country to the
enemy. It was the beginning of the famous May Fourth movement of 1919, where the most senior of modern China's leaders
first underwent their revolutionary baptism of fire.

To Chou in Kyoto, who received full details from Ma Chun, a
fellow Nankai student who had remained in Tientsin, the news
was explosive. Returning immediately to China and Nankai University (newly established extension of Nankai School), he
joined Ma in leadership of the Tientsin Students League. Its
girls' division, the Tientsin Women's Patriotic Association, included an energetic and attractive young leader named Teng
Ying-ch'ao—later to become Chou's wife—at whose widowed
mother's house in the French Concession the group would hold
strategy sessions. Teng, like Chou then in her late teens, had attended Girl's Normal School in Tientsin, and there had helped
organize a Society of Awakening which later supported the demonstrations under Chou's leadership. She solicited funds for their
activities and marched in student demonstrations—girls in the

center, men surrounding them so they would be the first arrested by the police.

Amid a storm of student strikes that finally compelled the government to refuse to sign the Versailles Treaty, which had leased Chinese territory to Japan, Chou was taken by Ma to an editorial meeting of the college paper. There he argued so persuasively for a language change from classical Chinese to modern vernacular that he was promptly chosen editor-in-chief. The paper's masthead bore in English an intriguing Lincolnesque slogan: "Democracy: of the people, by the people, for the people"— probably a fair expression of the youthful editor's views at that particular moment.

But history was racing on, and China's thinking was racing with it. Chou's editorials, conceived early each morning over a hasty breakfast of soybean milk and thrashed out at a later staff conference, began to lash out at the Versailles Treaty betrayal, at the country's warlordism, her abysmal poverty and ignorance, the exploitation of coolie and child labor, and the staggering toll of famine and flood. They pilloried the feudal family system with its dictatorship of the old over the young, and bitterly denounced the economic slavery imposed on China's poverty-stricken masses by the Japanese- and British-owned textile mills in Shanghai.

Such conditions are, of course, the classical breeding ground of revolutionaries, and many of Chou's associates were joining Marxist study groups in Shanghai and Peking. Chou, with his mandarin background, was doubtful whether China's revolution would have to duplicate the violent Soviet model. Nevertheless, Moscow's experience exercised a magnetic attraction, and one day the young man took several of his colleagues to call on Sergei Polevoy, instructor in Russian at Peking University, who happened to be doubling as Comintern representative in Tientsin.

The encounter marked another turning point. Soon afterward, in September 1919, Chou's call for a nationwide campaign of student agitation triggered a police raid on his newspaper's office. Ma Chun was clapped into prison, and when Chou with increasing bitterness started to agitate for his release, the paper was suspended. Chou thereupon headed a student delegation to the Governor demanding dismissal of the Police Chief, and, along with the entire group, was himself promptly jailed for his pains. Thus the battle was joined.

Confined in a cold, damp, windowless police stockade, Chou organized a hunger strike, held classes in social problems for the prisoners and continued from his cell to direct the nationwide student revolt. Possibly it was during this four-month winter's incarceration that the well-bred Confucian intellectual finally decided to become a professional revolutionary. When queried years later by one of his former schoolmasters as to why he had turned Communist, Chou replied with a smile: "You yourself once gave me advice in school. I could not bring myself to get out of bed on cold winter mornings until you told me to bounce right out, and then I would feel all the warmer for having had a dash of cold. Joining the Party was much the same. It was chilly at first, but much warmer later because of the chill."

On his release from prison young Chou found that China's youth had become the conscience of the nation. He determined to make them the spearhead of a new order. In the autumn of 1920, while U.S. Presidential candidate Warren G. Harding was successfully campaigning across America on a platform of "Back to Normalcy," the twenty-one-year-old Chou En-lai sailed for Europe in the Messageries Maritimes French liner *Porthos* to complete his studies and prepare himself for revolution.

A voyage to Europe from the Far East in those immediate post-World War I days was for young Asian idealists like Chou a traumatic experience. Western imperialism enveloped Southern Asia and the Middle East. The French ran Indo-China; the Dutch, Indonesia; the British, Singapore, Malaya, Ceylon, India, Egypt. To many of the Asian countries, colonies of the West, millions of Chinese had emigrated seeking their fortunes in the foreign-managed plantations and mines where Europeans scorned manual labor. As in Shanghai, yellow- and brown-skinned natives existed in squalor alongside their own handiwork —the palatial offices and homes of their white masters.

Arriving in Paris, Chou's first impression, despite the Great War's legacy of crippled veterans, widows and orphans, was of its charm. "Paris beautiful," read a postcard home to China. "Many friends, many sights. Would you like to come?" The new arrival spent the first weeks studying French, then crossed the

Channel for a brief look at England, dishwashing in a London hotel to support himself, then restlessly returned to Paris.

A Chinese student educational program had been under way in the French capital since 1903, the political diversity of its members reflecting the ideological turmoil of the day. Then came World War I and the importation of thousands of Chinese laborers to aid the French war effort. Since the Russian Revolution of 1917 and the end of the War, a Communist-oriented group had grown rapidly among both workers and students, and Chou was quickly diverted from his studies to active planning of a Chinese Communist Youth Corps in Europe. His record as a political polemicist in Tientsin and leader of student strikes had already given him a reputation among overseas Chinese and he was quickly enlisted in the cause, supporting himself by writing for newspapers back in China, working in Ruhr coal mines and as a mechanic at the Renault automobile works at Billancourt. When the Peking government, supported by the French, sponsored a new university for young Chinese at Lyon, Chou led his Chinese Communist student compatriots in a demonstration to demand equal right of entry. (Peking had been discriminating against those already there by sending out others considered more acceptable.) In the fracas, the French police arrested over a hundred young demonstrators, jailed them for three weeks, then deported them all to China. All but Chou. Imprisoned with the rest, he managed to escape deportation and returned to the French capital to continue harassing the government and planning student strikes to further embarrass the Chinese Legation in Paris.

In Berlin, a smaller Chinese student group made up in action what it lacked in size, and from the autumn of 1921 through the summer of 1922, Chou shuttled back and forth between the two capitals. By now he was getting some Comintern financial support and was able to maintain a certain style in clothes and lodging.

He was also developing a long-range romantic attachment. One evening a fellow student from Nankai days dropped in, commented on his somewhat affluent circumstances, and after a general conversation, asked as he got up to go: "Have you made any new discoveries lately?"

Chou's response was curt. "You mean girls? No."

"I don't believe it. Not with a handsome young man like you and your setup here."

"I don't think I want to get involved. It's better to stay single. You get more done that way."

"How about Teng Ying-ch'ao? Haven't you been writing to her every other week?"

"How did you know?"

"She told me. You know, once in a long while I also receive a note from her." With that the friend left.

Chou's outstanding Berlin recruit was Chu Teh, who would later start his road to fame as founder and longtime head of China's Red Army, still at ninety and until shortly before his death in July 1976 retaining membership in Peking's Politburo. General Chu Teh, then thirty-six and with a reputation as a particularly unsavory former Kuomintang militarist, opium addict and lover of wine and women, had become disillusioned with his old life in China, had decisively changed his ways, had applied in Shanghai for Communist Party membership and been turned down, and now in desperation had made the long journey to Europe to seek a new future for himself and his country.[9]

Arriving in France in 1922, two years after Chou En-lai, Chu Teh's first impressions gave no more hope than his bitter years in Asia. "Everywhere," he wrote in later years, "I saw a dark world of suffering. China was not the most miserable land on earth. It was one of many. The problems of the poor and subjected are the same everywhere. I saw that Europe was not a paradise of modern science, as I had thought. French workers were better dressed and better fed than Chinese, yet they were haunted men. I tramped the streets of France from morning till late at night and visited the battlefields of the great European War. France was one of the victors, yet everyone talked of the miseries of the war, and maimed veterans, widows and orphans moved like broken shadows against a background of past greatness."[10]

Eventually Chu Teh heard from a friend about young Chou

[9] Agnes Smedley, The Great Road: The Life and Times of Chu Teh. Unless otherwise documented, this is the chief source of facts on Chu Teh's life.
[10] Ibid.

En-lai's growing prestige on the Continent, and finding himself in Germany, journeyed to Berlin for an interview. It was October 1922, and the ex-warlord went directly to Chou's address. His biographer describes the scene:

> When Chou En-lai's door opened, he saw a slender man of more than average height with gleaming eyes and a face so striking that it bordered on the beautiful. Yet it was a manly face, serious and intelligent, and Chu judged him to be in his middle twenties.
>
> Chou was a quiet and thoughtful man, even a little shy as he welcomed his visitor, urged him to be seated and to tell how he could help him. Ignoring the chair offered him, Chu Teh stood squarely before this youth more than ten years his junior and in a level voice told him who he was, what he had done in the past, how he had fled from Yunnan, given up opium smoking, talked with Sun Yat-sen, been repulsed by Chen Tu-hsiu in Shanghai, and had come to Europe to find a new way of life for himself and a new revolutionary road for China. He wanted to join the Chinese Communist Party group in Berlin, he would study and work hard, he would do anything he was asked to do but return to his old life, which had turned to ashes beneath his feet.
>
> As he talked, Chou En-lai stood facing him, his head a little to one side, as was his habit, listening intently until the story was told, and then questioning him.
>
> The questioning done, Chou smiled a little, said he would help him find rooms, and arrange for him to join the Berlin Communist group as a candidate until his application had been sent to China and an answer received. When the reply came a few months later, Chu was enrolled as a full member, but his membership was kept a secret from outsiders.

On returning to Paris from the historic encounter with Chu Teh, Chou immediately threw himself into a double task. He established what became known as the Chinese Communist Youth Corps in France as a recruiting agency for the Communist Party proper, and himself took charge of its ideological training. He

also, as an Executive Committee member of the Corps, became a
founder of Europe's first branch of the Asian Party and editor of
the official publication *The Red Light* (Ch'ih-kuang). As in
Tientsin, Chou's articles—written under the pseudonym Wu Hao
—covered the gamut of revolutionary issues and were eagerly absorbed by the large and diverse group of young Chinese expatriates in Europe at that time.

During the next two years (1922–24), following the departure
of his closest Communist colleagues for study at the Far Eastern
University in Moscow, Chou emerged as the senior CCP[11] leader
in Europe and the recognized arbiter between the forty-odd
competing factions among Europe's turbulent Chinese youth.
Considering the various social, political and educational backgrounds of these hundreds of expatriates, ranging from students
with aristocratic and cultural backgrounds to graduates of the
wartime "Coolie Corps" with their laundrymen and restaurant
workers from all parts of Paris, Chou's attempts at mediation can
only be considered heroic. Practically all were hard-pressed
financially, and were consumed by bitter frustration over their
continuing personal and international plight. All were visited
equally by Chou and looked to him for understanding and leadership.

From the confusion three main groups of revolutionary expa-
triate Chinese emerged: The Paris branches of the Communist
Party of China led by Chou, the fledgling Kuomintang founded
by Sun Yat-sen, and a radical nationalist faction called the
Young China Party. The latter group opposed both the CCP and
Kuomintang (KMT) chiefly because both were then allied with
Moscow's revolutionary Comintern. Chou defended this alliance
and acceptance of Comintern financial aid on the grounds that
the world situation demanded help from Russia.

At one meeting, still clad in the soiled overalls of his auto-
worker job, and provoked beyond endurance, Chou let himself go in a rare display of invective against the "ivory-tower
dreamers of the *petit-bourgeois* Young China gentlemen." Speaking with emotion, he charged that "they [the Young China
Party] talk and talk about petitions and strikes, but when there
is a demonstration, who march at the head of the column to face

[11] Chinese Communist Party.

the guns and clubs of the police, get beat up, arrested, jailed, and even butchered? It is we, the KMT cadres, not they! They talk about assassination and terrorism, but it is the KMT comrades' blood that is shed, not theirs."[12]

Amid all the turmoil, the twenty-five-year-old Chou would occasionally exchange his overalls for his austere student jacket and spend an evening visiting some of the wealthier students in the city's Sceaux division. An expert amateur cook, he would take possession of the kitchen, prepare some of his favorite Chinese dishes, and relax over drinks and several hours of jokes and laughter. Apparently he always held his liquor well, and toward midnight would escort his comrades to their respective Metro stations.

The French years were formative ones for young Chou. "The united front Chou tried to achieve in Paris," writes Professor Hsu, "was not a complete success, but his approach became a respected hallmark of his later statesmanship. In a heterogeneous assembly his tact and quick thinking never failed to set him above the rest. Always the master of the situation, particularly a confused and violent situation, he chose the line for the crowd to follow. At times he did not hesitate to launch sharp attacks on his opponents, but immediately after the attack he always softened his voice to explain away the point in dispute, emerging in triumph as a resourceful peacemaker."[13]

These years abroad had been formative, too, for the hard core of the Chinese Communist Party leadership facing the long struggle ahead. Around Chou during his Paris years there grew up an extraordinary group of young Communist veterans who collectively were to contribute far more to the birth of the People's Republic than the celebrated group who officially founded the Chinese Party in Shanghai in 1921. Mao, it is true, was one of the original Shanghai group. But of the thirteen delegates present at that inaugural meeting, only he and Tung Pi-wu (later CCP delegate to the first United Nations Conference in San Francisco) survived to help bring Communism to power. All the others defected, were expelled, or simply dropped out. By contrast, the Party nucleus cultivated by Chou in Paris and Berlin

12 Hsu, *Chou En-lai,* pp. 42–43.
13 Ibid., pp. 43–44.

included many such as Li Li-san, early head of the Party, who later died for the cause after the long struggle with Chiang Kai-shek, together with a formidable array who went on to high office in the Communist state. Among the latter, besides Chou himself and General Chu Teh, already enlisted in Berlin, were Nieh Jung-chen (later Vice-Premier in Peking), Ch'en Yi (noted civil-war general and longtime Foreign Minister), Teng Hsiao-p'ing (later head of the CCP and in 1975 President Ford's nego-tiating partner after his rehabilitation by Chou earlier that year), Li Fu-ch'un (another Vice-Premier of the Peking regime), and Tsai Ch'ang (Li's wife and notable woman member of the Party's Central Committee). Not a bad crop of budding revolu-tionaries for one dedicated youth to have garnered during four brief years of labor in a foreign field.

By the time the leaves in Paris parks were beginning to turn in late 1924, Chou knew it was time to return home. He was tem-pered now in revolutionary action, and moreover had gained a firsthand grasp of the great world outside China that was to stand him in good stead for the next half century. Sun Yat-sen was now heading a fledgling Kuomintang-Communist coalition experiment in Canton, and he needed all the help he could get. Though China's warlord era was still at its peak in the North, and her revolutionary forces were meager, Sun had repudiated the reactionary and impotent Peking regime, and at Whampoa Military Academy, outside Canton, had commissioned a then unknown but experienced Japanese-trained general named Chiang Kai-shek to start welding the officer corps for a revolu-tionary army.

Impressed with Chou's credentials, Sun had urged him to take over the task of political training for Whampoa Academy, which he hoped would become China's West Point. The invitation, sup-ported by Moscow, was accepted with alacrity. At a Paris fare-well party tendered by Chou's youthful CCP and KMT associ-ates, toasts were drunk to the new China, souvenir photos taken, and the future Premier of the People's Republic was waved off eastward on his rendezvous with destiny.

CHAPTER III

SINO-SOVIET HONEYMOON

History can have few ironies more mind-boggling than the contrast between Soviet Russia's relationship to China at the time of Chou En-lai's return to Canton nearly fifty years ago—and today. Now the Sino-Soviet split, rooted deep in ideological rivalry far more than in the conventional hassles over markets or boundaries, rivals even the Arab-Israeli imbroglio as the most intractable international feud of modern times. Then, the two countries were on what can only be described by an eyewitness like myself as a honeymoon basis.

In Peking, the still warlord-controlled capital, Moscow had followed up its repudiation of the "Unequal Treaties" by being the first foreign power to raise its envoy to ambassadorial status—and, despite rigorous protests from Washington, the Chinese turned over to the new Soviet Ambassador the old Tsarist legation. In Canton the Kuomintang, comprising Communist and non-Communist wings, was in full flower as the world's first example of a "popular front." Sun Yat-sen's forthcoming successor, the thirty-eight-year-old General Chiang Kai-shek, had returned (December 1923) from a fact-finding visit on Sun's behalf to the U.S.S.R., declaring that Soviet Russia was the hope of the world's oppressed, and the South China city was liberally sprinkled with a couple of hundred Soviet advisers.

When a Chinese spoke of the Russians he would often throw out an arm in an instinctive and enthusiastic "thumbs up." The Soviet Mission Chief, Mikhail Markovich Borodin,[1] a forty-one-year-old international agent sent out personally by Lenin at Sun's request, was described to me by admiring Kuomintang leaders as "China's Lafayette." Arriving in the southern capital only the year before Chou, he became, during his three brief Canton years, the most colorful and formidable of those revolutionary pioneers who throughout the first half of this century, in far-off corners of the world, made the Communist power what it is today. Certainly at that time he was incomparably the most influential white man in East Asia.

When Sun Yat-sen died early in 1925, he not only issued his famous last message, expressing "my hope that the Soviet Union will find in a strong and free China a friend and ally," but added succinctly: "Remember, Borodin's word is my word."

Meanwhile, with Dr. Sun near death, Chou En-lai had arrived from France. One of his first personal moves on reaching Canton was to look up Teng Ying-ch'ao, the girl at whose Tientsin home he had once planned those early student demonstrations and who, like him, had since joined the Party. The years of long-range correspondence had finally borne fruit. "You might say," she has since commented, "that we fell in love by post." The two were married, probably early in 1925. There was no formal ceremony. The new relationship was revealed to a gathering of personal friends before whom the young couple repeated the "eight mutuals" of a Chinese Communist wedding, promising "to love, to respect, to help, to encourage and to consult each other, to have consideration for each other, to have confidence and to have mutual understanding."

Chou was twenty-six, his bride twenty-three. They rented a small house—one of only two homes they managed to enjoy for brief periods during the next violently peripatetic quarter century. Their only child died at birth a few years later when the expectant mother was in hiding from Chiang Kai-shek's police.

[1] John McCook Roots, "Mysterious Borodin Sways South China." See Appendix.

But marriage, though a genuine love match on both sides,[2] was very much secondary to the revolution. Moscow's Comintern, at an emergency session on January 12, 1923, had already proposed that the Chinese Communist Party, "while taking care not to lose its own revolutionary identity, should work through the Kuomintang to overthrow the warlords before concentrating on a proletarian movement toward socialism." Chou, therefore, on arrival had put himself immediately at the service of Sun and Chiang, formally joined the Kuomintang, and took up his post—one of the last appointments of the ailing Sun Yat-sen before he died—as Deputy Director of the Political Department at Whampoa Military Academy.

His young bride, Ying-ch'ao, meanwhile headed up the women's department of the joint Kuomintang-Communist forces in Kwangtung Province. She furnished their home in inexpensive but impeccable taste, made it a favorite rendezvous for both young and old among her husband's colleagues at Whampoa and at Chiang's and Borodin's headquarters, and had food prepared with the same style and care she always showed when arranging a home meal for her weary husband at the Premier's apartment in Peking during his quarter century of high office.

Chou's leadership qualities at Whampoa soon made him *de facto* head of political training for the entire Kuomintang officer corps. He thereupon proceeded to staff the Department with trusted Party comrades, while devising a political commissar system which ensured that every major military order had to be countersigned by one of his hand-picked political aides.

By the early summer of 1926 the newborn Kuomintang-Communist alliance under Chiang Kai-shek and Chou En-lai was on the verge of embarking on the task Sun Yat-sen had bequeathed them when he died—the invasion of the North. Feverish preparations were being made. Whampoa's cadet training school had graduated hundreds of young officers, with thousands more to follow (including the nineteen-year-old Lin Piao), disciplined both in military skills and Party principles. Soviet drill sergeants brought from Russia by Borodin dispensed technical advice on military tactics. But for the invasion itself, ideology was to be the

[2] In 1975 they observed their golden wedding anniversary in the Peking hospital where Chou lived for two years before his death.

key weapon, and Chou's Propaganda Department had been operating overtime to develop and diffuse it.

All this was completely new in China. For years past, when northern warlords needed either recruits or labor, the military would simply go out and impress any hapless coolie who came along. In Canton, for the first time in memory, the anti-warlord opposition was popular enough to attract volunteers. The young labor unions, and particularly Mao Tse-tung's newly created Peasant Institute, voted to take extra revolutionary tasks upon themselves. The first thing I saw during a visit to Whampoa Academy, built on an island in the Pearl River, was a sign in great gilt characters over the entrance: "He who seeks place or riches need not enter here." Indeed, one might say that the philosophy of personal sacrifice advocated by today's Peking regime for the past quarter century, and epitomized by the motto of the Cultural Revolution—"Forget Self; Serve the People"—had its earliest origins in the Canton of fifty years ago.

The Sino-Soviet "honeymoon" of 1924-26 has long since been forgotten in America. Indeed, it is so dimly recalled today (and never mentioned) even in Moscow and Peking since they have become mortal enemies, that it deserves substantial treatment here, the more so since young Chou was politically active at the time.

Two decisive factors were responsible for this early honeymoon era between the revolutionaries of China and Russia. First was the post-World-War-I policy of the Western powers, particularly the United States. Second was a pair of remarkably gifted and dynamic "old Bolsheviks" of the Lenin breed—the Canton-based Borodin, mentioned above, and his Moscow-based opposite number, Karl Radek, who concurrently ran the newly christened Sun Yat-sen University in the Soviet capital, elite training center for China's Communist youth.

First the policy. As already noted, the Western-trained physician Dr. Sun Yat-sen had emerged from the anti-Manchu Revolution of 1911 and the 1914-18 war as the one clear, authentic voice of republican China. Trustingly, Sun looked to the Great Powers assembled at Versailles to put his struggling nation on her feet. But at Versailles, China and Indo-China received the same treatment as the Arabs—near total indifference, bordering on contempt, to their legitimate rights—and not even a T. E.

Lawrence to plead their cause. Not only was no help forth-coming, but, adding insult to injury, Japan was given legal title to the territory in China's Shantung Province, birthplace of the sage Confucius, which Germany had seized by force twenty years before.

In desperation Sun Yat-sen turned to America, whose Senate had just voted down the Treaty of Versailles. But America's brief mission to save democracy had ended. Its rejected spokesman, Woodrow Wilson, had retired into a crippled and embittered old age. Isolationism reigned supreme. A prosperity-bent United States seemed totally oblivious of the stakes involved—much as in later years we were blind to the cost of our gratuitous aliena-tion of President Gamal Abdel Nasser of Egypt over the Aswan Dam, and of President Julius Nyerere of Tanzania over the Tan-zam Railway.

As a last resort, Sun tried briefly to interest a group of Ger-man ex-officers, unemployed since their country's defeat and devastation in World War I. But this too came to nothing. Only then did the frustrated Chinese statesman consider an appeal to Moscow and, in January 1923, the die was cast in a series of key conversations with the Soviet emissary Joffe at Sun's Shanghai residence. As a result, Sun Yat-sen decided to send his young military aide, Chiang Kai-shek, to Moscow to see what the Krem-lin would offer.

Predictably, the Kremlin offered everything: money from its own scanty treasury, an elaborate student-exchange program, technical aid, military advisers, economic advisers, and finally—as the second decisive factor noted above—the services of Lenin's two master propagandists, Mikhail Borodin and Karl Radek.

When, on arriving as a foreign correspondent fresh from Har-vard, I first heard the name of Borodin in the cool, privileged recesses of the Shanghai Club, it meant no more to me than to anyone else outside treaty-port Asia. But the circumstances of the day were such as to alert even a fledgling reporter to the likelihood of a story. For the name was being shouted at the top of his lungs, between gulps of a double whiskey, by an irate "old China hand" who was passionately informing a cluster of fellow patrons lining the longest bar in the world that "this bloody Bolshevik" was back of all Britain's current woes in the Orient, and ought forthwith to be run into the Yellow Sea.

I soon discovered that, although every member of the British, French and American community in Shanghai had heard of Borodin, and detested what they heard, not one had ever met the man. Strangely enough, considering the chaos in Western trade produced by the elusive Russian, this seemed due not so much to ill will as to lack of imagination. It had simply not occurred to anyone to try. And when I proposed doing so, the cursing, after a startled crescendo, slowly subsided, and a rumble of bemused alcoholic wonderment sped me on my way to Canton.

Borodin's reputation among treaty-port foreigners hardly prepared one for the reality. I had imagined a small, furtive man, shifty-eyed and sinister. Instead, after duly presenting my introduction,[3] conveyed by the Russian's Vietnamese secretary, later known to the world as Ho Chi Minh, I found my hand being pumped by a burly six-footer clad in crumpled white jacket and trousers, with a shock of unruly black hair, a neat handlebar mustache and a booming voice that bade strangers welcome in heavily accented but fluent and idiomatic American English.

Seated at tea in his small, severely furnished waterfront office, I rapidly recalled the few hard facts about this legendary figure that Western journalists had so far pieced together. As with all old Bolsheviks, there was little enough to go on. He was said to have once served time in a Glasgow jail, and earlier appeared to have taught school in Indiana and Chicago. None of our China Coast correspondents' fraternity of those days had heard anything but rumors about the Comintern, and they did not of course know that for a decade before the Revolution Borodin had been one of the International's earliest underground couriers to the United States. The reputed closeness of his association with Lenin seemed borne out by the fact that Lenin had personally picked him for the China job. But just what that job was, why he had taken it and what he expected to achieve in it were matters everyone in the Far East was discussing, and I still could hardly credit the luck that had placed a novice reporter like myself in the way of getting the answers.

[3] Given me at an earlier interview in Canton by Chiang Kai-shek, still at that time (June 1926) officially in a "popular front" alliance with Borodin, who was his Sun Yat-sen–appointed Soviet adviser. He was also, though to a rapidly dwindling extent, in private accord with Moscow in their common opposition to the northern warlords.

Eagerly and rather pompously I put my first question:

"They say, Mr. Borodin, that you are here to take over China. I am sure my paper would be interested to know if this is true; or if not, just why you have come."

The Russian flung back his head and laughed.

"That's easy," he replied lightly. "If you say my colleagues and I plan to take over this country, the answer is no. But if you say we believe that our idea will one day take it over, the answer is yes. China has suffered for hundreds of years. She wants help. She has asked us for it and we intend to give it. That is why I am here. Have you any objections?"

I thought of the modest goals in life so recently shared with the more easygoing of a delightful group of Harvard classmates —goals composed in more or less equal parts of making our first million on Wall Street, casting our first vote for the Republican ticket and breaking 100 at golf.

"No," I countered, with an effort at nonchalance. "No objection. But do you have any notion what you are taking on? I was born here and I know. How many people do you think live in this country?"

"About five hundred million. Why?"

"Don't tell me you seriously mean to take over a fifth of the human race. In the first place, you are too few. You're only a handful with no knowledge of the land or the language. You'll never do it in a thousand years."

"Oh yes, we will," came the cool rejoinder. "All we need is a little time."

Borodin's dark eyes regarded me appraisingly. He decided to press the attack.

"You forget, young man, that I am not here for my health, or I would not be working in this barbarous heat. I don't spend my time at the bars and the races like the English and French. I am not interested in a career or a fortune like the Americans. I serve an ideology. And with an ideology it is not numbers that count. It is dedication. You Americans would not understand that. I have lived many years in your country[4] and I know what goes

---

[4] Roughly 1907–17, under various pseudonyms, shuttling chiefly between Chicago and Mexico City, where he enlisted for the cause the young M. N. Roy, later cofounder of the Communist Party of India. At the time of Russia's October Revolution in 1917, Borodin was briefly appointed Soviet

on. You concentrate on comfort and personal success. Aside from trade deals and missionary converts, you're not really interested in these Asian countries, or some of you would be in my place right now. You had the chance. But you don't care. I do. I'm interested in China. I want to help her find something that will change things."

Dimly I sensed that this extraordinary man had somehow succeeded in reversing the usual journalistic pattern. He was now interviewing me, and in terms that my editors might well find as embarrassing as I did. I tried a more conventional tack.

"Do you enjoy your work in China, Mr. Borodin?"

"Enjoy!" he echoed scornfully. "A bourgeois question. It is not a matter of whether we enjoy our work here. The work is necessary. That is all that counts. It is of course far from the friends, the concerts, and the theater that mean so much in Moscow. But long ago I made up my mind that Communism alone held an answer for the world, because Communism, unlike modern religion, insists on changing things. And I decided I would go wherever I could help most in the fight. The Party decided I could help most in China. Therefore I was glad to come. Nothing else matters. Does that answer your question?"

Another of our many exchanges stands out in my memory. One evening Borodin, for some reason, had got onto the highly controversial subject of missionaries in China. He was standing looking out the window at the junks lazily sailing by against a brilliant Pearl River sunset. I was sitting, notebook on knee, questioning him with the unconscious arrogance of the privileged young Westerner amid the squalor of the East.

After a long silence, Borodin, still gazing out the window, began murmuring, half to himself. "You know," he mused, "I used to read the New Testament. Again and again I read it. It is the most wonderful story ever told. That man Paul. He was a *real* revolutionary. I take off my hat to him!" He made a symbolic gesture, his long black hair falling momentarily over his face.

Another long silence.

Consul-General in Mexico, returning soon thereafter to Europe, and eventually to Moscow to join forces with Lenin and be sent by him in due course on the fateful China mission.

Then suddenly Borodin whirled, his face contorted with fury as he shook his fist in my face.

"But where do you find him today?" he shouted. "Answer me that, Mr. Roots. Where do you find him? Where? Where? Where?"

Then furiously, triumphantly: "You can't answer me!"

Unnerved by this outburst, I sat speechless, then quickly changed the subject.

Later that week he brought up the matter again. This time he was very quiet.

"You must understand, Mr. Roots," he explained, "that with a revolutionary, his life is not his own. That is our pride. That is our strength. And because our opponents cannot match our sacrifice or our faith, they are powerless to stop our advance. For this reason Communism will win. Of course there are disappointments. But one must be able to take the long view. I may not live to see the final victory. But it is sure."

Borodin did in fact live to see the victory, though not to participate in it. In 1927, when Chiang Kai-shek broke with the Communists, the Soviet adviser was forced to flee with his family and his meager possessions across the Gobi Desert back to Russia, where Stalin blamed him for the failure of China's Revolution and kept him in obscurity for the rest of his days. Meanwhile the Chinese Communist Party, many of whose leaders he had helped to train, survived every trial of the next two decades and in 1949, as everybody knows, took over the country. Two years later, in far-off Moscow, Borodin died.[5]

When I was last in the Soviet capital, his son Norman, who in my Canton days was a young teen-ager and is now a Novosti Press Agency columnist, took me with his wife and daughter to the niche in the wall of the Novodedichi Cemetery outside Moscow, which holds the ashes of his parents and hundreds of other old revolutionaries who, in the books of the ruling Politburo, don't quite rate the more prestigious Kremlin Wall. Nearby are

[5] To examine in more detail the character of this man who worked closely with Chou En-lai and influenced irrevocably the course of Chinese history, see my article, "Mysterious Borodin Sways South China," reprinted in full in the Appendix. Confirmation of many points of detail may also be found in *Personal History*, the first book-length work of my old friend Vincent Sheean, to whom I had later given an introduction to the Russian and who saw him the following year.

headstones marking the graves of Stalin's young wife—and, more recently, of Nikita Khrushchev.

It was through Borodin that I met the fabled Karl Radek. Following my 1926 summer in Canton, the Soviet adviser handed me a letter of introduction, along with the coveted Russian visa for which other Western correspondents in Asia had waited vainly for months. I left immediately and, following the ten-day train trip across Siberia, found myself one September morning dashing up the steps of Moscow's Sun Yat-sen University, mentioned earlier, and rapping firmly on the door marked "Rector."

It was opened by a short, stocky man with a simian face, high intellectual forehead, thick-lensed glasses, and a smile which completely filled the space between two enormous sideburns. I had of course heard of Radek, the legendary exile who shared Lenin's compartment on the sealed train in which, during the spring of 1917, the German General Staff sent them from Zurich to Petrograd to start the Russian Revolution.

Borodin's letter moved my host to roll out the red carpet. Radek introduced me to his three hundred students from all over the Far East (including, I discovered later, Chiang Kai-shek's son, Chiang Ching-kuo). These were mainly alert young Chinese, who were as delighted as the Russians were nervous to discover that I spoke their language. Radek showed me through lecture rooms vivid with charts illustrating the materialist interpretation of history, the doctrine of the class struggle, the rise of British and American imperialism, and practical revolutionary tactics such as how to infiltrate an army, dominate a government, capture a conference, liquidate the landlords, enlist the peasants, win labor. On many evenings, classes were adjourned to the Moscow Art or Meyerhold theaters for a series of indoctrination propaganda plays. I saw one that caricatured British foreign policy in the Orient—Britain, not America, was then the chief enemy—which was calculated to leave the innocent onlooker limp with rage and wondering if there could ever have been such a thing as a decent Englishman.

It had never been any mystery why Moscow should take more than an academic interest in China's nationalist movement: the Soviet Government, to secure an ally; the Third International, a convert. But I had often wondered how they ever contrived to interest the Russian people in this military campaign of a foreign political faction thousands of miles away. I wondered no longer after seeing the play.

The title—*Roar, China*—well describes this brilliant piece of revolutionary stagecraft, based on just enough truth regarding Western exploitation of Asia's masses to lend it plausibility and impact. As a spectacle, acted with passionate intensity on the curtainless Meyerhold floorboards, the play gripped the audience from beginning to end. As a breeder of class and race hate it was superb.

The scene is laid in a Chinese village on the upper Yangtze, with a swarm of coolies squatting near the riverbank. Beyond this group the *Cockchafer* (it was hardly coincidence that the name was that of the British gunboat that had shelled Wanhsien two weeks before) stands against the current, with its bridge and turret and six-inch guns raised well above the stage.

An American oil merchant, in daring sports costume, rushes in and orders the coolies to unload his cargo. They haggle over payment and, through an officious comprador, or middleman, he appears to name a satisfactory figure. The coolies hurry through the job and gather, a panting, sweating crowd, to receive their pay. Meanwhile the merchant has reconsidered and finally offers a price far below what they had been led to expect. There is a howl, of course, but the comprador manhandles several of them, the American withdraws in lofty contempt, and the coolies, all except one or two, sulkily accept their few cents apiece. Two foreign tourists—father and daughter—arrive, and the father holds out a shining dollar to induce one kindly old Chinese to face the daughter's outstretched camera. The gray-haired laborer raises wondering eyes toward the biggest sum of money he has ever seen, the shutter clicks, the dollar is withdrawn, and the foreigners depart in glee.

After a night of dancing and carousing with British officers and their wives aboard the *Cockchafer*, the American hails a sampan to take him ashore. Halfway across, a dispute starts over the fare. The American rises to strike the boatman and in so doing loses his balance, topples into the muddy current and is drowned. Terror-stricken, the sampan man tells the awful news to his fellow villagers and escapes into the hills.

Meanwhile, the *Cockchafer* bears down on the village with decks cleared for action. "One American is worth at least two

Chinese," the British commander has reflected. An ultimatum! For default in finding the guilty man, the village must surrender two members to the naval authorities before sundown as reprisal for the foreign life lost.

In a heartrending scene, the villagers discuss their plight. Finally, the old man who had been deprived of the dollar offers himself as one of the victims. "I am old," he sobs, "and of no more use in the world. Besides, I have a son to carry on the family name. I will give myself to satisfy the foreigner." His son tries to dissuade him, but to no purpose. Aboard the *Cockchafer* the city magistrate, a proud mandarin of the old order, kneels before the British commander to ask a commutation of sentence. With him kneels the interpreter, a young American-trained Chinese. "One is enough," they beg. "The old man has volunteered. Let it be life for life!" The Englishman smiles sardonically and turns his back. The young Chinese springs up and shakes a trembling fist. Bluejackets jump forward, and the two are hustled off the ship.

That afternoon lots are drawn for the one who must accompany the old man to death, and the lot falls on his son. Armed British sailors guard the place of execution and the *Cockchafer* officers, who attend in a body. A foreign priest supports a towering cross with the inscription "Peace on Earth, Good Will to Men," and by his side an American reporter crouches with his camera stripped for action. The prisoners, pinioned together with a great wooden yoke, arrive under escort.

Frantic, the mother and child of the young man throw themselves at the feet of the British commander, imploring mercy. The gold-braided figure shakes his head. A woman missionary steps forward to remind the mother and child of their Christianity. They must be reconciled to God's will, she says.

The coolies rush the British, but a row of gleaming bayonets quells the outburst, and the executioner makes ready. The victims are strapped, each to a post, and blindfolded. Strangle cords are looped around their throats. When all is ready and the cameraman is in position to catch the fatal moment, an order is shouted. The cords are tightened, the camera clicks, and two limp yellow figures tell the tale of British justice.

"How are we to save ourselves from these imperialist cutthroats?" shouts a ragged coolie as the *Cockchafer* steams away. The young student who served as interpreter for the city magistrate the day before leaps upon a bench, arms raised in fierce denunciation. "There is only one way. Follow the example of the laborers in Canton and Hankow. Organize! You cannot beg justice. You must force it!"

I can still see, as the lights came on, the outraged faces of the red-bandannaed Soviet Komsomol[6] girls in the front rows, and the grim ranks of Asian youth surrounding me. For a full two minutes there was neither sound nor movement in the theater. Then the audience filed silently out.

Back at Sun Yat-sen University the briefing was resumed. An intensive two-year course, my host explained, was the minimum needed to produce hardened ideological fighters. He praised the Chinese as apt pupils, told eagerly of similar schools for other Asian trainees, as well as for German, French, Italian, Spanish and British Communist leaders, and asked if I, as a fellow Harvard man, did not feel proud of young John Reed, earliest Comintern immortal, whose ashes lay imbedded in the Kremlin Wall.

My farewell to Radek produced a memorable scene. On the University steps the Soviet Union's most versatile propagandist gripped my hand. Then his eyes took on the faraway gleam one used to see in so many "old Bolsheviks." "Mr. Roots," he said, as if reading my mind, "these young men and women may not impress you much now. But come back in twenty years and they will be running China. You will see! You will see! Goodbye, goodbye!" And the face of Karl Radek, who had never set foot in Asia, expanded in a grin of apocalyptic assurance—that same confident, ebullient, militant grin which observers once noted about Lenin, and which later, before he fell from grace, became the special symbol of Nikita Khrushchev's faith in a Communist future.

Radek's sensational prophecy struck me at the time as pure and simple bombast—so much so that I did not even trouble to file a story on it, or even to report the incident in a long series of articles in the American press. Yet twenty-two years later Communist troops, having conquered the North, were pouring south across the Yangtze River, and by the autumn of 1949—

[6] Young Communist League of the Soviet Union, generally corresponding in Russian revolutionary history to the Red Guards of recent years in China.

twenty-three years after the Radek pronouncement (and long after his own death in a Stalin purge)—graduates of Sun Yat-sen University were among the leadership group who founded the People's Republic of China.

So much for the Sino-Soviet honeymoon—a far-off era which formed the background for Chou's and the Chinese Communist Party's emergence on the world scene. It was an intensely germinal era, almost wholly neglected in histories of Chinese Communism, but which, in the current kaleidoscope of international politics, might just conceivably re-emerge one day to haunt the regime of a Henry Kissinger successor.

CHAPTER IV

CHAPTER IV

SINO-SOVIET SPLIT

Like many honeymoons, that between Communist Russia and Communist China had its stormy moments. From the beginning the alliance was frankly a marriage of convenience, and it is only surprising that it lasted as long as it did—1923 to 1927—four years of increasing bitterness and frustration, with only the common antagonism toward the West and toward the northern warlords to hold it together.

My own interview with the new Commander-in-Chief General Chiang Kai-shek in the early summer of 1926 was to be, I was told, the last before he left for the North at the head of his troops. Apparently, it was also the first given an American correspondent. Certainly, as far as the world press was concerned, he was still almost completely unknown.

Though divorced from his first wife, Chiang was not yet married to Soong Mei-ling. He had already fathered a son—the seventeen-year-old Chiang Ching-kuo, whom I was to meet later that autumn at Sun Yat-sen University in Moscow, and who became Premier of the Republic of China government in Taiwan.

General Chiang Kai-shek was at that time not yet forty, and in the manner of so many Chinese still looked to a Westerner incredibly youthful—so youthful, in fact, that, since he was not in uniform, I mistook him for the houseboy. I had telephoned one Saturday for an appointment, and though he was then due to leave for the North on Monday (the departure was later postponed a few days), he agreed to receive me at once, and I dashed over through Canton's steamy summer streets to the secluded little house that served as home and headquarters.

"Is the General at home?" I inquired of the slim, clean-cut young man who opened the door.

"I am the General," he replied without embarrassment, and promptly led me inside to sip tea and study the military map that completely covered his study wall. It showed in outline the road his armies were so soon to follow—to Changsha and my old hometown of Wuhan on the Yangtze, and concurrently to Shanghai and Nanking.

Chiang, clearly under the spell of his visit to Russia, still talked the language of revolution, used Communist phraseology, and spoke with great reverence of his mentor, Sun Yat-sen. He confirmed to me that Dr. Sun, in the last days of his life, in early 1925, had not only stressed the importance of the Soviet Alliance, but had also redefined the third of his "Three People's Principles"—People's Livelihood. "It is socialism," Sun had explained, "or you could call it Communism."

Before we parted, Chiang spoke warmly of Borodin, scrawling the brief introduction mentioned earlier and thus setting up the interviews recorded in the previous chapter. Significantly, he did not more than mention Chou En-lai—clearly the chasm of political philosophy between them was already wide and deep. But I ran into the CCP leader several times that Canton summer of 1926, going or coming from Borodin's office or at the Whampoa Academy where he taught.

In July, Chiang headed north with the Kuomintang Revolutionary First Army. With him went Borodin, together with General Gallen, chief of the Soviet military advisers (originally sent by Lenin to accompany Borodin), who had increased in number to about two hundred and were scattered throughout the Kuomintang forces. They were mostly volunteers from Russia's Red Army, but they were supposed not to talk politics. Their work was technical. They furnished aviation experts, strategists, artillery instructors and drill sergeants, and much credit for the efficiency of the Cantonese forces under Chiang in a purely military sense must go to them. When I visited Peking in August, one of the northern warlords had three thousand "White Russians"— Tsarist refugees from the Soviet regime—incorporated into a crack division of his troops. Their position was akin to that of the Hessians who fought with the British in 1776 against the American revolutionaries. But the Soviet experts attached to Chiang's forces were different in that their position was purely advisory, like that of Lafayette, Steuben, and others who gave their services to Washington. They were not formally enrolled in the KMT forces, and under no circumstances were they to fire on any Chinese.

The route of General Chiang's expeditionary force extended over eight hundred miles along one of the ancient highway links between Canton and North China. There were one hundred and forty miles of railway on the southern section of this line of march, and a two-hundred-and-twenty-mile strip just south of the Yangtze. Aside from this, the rest of the journey—a distance of some four hundred and fifty miles—had to be made overland and on foot; there were difficult mountains to cross, and the old flagstone highway dating back a thousand years had never been intended for anything more speedy than wheelbarrows or sedan chairs. Only a few weeks before, I had myself traversed this route in the opposite direction. The chief highway interest was an occasional sedan-chair caravan bearing some high official to or from the capital. I recall covering over fifty miles one seemingly endless rainy day. With my pack I averaged about three miles an hour, arriving exhausted late at night at my destination and with a new respect for the Chinese foot soldier who had to carry his rifle as well.

The National Revolutionary Army had no big guns. Even if they had had them, they obviously could not have been dragged over hundreds of miles of mountain, plain and river. The immediate and dramatic success attending their early advance was principally due to a unique factor that had already come to distinguish the growing Communist element among the Nationalist forces. This factor was an innovative idea that put the ignorant masses not last, as in the North, but first. The country people recognized in such an attitude the antithesis of the feudal "war-

lordism" that for a decade had enslaved their manhood, outraged their womanhood and confiscated their meager earnings.
It would not be peace and order all at once for them under
southern rule, but if there must be authority—and everyone knew
the nation needed a firm hand—it would be the authority not of a
few self-seeking militarists but of men and women like themselves.

The ovations that greeted the revolutionary troops during
their advance north into Central China were quite spontaneous.
A letter from an officer-graduate of Whampoa Academy to a Chinese friend at Sun Yat-sen University in Moscow, gives a glimpse
of what was going on between Canton and the Yangtze River
during that strenuous August of 1926:

> Our units proved vastly superior owing to their rela-
> tively greater political consciousness. . . . This was evi-
> dent from the very beginning when, during our ad-
> vance into new territories, the population manifested no
> fear but greeted us with open arms. I am writing as a
> witness of the triumphal welcome given to the National
> Armies by the local population. Tired out by the long
> day's march on foot (our only means of locomotion), I
> was daily obliged to address the people in the name of
> the Kuomintang and on behalf of our generals. What a
> pity I am not an artist that I might transcribe these
> wonderful night welcomes when the people, hearing of
> our coming, flocked out from miles around with colored
> lanterns, national music and singing. There is no other
> army in China which devotes such attention to political
> work, appeals, illustrated placards. Pamphlets are being
> printed in millions of copies, and there is not a remote
> hamlet through which the National Army has passed
> where these placards, appeals and revolutionary orders
> of our generals are not posted.[1]

In these days of the northern expedition, Chou En-lai first
gave promise on a nationwide scale of those extraordinary qualities which, for half a century to come, contributed so much to
holding together first the Communist Party, and then China.

[1] John McCook Roots, "The Canton Idea," *Asia*, April 1927, p. 349.

He began by supplying the indispensable liaison between the KMT's General Chiang, Borodin with his Soviet colleagues, and Mao Tse-tung, who was never enamored of either the Russians or the city proletariat, with his budding Canton Peasant Movement Training Institute. Because of this versatility, Chou was the only man who, from the beginning, consistently held top posts in the three key fields of Army, Party and Government.

Chou's army experience had begun as early as 1925, when Sun Yat-sen himself appointed him Political Commissar, under Chiang, of Whampoa Military Academy. Thereafter, for over fifty years, he held a permanent place on the CCP's military commission—a service for which the CCP was later to pay him tribute as having laid the foundation for China's future Red Army.

Chou's party pre-eminence had come even earlier. Indeed, he was already a high-ranking Party cadre when Mao, holding lesser posts in Hunan, at one point came close to expulsion from the Communist ranks. Chou's government experience, of course, had to await the creation of the People's Republic in 1949.

Chou's revolutionary concepts for the next few years closely paralleled Moscow's, and were to bring him at one point (August 1932), along with most of China's Communist leadership at that time, into direct confrontation with Mao. Only two and a half years later did his changed views bring him to the position which he was to hold until his death four decades later as Mao's closest colleague and supporter.

But before the key relationship with Mao could be further defined, the Chou-Borodin alliance of expediency with Chiang against the warlords had to be resolved. Each side knew exactly where the other stood. And although Mao had his differences with the Russians—and at that time even with Chou—these were nothing compared to the irrepressible and inevitable antagonisms implicit in the relations of both of them with Chiang Kai-shek and the Kuomintang's conservative and increasingly reactionary right wing.

It was as if both schools of Chinese Kuomintang politics, right and left, were reminding each other that, although each realized an eventual clash was inevitable, each also knew a wider arena was necessary for such a clash, and had agreed, while advancing toward a common goal, to postpone it.

The day of reckoning was, in fact, imminent. By the time I had left Canton for Moscow that summer of 1926, both the right-wing Kuomintang generals under Chiang, and their left-wing counterparts accompanied by the Borodins and the Soviet advisers, were moving northwards. Chou had already proceeded northeast to Shanghai. The Borodins, with the Kuomintang left-wing forces, headed directly for Hankow, where they remained with the Communist and more liberal elements of the expeditionary forces. All across the trans-Siberian express route to Moscow, to the delight of my Russian fellow passengers, victory bulletins continued to pour in from Central China, and were the first subject discussed by a jubilant Karl Radek in the Soviet capital when I arrived.

Meanwhile Chiang wheeled northeast toward Nanking and Shanghai to join up with Chou. The teeming metropolis of Shanghai, the major industrial target in largely rural China, was the key common objective for both Chiang and Chou.

Chou, first on the spot and already well-entrenched, had the initial advantage. He commanded the loyalty of thousands of workers whom he had spent months organizing into fighting units. He knew that if he let Chiang take over Shanghai without resisting him, he would be betraying the revolutionary cause of these workers. Since he and Chiang were still allies, it was a dilemma.

As Chiang's troops drew nearer, Chou launched a series of general strikes. But his workers were poorly armed and trained, and by the spring of 1927 it seemed likely that the General's disciplined troops would carry the day.

Chiang Kai-shek, for his part, was also faced with a dilemma. He knew he could never control Shanghai without the help of its banks, commercial establishments and foreign support. These international bankers, traders and foreign-backed political leaders, to whom of course Communism was anathema, had warned the General that he must either break with Chou or forfeit all support from them and their foreign allies.

This, Chiang realized, he could not afford to do. Furthermore, he knew from his Canton experience that the ultimate Communist aim was to take over the Kuomintang from within. The KMT-CCP alliance had always been an uneasy one. He decided the time had come to end it.

Chou, of course, was wholly unaware of Chiang's *volte face*. On March 20, 1927, as darkness came over the city, he personally mobilized three hundred labor supporters and stormed the post office, police headquarters and ordnance depot. Seven of his armed columns had spread throughout the city, capturing the railroad station. This meant that Chiang's expeditionary forces, which had been rapidly approaching the suburbs, could not enter the city as planned. For three weeks Shanghai was shaken by sporadic strikes and armed clashes.

Chiang Kai-shek eventually arrived in Shanghai by gunboat. At 4 A.M. on April 12, his forces, which had been marking time outside the city, entered with orders to shoot every armed man on sight. Dumbfounded at being attacked by their presumed allies, Chou En-lai's poorly equipped and ill-trained labor-union squads fought back as best they could. But they were no match for regular troops.

Thus began the general massacre of Communists which officially launched China's long and agonizing civil war—not the original Kuomintang-Communist joint attack against the warlords, but the far more basic and bitter life-or-death struggle between the erstwhile allies: the Kuomintang under Chiang Kai-shek, and the Communists under Chou and Mao. This civil war was to continue intermittently, with prodigal barbarities on both sides, till the ultimate Communist victory nearly a quarter century later.

Chiang's "bloodbath" phase of the civil war lasted a full year (1927–28), and in that period reduced the total Chinese Party membership from sixty thousand to ten thousand cadres. For weeks in Shanghai the tumbrils could be heard making their nightly excursions to the execution grounds in the suburb of Lunghua. For Chou it was an incalculable loss.[2] These were the cream of his comrades—the men and women who would have

[2] Edgar Snow, *The Battle for Asia*, pp. 124–25.
"Chiang's Nanking Government made it a crime punishable by death to be a Communist or a member of any organization or union considered as such by the 'purified Kuomintang.' Thousands of radical leaders, students, officers, soldiers, and members of workers' and farmers' unions were killed . . . The Communists went about redistributing the land and organizing local workers' and peasants' governments, while Chiang Kai-shek went after them, bringing back the landlord system, . . . and executing the rebels and smashing their unions."

been running China after 1949—and the Party's top leadership
would have to be largely reconstituted.

Chou En-lai himself was fortunate. During the first hours of
the purge, disguised and under an alias, he found shelter in the
building of the city's chief newspaper, the *Commercial Press*, escaping from his hideout only moments before a KMT search
party, hot on his trail, reached the building. Eventually rounded
up, along with many other suspects, he was imprisoned by General Pai Ch'ung-hsi and told he would be shot in the morning.
Toward midnight he felt himself being shaken awake and recognized one of his former Whampoa cadets, who silently beckoned
him to follow. As they emerged into the dark Shanghai streets,
the sentries ostentatiously looked the other way. Deftly dodging
Chiang's police, who had posted his picture all over Shanghai,
Chou escaped upriver to Hankow.

Chou's principal Communist colleagues suffered a tragic fate.
Two dozen of his oldest comrades, many of them members of the
Shanghai Municipal Council, were rounded up, tortured and
shot.

By contrast, these were landmark years for the Commander-in-
Chief personally. On December 1, 1927, Chiang Kai-shek married Soong Mei-ling, the beautiful daughter of one of the
wealthiest businessmen in China. Chiang's fiancée, whose father
had been a prominent Christian convert until his recent death,
was eager that the General accept the family's religion.[3]

This was in fact the way it worked out. The two were married; Chiang studied the new creed apparently with zeal and
sincerity, and eventually adopted it as his own. It lasted a lifetime—until his death at eighty-seven—and seems, on the personal
level, to have been considerably more than the conventional faith
of many Western statesmen. Churchill records in his memoirs of

---

[3] My father would occasionally tell privately the story of the courtship
as he had learned it from the couple themselves: The young general had
come to the redoubtable Madame Soong, a devout church-goer of the
old school, to ask for her daughter's hand. "Are you a Christian?" she asked.
"I cannot allow my daughter to marry a non-Christian." Looking her straight
in the eye he replied, "Madame, are you trying to bribe me into becoming
a Christian?" The old lady, duly impressed, said, "No, I am not," to which
he responded, "I promise you one thing. If you let me marry your daughter,
I will make a thorough study of your religion and, if I find it has the
answers for my country, and for me personally, I will become a Christian,
and under no other circumstances."

the wartime Cairo Conference his amazement at seeing the light go on in the Generalissimo's hotel bedroom at Mena House near the Pyramids regularly every morning at 5 A.M. It was the Chief of the Chinese Delegation, with his Bible, at his early-morning devotions.

Chou meanwhile had reached Hankow in late April, and set out to consolidate his forces with Borodin, Ch'en Yi (later Peking's Foreign Minister), and others at the famous Yangtze River port.

Starting point of the 1911 revolution which overthrew China's Empire, the great industrial city where I was born and raised was now in a fever of fresh revolutionary activity. Wang Ch'ing-wei, first KMT government head after Sun Yat-sen and chairman of the left-wing Hankow government, had just denounced Chiang Kai-shek for his Shanghai purge. Chiang had responded by outlawing the Wang regime and, on April 18, setting up a new national government at Nanking.

Mao Tse-tung meanwhile had organized two million peasants to seize land in the Hunan-Hupeh area surrounding Hankow, setting up "people's courts" to try the landlords and local bosses who refused to surrender their property. Militant labor unions had been formed in the cities to instigate insurrections.

Such upheavals, nurtured and spread throughout the winter and spring of 1926–27, increasingly alarmed the international community of Hankow, confined within the five-mile-long narrow strip of riverfront that formed the five foreign "concessions" —British, ex-Russian, French, German and Japanese. Letters from home (my father had remained in Hankow, but my mother had been evacuated along with most foreign women and children) had told of the daily demonstrations, the attack on the British municipal buildings near our house and the ferment among our own servants and Chinese friends.

The Bishop's house was frequently visited by foreign correspondents keen to get the latest news—among them my colleague Vincent Sheean, whose Hankow experience formed the main theme of his first best-seller, *Personal History*. Anna Louise Strong, the mercurial American writer-revolutionary, shuttled back and forth between her varied sources of information— government offices, newspaper desks, Father's dinner table and the rooms where Mikhail Borodin held counsel. She and the mysterious Russian were known among most foreigners as "the unpredictable Bolsheviks."

Chou En-lai, on the other hand, was then virtually unknown to foreigners and Chinese alike. His work lay with the Communists and others around Borodin who were concerned with policy and strategy. For this he needed all his innate diplomatic skill. Moscow's directives were urging the CCP to ally themselves with the left-wing KMT. Many military leaders, enthusiastic about the KMT but not necessarily about Communism, had been pressuring the government to use violence. As a result, Communist-led strikers had latterly been mowed down or arrested on orders of Wang and his Hankow government.

Chou's comrades were naturally indignant. "Are we to accept their spitting and beating without any right to speak up in protest?" said one. "Are we somebody's concubine?"

"Comrade Liu," Chou replied, "we must be patient—very patient. For the sake of our revolution we can play the role of a concubine, even of a prostitute if need be . . ."[4]

Meanwhile in Moscow, Stalin's policies were winning against those of Trotsky, and the long arm of the Comintern reached out, in effect directing the Hankow comrades to do the impossible. Urged to seize political leadership from the KMT, infiltrate their army with as many Communists as possible, and accelerate the peasant confiscation of land, Chou finally realized the depth of his dilemma.

"If we break with the KMT," he said, "it would help our worker-peasant movement, but militarily we would suffer." He needed time—to demonstrate obedience to KMT leaders while strengthening his infiltration into their army. Reluctantly he directed his comrades to lay down their arms and take orders from the KMT government.

It was already too late. The Comintern envoy, M. N. Roy—a Trotsky man opposed to Borodin—had shown the secret Moscow directive to a shocked Wang Ch'ing-wei, and the Communists were doomed. On July 20, 1927—only a brief three months from the time he escaped the Shanghai purge—Chou was forced once more into hiding as the ruthless hunt began. The streets of Hankow were bathed in blood and heads rolled on the boule-

[4] Hsu, *Chou En-lai*, p. 69.

vard by the tree-shaded bund where the British and American Navy bands of my boyhood, bagpipes skirling and horns blaring, had once paraded to church on a Sunday morning from their gunboats in the river.

Chou took refuge in the British Concession, and I have been told authoritatively by a former Hankow resident that the future Premier once confided to the widow of Dag Hammarskjöld's Swedish interpreter that he owed his life to my father. Certainly Father had never told any of our family—as indeed he would not. Far from emphasizing political points of view, the Bishop was a concerned and compassionate man who, in earlier years, had offered the sanctuary of our home in the British Concession to other endangered Chinese, including a number of Sun Yat-sen's associates in the 1911 Revolution. Though my father never spoke of these things, the facts about Chou would undoubtedly have been known by at least one or two of Chou's Hankow friends.

Escaping from this brief hideout in Hankow, Chou fled downriver to Nanchang, capital of Kiangsi Province where, on July 25, he rejoined General Chu Teh, just returned from Germany. The two men, now freed from all obligations to the Kuomintang governments of Nanking and Hankow, prepared at last to launch the Chinese Communist Party on its eventful independent career.

Chou and Chu Teh's Communist uprising in Nanchang was set for midnight on August 1, 1927. With the support of the local army commander, their new government maintained itself for two days before being overwhelmed by the Kuomintang's superior forces and compelled to flee south. Their retreat that summer of 1927 was a rout. Their forces were scattered. Their supplies and funds lost, Chou, with a fever of 104, sick, penniless and in rags, barely managed to make his way to the coast and escape by sampan to Hong Kong. Chu Teh eventually joined Mao in the West in Chingkangshan.

But though the Nanchang operation was, by any conventional standard, a debacle, in the perspective of the years it was to prove historic. By this desperate action Chou En-lai and Chu Teh forever broke the parasitic bonds that bound the Communist Party to the Kuomintang, and gave the party its independent existence on the Chinese political scene. Ever afterward, August 1 has been celebrated among China's Communists as Red Army Day.

Characteristically—Chou En-lai was always the most resilient of men—only a brief recuperation was needed to fit him once more for the fray. Summer had hardly turned to autumn before he was back again in Shanghai, settled in an "underground" establishment with his wife Teng Ying-ch'ao, continuing to plot and plan as if no setbacks had ever occurred. Mao, with Chu Teh in Mao's "Kiangsi Soviet,"[5] was beginning finally to give the Chinese brand of Communism, as distinguished from the Russian, its own distinctly rural—and ideological—stamp.

The iron hand of Stalin,[6] however, was to continue for several more years to weigh heavily on the Chinese comrades. The Soviet dictator and his colleagues treated all Asians with condescension, particularly the Chinese, whose ancestors had, in fact, been an exceptionally superior human breed for some four thousand years—the longest continuous record of independent civilization on earth.

It followed naturally, in Moscow's thinking, that the strategy in China was a mere appendage of the overall Moscow plan, and that the comrades in that country were dispensable and expendable at the whim of their master in the Kremlin. Thus, when Stalin happened to need a foreign-policy coup—as he did in December 1927—the word went forth and a commune was hurriedly set up in Canton. Unhappily, due to impossible local conditions of which Moscow knew little and seemingly cared less, it was able to maintain itself for only two days—the eleventh and twelfth. It then promptly collapsed, but only after the slaughter of many more Chinese Party members.

The loss in a single year, however, of five sixths of China's carefully nurtured sixty-thousand-member Communist Party was more than even Stalin could put up with. In the summer of 1928,

[5] This early center of Chinese Communism, initiated by Mao some time before the Long March, has been described by a leading French scholar as "the key experiment of the Chinese Revolution." For a fuller description, see Bianco, Origins, pp. 61, 63–64.

[6] For a penetrating analysis of the influence of Russia's Stalin-Trotsky feud on the Kuomintang-Communist struggle in China—and Stalin's costly misreading of the situation—see Fairbank, United States and China, pp. 228–32.

1. Young Chou in his late teens in 1919. It was in these Tokyo-Tientsin years that he became a noted student leader and "first encountered Marxism and began furiously to ponder China's past."

2. Chou En-lai in Paris in 1922, where he founded the Communist Youth Corps. During these early years in France, Germany and England he enlisted many future leaders of the Peking regime and formed his unique lifelong understanding of the West.

3. In Canton during the Sino-Soviet honeymoon of 1925–26. In Kuomintang officer's uniform he worked closely with the youthful Commander-in-Chief, Chiang Kai-shek, Soviet Adviser Borodin and his aide, Ho Chi-minh, and was political instructor at Whampoa Military Academy, southern China's West Point.

4. At the end of the famous six-thousand-mile Long March (Oct. 1934–Oct. 1935), a gaunt and bearded Chou En-lai was photographed by American journalist Edgar Snow, who had penetrated China's Civil War blockade to interview Mao and Chou.

5. The Sian Incident, December 1936. Chou at Yenan airport on his return from the dramatic "kidnaping" of Chiang Kai-shek which initiated China's "United Front" against Japan—a major factor in the Allied victory in World War II.

6. Red China's "Big Three," from right to left, a lean and rangy Mao Tse-tung, an ebullient Chu Teh, and a now beardless Chou in Yenan prior to Japan's Marco Polo Bridge attack in mid-1937, which launched her invasion of China and a decade of desperate Chinese resistance.

7. Chou and his wife Teng Ying-ch'iao in Hankow, March 1938—"the high-water mark of the United Front." Chou autographed this photo and presented it to the author's father after their series of intimate private talks.

Chou and his then closest colleague, Li Li-san, were summoned to Moscow.

Stalin and the Soviet Politburo, however, were both ignorant of Chinese conditions, and scornful of China's Asian leadership. The two Chinese comrades were called before Bukharin, upbraided for their failure in the cities and, oddly enough, admonished not to change this city policy, but simply *to push it harder*. In other words, they were to go home and continue to establish Soviet regimes throughout China, build up a united Red Army, and win over the masses of the people in anticipation of "an upsurge of the high tide of world revolution which is imminent."

Faced with Moscow's ill-informed and self-defeating directives, Chou and Li returned to China and to three years of relentless activity under humanly impossible conditions. They and their comrades in the Central Committee had no secure base of operation in Shanghai, where their clandestine organization was under daily threat from the Secret Police.

While Li Li-san was secretary-general of the CCP, Chou as head of its organization department was charged with rebuilding a Party which had been virtually wiped out during Chiang's year-long "white reign of terror." At the same time he headed up the military department with official responsibility for recruiting a Red Army in the provinces. The major bulk of this potential strength lay in widely scattered Communist units—one of them under Mao Tse-tung—operating out of remote inaccessible areas. The motley origins of this embryo Red Army—ex-bandits, defected KMT troops and landless peasants—urgently necessitated a political indoctrination and retraining as important as their reoutfitting. Yet communication with these units was a nightmare filled with the threat of death, its lifeline the secret supply route along the Yangtze River. Chou was responsible for the security of this lifeline.

In addition to Moscow's myopic dictates, the Chinese Communist Party itself was also faced with internal disintegration as its clashing personalities erupted into intense intraparty strife. Mao Tse-tung in the rural areas disagreed with Li Li-san and his urban Central Committee. Li Li-san disagreed with the Comintern in Moscow. Chou's task demanded a reconciling of opposing elements while upholding the theoretical correctness of Moscow's leadership. At times he had to reprove Mao and apologize for Li, while trying to prevent the liquidation of hundreds of troops, their commanders and even some Central Committee members in the violent fratricidal upheavals.

Chou's chief problem, however, was how to interpret Moscow's ambiguous directives, alternating as they did between a watchful "wait and see" policy and a demand for armed insurrection. On June 11, 1930, Li, "China's self-styled Lenin," won over the Central Committee in Shanghai to his belief that the "revolutionary high tide" was imminent. Orders were issued to all Communist military forces in the countryside to march on the urban areas and seize national power. Mao Tse-tung, as opposed as ever to Moscow's "city strategy," reluctantly complied, obediently attacked Changsha, and promptly lost two thousand more Party cadres slaughtered in that city alone.

Though China's Communist leadership preserved a public display of unity, it seems this bitter experience privately convinced Mao that, for many reasons, the Chinese Revolution had to take a different path from the Russian, and that if his own Chinese comrades did not come to understand this, he might one day have to go it alone. In fact, as everyone knows, Mao's views were to prevail sooner than anyone had expected.

Meanwhile Chou En-lai's stature grew—as it had already begun to develop first in Paris and then in Canton—as the one harmonizing personality on China's Party scene. When he again visited Moscow in the summer of 1930, he was met this time by top Soviet officials and treated as the acknowledged leader of Chinese Communism. The youth of Sun Yat-sen University, it should be noted, though influential later, were still too young to count in policy decisions back home.

On his return from this second official visit to Moscow, Chou issued a thoughtful document, celebrated in Party history as the Shao-shan Report, analyzing the current situation and making clear the secret of his genius for getting Party rebels to work together. The secret seems to have been the simple, but rare, virtue of being candid about his own personal errors. In one notable passage Chou states: "It is clear there has been some difference between the Comintern and the [Chinese] Central Committee in their evaluation of revolutionary readiness throughout the country . . . The Central Committee made exaggerated and inaccurate estimates of the speed and degree of development of the revolution, planning again on the basis of a situation that was yet to come. These tactical mistakes were made. *I myself committed mistakes* [italics added]. We accepted the criticism of the Comintern and point out that Comrade Li Li-san should shoulder more responsibilities in ideological interpretation, but we must not tolerate irritating remarks made by other comrades aimed personally and individually at Li Li-san . . . We should carry out self-criticism on a collective basis."[7]

Characteristically, Chou backed Li, both as titular head of the Party and because of his demonstrated ability, though the latter's ambitious and overbearing attitude increasingly alienated everyone else. At a subsequent conclave when Li was forced to recant, Chou typically redistributed his Shao-shan Report with a simple and disarming comment: "I am releasing it so that our Party can identify and recognize my error; and I myself shall also criticize this persistent, serious error in our Party organs."

In the midst of all this deadly dangerous clandestine activity, pursued relentlessly by General Chiang's police and with an astronomical price on his handsome head, Chou and his wife managed to live a wholly different side of their multifaceted lives in the house of his foster parents on Seymour Road in Shanghai's foreign Concession. Here, in the quiet protected area patrolled by the foreign-controlled Settlement Police, the young couple could come and go as unobtrusively as scores of other Chinese who could afford such a standard of living. As a schoolboy in Shanghai, I would often pass these long-gowned, elegantly groomed gentlemen and their ladies, dismounting from their rickshaws, or being driven off by uniformed chauffeurs. Those who dressed in the Western-style suits and ties were hard to distinguish from the foreign businessmen whose pattern of life gave this part of the city its European and often British flavor.

Chou's sister-in-law, Ma Shun-yi, who had married his profligate foster brother En-chu, under the old custom by which the Chinese wife is picked by his parents, openly admired and envied Chou and Teng, who had married for love and showed it. Ma's recollections of this period in Shanghai are invaluable for the picture they give of a side of Chou previously unknown. She and her family had no reason to connect him in any way with reports of Communist activities throughout the country which were beginning to appear from time to time in the press. Certainly not with the gruesome evidence, later unearthed by the police in the French Concession, of several persons clearly buried alive and probably in revenge for some grave act of Party apostasy.

Shun-yi envied her brother-in-law for having traveled and studied abroad and admired him for his apparently important work in "the government." Like most women of her class, she would have no interest in the specifics of his type of government work. To the servants of the household he was their Seventh Young Master, who could do no wrong—unlike her husband, their Thirteenth Young Master, who seemed to cause nothing but trouble.

Her memories of Teng Ying-ch'ao are of an attractive, warmhearted young person, vivacious, much given to laughter and chatter. She found it impossible to be bitter herself when she remembered how Ying-ch'ao would reach out under the dining-room table and squeeze her hand gently in sympathy. When she felt most depressed, En-lai's brotherly concern and understanding helped her bear with her own fate. She remarked especially on the childless Chou's solicitude for her own youngsters.

One evening he had turned to her and said: "Last night I woke up hearing one of the children crying. Was it the older or the younger one? Are you sure they have enough to cover them at night?"

"It was the younger one," replied Shun-yi. "I guess it was just a stomach upset. He was all right this morning."

"We had better make sure," said Chou, and turned to his wife. "There is an extra new quilt on our bed. After dinner, take it over and put it on the children's bed."

"The quilt won't do. The children just kick it off in their sleep," said Teng. "I am just finishing knitting a sweater, and with a little sweater on, the children will never catch cold at night."

Chou's foster mother, who was very dear to him, had often noticed his special devotion to her son En-chu, and how hard he tried to get him to give up the bottle and turn over a new leaf. Many evenings he would announce they were both going to the theater. What she didn't know was that En-lai was secretly taking En-chu to Communist Party meetings in hopes that a new dedication would counteract old bad habits.

Another thing that impressed her was that every morning En-lai swept his own room, though she had urged him to let the servants do it. As for his cooking—Hsiang-yu (her name for Chou) "does very well in the kitchen," she remarked. "You girls had better not try to compete. I have tasted his cooking several times."

Perhaps what touched the old lady most deeply was Chou En-lai's reverence for his deceased grandfather. When the patriarch's birthday arrived, En-lai as eldest son took charge of preparations for the customary family memorial service, ordering the supplies and supervising the servants in erecting the altar. Before personally lighting the candles and incense sticks, he gave everything a final inspection, then arranged the cushions before kneeling at the altar. With great reverence he then burned three pieces of yellow paper carrying messages to the spirit world. And as the last piece flickered out, the old matriarch, known in the family as a sharply critical person, remarked to Shun-yi: "Hsiang-yu knows all the rules, and he does everything just right!"

This part of Chou's and Teng's Shanghai double-life took place in late 1928 and 1929. Chou's female in-laws apparently believed that, like most sons of gentry families who had successfully negotiated the old imperial examinations, he was waiting for a new government assignment and, when away from home for extended periods, was likely visiting one or other of the many members of the Chou clan.

Nor did they suspect anything when Chou and his wife finally, late in the spring of 1931, left home for good. For they did not see him disguise himself in a priest's black robe, with a long, dark beard, and board a small coastal vessel that landed him at an obscure port on the Fukien Coast, en route to Juichin to join Mao Tse-tung, Chu Teh and others at the capital of the Kiangsi Soviet.[8]

[8] When Chou En-lai disappeared from Shanghai, it was assumed by most that he was dead. A young American vice-consul named Edmund Clubb arrived that same spring in Hankow and, a year later, submitted a voluntary confidential report to the American Legation in Peking entitled, "Commu-

The next three to four years were critical for the Communist Party of China. Not only were Mao and Chou, isolated deep in the hinterland, cut off from all direct contact with Moscow, but Mao had reached two basic decisions for the future. One was, in essence, that since China was 80 per cent a nation of peasant farmers, with only a relatively infant industry, her revolution, unlike Russia's, must be essentially agricultural rather than proletarian. The second was that, long before any of his chief colleagues, Mao had come to favor a strategy of retreat, rather than a continuation of the suicidal attempt to meet the overpowering Kuomintang offensives with repeated and ineffectual counteroffensives. Consistently overruled by his colleagues, Mao, though loyally co-operating with Party policy, adhered to his own views on both counts.

The years following Chou En-lai's arrival at Juichin were chiefly important in bringing him gradually to the same conclusions as Mao.

Chou did not capitulate at once, or easily. With a long experience of travel abroad, he had firsthand knowledge of Moscow and the Soviet Union. Mao knew neither the Russians nor their country. In fact, he had yet to set foot outside China proper. But he possessed, above all his Party colleagues, an intuitive understanding of the Chinese people, their hopes and their needs. His mind was by now finally made up to act on his beliefs—if necessary, alone. Since Chou En-lai, no less dedicated, was a fair and open-minded man, he was gradually drawn to Mao's thinking. Eventually, as we will see, Chou resolved to make common cause with him.

Chou's decision was hastened by events. Chiang Kai-shek, aided by expert German advisers,[9] spent those three years in no less than five "annihilation" campaigns against the dwindling Communist forces. In April 1934, had come a disastrous Communist defeat on the Fukien-Kiangsi border. The forces of Chou and Mao left four thousand dead on the field, which, with

nism in China." This important document presents at the end a "List of Revolutionaries" and among them the following: "Chou En-lai—Chairman of Organisation Committee of CCP, executed in June 1931." See Clubb, *Communism in China: As Reported from Hankow in 1932*, p. 116.

[9] These had eventually replaced Chiang's Soviet advisers after his 1927 split with the Communists.

twenty thousand wounded, effectively crippled the main Red Army.

All this of course had a shattering military effect—even the Communist press admitted that desertions had become more deadly than Kuomintang armies. Their soldiers would commit suicide by putting a rifle to the throat and triggering it with a toe. But even more serious was the disharmony within the Communist ranks. Mao himself that summer was expelled for the third time from the Central Committee, barred from Party meetings, and even (on orders from Moscow) placed for a time under house arrest. Physically he was in bad shape, with a fever of 105°, and disheartened by the final failure of the offensive strategy he had all along disapproved.

During that summer of 1934, several Communist diversionary thrusts were made to confuse the enemy. Some partially succeeded, but others failed, and their leaders were exhibited in cages by the Kuomintang and then beheaded. Finally, in a climactic fifth campaign, Chiang Kai-shek directed a million men, heavily equipped with planes and artillery, in a furious four-pronged assault. By early autumn of 1934 it had become clear that the results of seven years of Mao's careful nurturing of his Central China base were about to be totally destroyed.

It was then, on the night of October 2, in a hurriedly assembled field conference within earshot of the approaching enemy guns, that Chou, Mao and Chu Teh met to decide what to do. There had been strong sentiment in favor of fighting a final battle with the enemy, but Chou reacted firmly against it, urging, out of his own experience, immediate withdrawal. Mao backed him strongly. None could see far ahead. They decided to move to Hunan, then possibly to Szechuan, Chu Teh's home in the Far West. Beyond that, no one could tell.

CHAPTER V

COMMISSAR OF THE LONG MARCH

Through the centuries large bodies of men have traversed large distances together, for many reasons, under differing conditions, with varying results. On the record, by any standard, the journey of the Chinese Communist army in our own era, known simply as the Long March, was incomparably the longest and most arduous, until recently one of the least known, and now generally recognized as perhaps the most historically pregnant of them all.

Edgar Snow's vivid vignette in his *Red Star Over China*[1] forty years ago is still the best: "Adventure, exploration, discovery, human courage and cowardice, ecstasy and triumph, suffering, sacrifice and loyalty, and then through it all, like a flame, an undimmed ardour and undying hope and amazing revolutionary optimism of those thousands of youth who would not admit defeat by man or nature or God or death—all this and more seemed embodied in the history of an odyssey unequalled in modern times."

Or in ancient times either. Snow notes that Hannibal's famous crossing of the Alps "looked like a holiday excursion beside it," while the military analyst General Samuel B. Griffith called it

[1] P. 177 (1938 ed.).

"an even more majestic achievement than the retreat of the ten thousand Greeks under Xenophon." He might also have pointed out that the men of the Red Army covered six thousand miles to Xenophon's one thousand, marched for a year instead of four months, and that far greater numbers were involved.

The English historian Dick Wilson summarizes the deep and enduring effects of the March on China's Communists themselves. He writes: "Their suspicious attitude toward the Soviet Union and their fierce independence of Moscow's tutelage; their distrust of the city as a modern institution and of urban life as a corrupting and demoralizing force; the unity, discipline and secrecy which characterized the conduct of their Party's affairs and their government's operations for so long; their idealism and simplicity, and their preference for the guerrilla ethic over the values of the technocrat; the long ascendancy of Mao Tse-tung over the Chinese Communist Party and in so many sectors of the world Communist movement as a whole—all these have their roots in the Long March."[2]

The decision to march has been much debated and many facts are still obscure. The one thing certain is that it was done as a move of desperation, under intolerable pressure, as a last resort, because not to retreat would have meant annihilation. The pride of international Communism, China's Kiangsi base, was to be abandoned, and the future looked bleak indeed.

From October 1934 to October 1935, Mao's and Chou's ragged, retreating, beleaguered troops disappeared from public view. But when the surviving eight thousand of the original ninety thousand arrived at the Caves of Yenan in the far Northwest, the tide of China's civil war—though anything but clear at the time—had turned irrevocably.

The physical start of the Long March proper has been recorded by Mao's orderly: "Around five o'clock on the evening of October 16, Mao and about twenty others left Yutu (southwest of Nanchang in Kiangsi) by the North Gate, and then turned to the left towards the river, which was all yellow, roaring and foaming as though calling on the armies to advance. Soon the sun set and the gusts of bitter wind chilled us. The Chairman wore a gray cloth uniform and an eight-cornered military cap,

2 Dick Wilson, *The Long March*, 1935, p. xv.

with no overcoat. He walked with enormous strides along the river bank."[3]

As far as the Kuomintang forces knew, this retreat by Mao, and another led by Chou, were only two of many Communist thrusts. The secrecy of the entire operation duly misled Chiang's intelligence, and the Generalissimo did not realize the size and direction of the true breakout till a full month later. By then the Mao-Chou-Chu Teh main force had passed through the imprisoning enemy lines to the west. The Communists, favored by heavy rain and clouds hiding the moon, traveled at first only by night, but soon were forced to operate around the clock. Over one seventy-two-hour stretch they alternated four hours on the march (at nearly four miles an hour) with four hours' rest. Finally they penetrated the last line of the Kuomintang forces. They had broken the blockade.

As the main force moved on, the wounded, numbering some twenty thousand, had to be placed in the care of peasant families, while General Ch'en Yi (later Foreign Minister in Peking) and a number of senior Party members were left in charge of a small protective force. Several of these leaders, including Mao's own brother, were eventually caught and beheaded by the Kuomintang. Perhaps the sternest test concerned the families of the marchers. Most wives and all small children had to be left behind. Many of the women were eventually executed by the KMT troops, and when the Communists came to power fifteen years later, a diligent search for the children was made by the Red Army. None were ever found.

Chu Teh later reported: "We left many of our ablest military, political and mass leaders behind. One was the chairman of the All-China Federation of Labor who was captured and beheaded by the Kuomintang seven months later. Ho Shu-heng, Commissar of Justice, and Chu Chiu-pai, former Secretary of the Party and now Commissar of Education, were also left behind because Ho was in his middle sixties, while Chu was slowly dying of tuberculosis. Chu Chiu-pai had been one of the leaders of the cultural renaissance and a member of the Central Committee of the Kuomintang under Sun Yat-sen's leadership. Ho and Chu were to be smuggled to Shanghai. Eight months later they were cap-

[3] Ibid., p. 74.

tured by the Kuomintang and beheaded at Lungyen, together with a number of women leaders."[4]

Nearly thirty-five women, wives of higher officials, were on the March, including Chou's wife Teng Ying-ch'ao, who developed tuberculosis during the rigors of the retreat. Amazingly, she survived, and her eventual recovery from the disease was credited in part to the five months she spent afterward resting in an isolated temple. Mao's second wife, Ho Tzu-chen, was pregnant at the start and wounded later by enemy planes with sixteen pieces of shrapnel in her body.[5] She bore Mao a third child in Yenan before going to Russia for treatment in 1937.

Outstanding among the women marchers was K'ang Ke-ching,[6] the redoubtable wife of Chu Teh. With her weapons and knapsack, she also on occasion carried a wounded soldier on her back. She always had three or four rifles with her "to encourage the others." Once when visiting a village on official work, her party accidentally met the enemy and had to fight. K'ang Ke-ching was spontaneously chosen commander by the three hundred men there. "I was the only woman," she explained. "We fought for two hours; then the enemy retreated. I don't know whether I killed anyone or not—I could not see the results of my shooting. But I am a very good marksman. I must say this was a happy day for me."[7]

Of the marchers, some 28 per cent were Party members, 68 per cent were peasants and 30 per cent were proletarian workers. Most of the force were under twenty-three. They were an enthusiastic lot. Snow described them in Yenan as "perhaps the first consciously happy group of Chinese proletarians I had

[4] Smedley, *Great Road,* p. 309.
[5] Helen Foster Snow (Nym Wales), *Inside Red China,* p. 178.
[6] When my sister Frances first met K'ang Ke-ching some three years later (1938), she reported Chu Teh's young wife as giving the impression of a teen-age sports enthusiast. Clad in a captured Japanese overcoat, she strode through the villages, laughing and calling out to everyone she met. Her sense of fun never left her. She delighted in teasing her famous Commander-in-Chief husband (who was then fifty-four to her twenty-two but looked nearer three times her age). When Frances saw her again thirty-four years later (autumn of 1972), K'ang Ke-ching's hair was graying, but her cheeks were as bright red as ever and she bubbled in the same old way. "Who would have thought thirty-four years ago," she laughed, "that today we'd be walking arm in arm down a corridor in the Great Hall of the People?"
[7] Snow, *Battle for Asia,* p. 6.

seen."[8] They would sing at the slightest pretext and had a huge repertoire of propaganda and folk songs.

They needed all their youth and high spirits, for the march was a rigorous ordeal. One army group marched for twenty-seven consecutive days without a single rest day, twice marching straight through the night as well as through the preceding and following days. One day they covered fifty miles. The average daily march was nineteen miles over the whole year. They crossed eighteen mountain ranges, five of them permanently snow-capped, twenty-four rivers and twelve provinces. They captured by assault sixty-two cities and towns along the route, besides breaking through the opposing forces of ten different provincial warlords. Dr. Nelson Fu, a Christian doctor who was Mao's personal physician as well as medically in charge of the entire army, remarked on one feature unique among the world's armed forces, East or West: "So far, only ten of our soldiers have become infected with syphilis, as we are very strict on this matter. About 90 per cent of our soldiers are sexually inexperienced. We have no problem of immorality as the men are too tired and too busy . . ."[9]

"Once in enemy territory," according to the Chief Engineer at GHQ, "we often marched at night to avoid air raids. Night marching is wonderful if there is a moon and a gentle wind blowing. When no enemy troops were near, whole companies would sing and others would answer. If it was a black night and the enemy far away, we made torches from pine branches or frayed bamboo, and then it was truly beautiful when at the foot of a mountain we could look up and see a long column of lights coiling like a fiery dragon up the mountainside. From the summit we could look in both directions and see miles of torches moving forward like a wave of fire. A rosy glow hung over the whole route of march . . .

"When hard-pressed by superior enemy forces, we marched in the daytime, and at such times the bombers pounded us. We would scatter and lie down; get up and march, then scatter and lie down again, hour after hour. Our dead and wounded were many and our medical workers had a very hard time. The peasants always helped us and offered to take our sick, our wounded

[8] *Red Star,* p. 59.
[9] Wilson, *Long March,* p. 73.

and exhausted. Each man left behind was given some money, ammunition and his rifle and told to organize and lead the peasants in partisan warfare as soon as he recovered. Sometimes one or two companies would become separated from our main forces during battle, but they merely retreated into the mountains and developed partisan areas."[10]

The conference at Tsunyi (January 6–8, 1935) in the Far West, between Kweichow and Szechuan, was decisive for Communist China's future. It began the eclipse of Soviet dominance over the Chinese Revolution. It started a major turnabout in the fortunes of Mao Tse-tung, raising him from semidisgrace to a decisive position in military and, later, political affairs. It initiated the close collaboration between Chou En-lai and Mao that dominated the country's affairs for the next four decades.

Chou himself was the moving spirit in Mao's elevation. With that rare mixture of political prescience and personal self-effacement which had marked his career from the beginning, Chou, in his main speech at Tsunyi, boldly made a clean breast of his own and the Politburo's past errors, chiefly in failing to appreciate Mao's emphasis on China's overwhelmingly agrarian character, and the consequent folly of following Moscow in stressing the urban proletariat instead of the peasantry. Therefore, though senior to Mao, he proposed that Mao be made Chairman of the Party.

Three major results followed Chou's initiative. First, Mao's being put in charge represented the upgrading of men who, unlike Chou and his colleagues, had never been out of the country and so possessed a wholly indigenous interpretation of the philosophy of Karl Marx. Second, Mao's new supremacy gave him, with his guerrilla training, the special confidence of Army Chief Chu Teh and other guerrilla leaders. Third, Chou discerned that Mao uniquely possessed the *style* of leadership needed for China's future—a style, remarks one historian, "that could grip the emotions as well as the intellect, that could identify, and plausibly exaggerate, the few elements of hope in an otherwise bleak prospect. Like Churchill after Dunkirk, Mao was a good man to have at the helm when things looked really hopeless. Like Churchill he knew the secret of appealing to the

[10] Smedley, *Great Road,* pp. 311–12.

deepest instincts of his countrymen and arousing their will to resist, to endure, to go on against all the odds."[11] Mao's closest Western friend, the late Edgar Snow, gave some revealing insights into the leadership qualities which led Chou to make his historic proposal:

> Mao's political intelligence explains his command of the Communist Party, but not the real affection in which he is held by the men of the army and the country people. In speaking, he has a way of presenting a most complicated subject so that even the uneducated man can seem to understand it. He is full of homely idioms and instances; he never talks above the heads of his audience but he never talks down to them either. There is a real flow of intimacy between him and the people; he always seems to be in contact . . .
>
> Mao can rarely speak long without making a homely wisecrack or epigram, and he seems to maintain his leadership by winning all the arguments. He is very well read and an accomplished dialectician in debate. He has an interesting technique. He seldom makes a frontal attack against opposition. He delivers a blow here, another there, he outflanks his opponent's case, he breaks down its defenses one by one, until gradually he has it completely encompassed and it falls apart before a last witticism or a telling stroke of logic. He likes people and their laughter and is at home in any group. He has a lively imagination. I remember once seeing him laugh till he wept when somebody described to him a comedy he had seen in Shanghai. It was an American movie—Charlie Chaplin in *Modern Times*.[12]

In retrospect, Tsunyi marked the point at which the mass retreat of the Red Armies ended—where Chou En-lai's political acumen initiated the moves that thereafter gave Mao's intuitive wisdom and Chu Teh's brilliant generalship their chance to turn the nadir of Chinese Communism's defeat into the prelude to its final nationwide triumph.

[11] Wilson, *Long March*, p. 105.
[12] Snow, *Battle for Asia*, pp. 283, 287.

Fittingly enough, soon after the Tsunyi Conference broke up, the Red Army penetrated into the border areas of Szechuan and discovered there a village named Maotai where the famous clear-white and extremely heady rice wine is produced. Today, as every foreign visitor to Peking or recipient of Chinese hospitality abroad knows, the Chinese will toast their friends in maotai as Frenchmen will in champagne, Britons in scotch or Russians in vodka. A legend grew among the Long Marchers that the unsophisticated Red Army youth who first entered the distillery thought the white liquid was for bathing and promptly soaked their aching feet in it. Apparently it was the German adviser Li Teh (his Chinese name) who discovered the truth, became quite drunk, and by the time the Marchers left Maotai, "there was not a drop of the 'foot water' left."

Hundreds of vivid personal incidents, many of them now unhappily lost to history, illustrated both the unprecedented hazards of the Long March, and the deep dedication of the marchers. Of these, two especially are worth recording in some detail. The first involves Chou, the other Mao.

One day in April 1935, Chou En-lai ordered the unit traveling with him to stop in a single-street mountain village in Central Yunnan for a brief rest. The village slumbered in the chilly darkness of an early spring night. A few families had fled to the mountaintops when Chou's unit arrived, but most of them remained. Chou ordered his men to retire early, to recover from travel fatigue and also to save lamp oil. Only his room, a kitchen corner borrowed from a bean-curd vendor, was lighted with a candle. He had a stack of maps to pore over and his radioman brought him a slip of paper from time to time. The strain of six months of eluding the close pursuit of hundreds of thousands of Chiang Kai-shek's men had begun to tell on everybody. Chou could see this, and yet the end was still nowhere in sight. Wearily he pushed the papers aside and walked out of the hut to stretch his legs.

"K'ou-ling! [Password!]" shouted a patrol soldier out of the darkened street.

"This is Chou En-lai," responded Chou. Preoccupation had made him momentarily forget his own order, but he did not need to correct himself, for the soldier immediately recognized his voice. Chou returned the soldier's salute and greeted him by name. "When you finish your shift," he said, reaching out a hand to feel the soldier's shivering shoulders under a tattered cotton padded uniform, "come to my room for a chat. There is some wood in the stove that will warm you up for a better rest." It was close to midnight when the soldier went to Chou's room. Chou sat him down near the stove and talked to him about his family. The soldier studied the dancing shadows on Chou's face. It was sallow and drawn, almost buried in overgrown hair and beard. His eyes had lost the luster which the man used to note before the March began.

"You don't feel well, do you?" the soldier said.

"Nothing too bad," said Chou. "The cold I caught shortly after we started last year keeps coming back. It is just a nuisance. Many of our comrades are much sicker than I—yet they carry on."

The conversation turned to the unit of comrades who had stopped at a small hamlet a few miles ahead. Earlier a runner from that unit had brought back a report about the capture of several rich merchants who were made to march along with the Red comrades. The soldier wondered if they were being held for ransom, since the commander was treating them well, sharing meals with them, and even offering his own good sandals to one of them whose shoes had been lost in the mud.

"It is not so much for their money," said Chou. "Of course, if they have money in excess of their travel expense to contribute, we would welcome it. But it is even more important for us to have friends. They are rich and influential people from Szechuan, where we are going. Cultivating a little goodwill by showing these men how our Red Army behaves is always good policy."

"What if they are antirevolutionaries?" asked the soldier.

"In that case—if we find out that is the case—we will know how to deal with them. Meanwhile they are getting an education. They are comparing their lily-white soft feet with our commander's feet—your feet and my feet—calloused, chapped, just like those of any one of our comrades. They will watch how our commanders eat and sleep just like any ordinary soldiers, but work harder and do more. Our iron discipline will convince them that we are soldiers of revolution, not bandits."

"That's fine, but I cannot help wondering why we add them to our burden when we have trouble keeping all we have got already."

"The commander told me that they choose to walk along with us, at least until they get out of this part of the country. With all the bandits and unruly reactionary soldiers around, those merchants on their own wouldn't have a chance now they have lost their hired bodyguards."

The radioman brought in another message and Chou moved his stool close to the candle to read it. The soldier stood up to leave. Chou called him back and said, "Tomorrow, when we move on, be sure to remind all the comrades of your squad to return as usual everything they have borrowed, the boards, doors, and what-not, that they used for beds, and the scissors, needles and thread borrowed from the womenfolk here—everything back to their owners!"

The incident involving Mao occurred about the same time—April 1935. It is recorded in the words of the Chairman's own personal bodyguard and orderly, Chen Chang-feng, and concerns the same critical period when the Long Marchers, facing the crossing of three nearly impassable rivers, came closest to utter failure.

"It was one April evening, I remember," Chen says, "that we reached the Golden Sand [Yangtze] River—we being the Ninth, First, Fifth and Third Red Army Groups and the Cadre's Regiment, all belonging to the First Front Red Army. The Central Committee staff was also with us. The Golden Sand River was the first big river after the crossing of the Wukiang. It was in spate, with angry dragon-headed waves. All the leaders were greatly concerned with the problem of crossing, as we had practically no craft. Chairman Mao, of course, was in the thick of these discussions, which went on all night.

"I was his personal bodyguard. Just before dawn I crossed with him. We had hardly landed when he was off to General Liu Po-cheng [the Chief-of-Staff] to plan the next stage of the march. I started searching for some place for him to use as a temporary office and home.

"It did not look hopeful. The riverbank was nothing but bare rocks, with a few holes in the cliffs, dripping with moisture, hardly big enough to be called caves. I sought in vain for planks or even straw to use for a bed. In the end I had to lay out a piece of oiled cloth and put the plank on that, feeling that that at least would give him something to lie down on—he had not rested at all the whole night. Come to that, he had had no rest for the last few days.

"My next task was to lay out his documents—maps and papers. Usually I did it with his secretary, Comrade Huang, whenever we made camp. We used to rig up some kind of table or desk. But Huang was still on the other side of the river. I couldn't think what to do. I tried pinning one map up on the side of the cave but it was no good—it was just sand and wouldn't hold the nail and there wasn't room to spread the documents out. Already I had wasted enough time. I was expecting Chairman Mao back from his conference any minute, and had not even got a drop of boiled water ready. I knew he would not eat after all he had been through. I put aside the problem of the documents and hurried out to see what could be done about the water.

"It was broad daylight when Chairman Mao returned and sent for me. When I reached the cave I saw that he was standing there, deep in thought.

" 'You have come back,' I said.

" 'M'm . . . Everything ready?'

" 'I have done what I can,' I said, pointing at the 'bed.' 'There are no boards to be found. Will you lie down for a bit? The water will be boiled in a minute.'

"I turned to go to see how the water was getting on, but he called me back.

" 'Haven't you found me a place to work?' he asked.

" 'Comrade Huang hasn't come over yet,' I said without thinking. 'I couldn't find anything to use as a desk. Why don't you have a bit of a rest and a drop of water first?'

"He took a step towards me as though he hadn't heard what I had told him and said, very seriously, but not at all angrily, 'The work's the all-important thing at a moment like this. Rest, or food, or drink, are trifles. Twenty to thirty thousand of our comrades are still waiting to cross the river there. Thirty thousand lives in peril!'

"I didn't know what to say, but stood there looking at him. I could feel my heart pounding. He came right up to me and patted my shoulder. 'Come on,' he said, 'find me a board or something to use as a desk before you do anything else.'

"I pulled myself together and ran off, and by hunting high and low found a small board which must have been used as a door for a cave mouth. Chairman Mao helped set it up, making it flat and steady, and spread out his maps and documents. Then I remembered the water: It must have boiled by now. I got up to go and fetch it when Chairman Mao called to me again.

"'I will have to give you some punishment, you know,' he said. Although the tone of his voice was mild and there was a kind look in his eyes, I felt the air very tense. I realized how I had failed in my job, and stood looking at him very miserably.

"'I want you to stay by me and keep awake.'

"I felt an uneasy smile come over my face and sat down opposite him. 'Right,' I said.

"He had got telegrams and documents all over the desk. The field telephone which the signal corps had rigged up was going all the time, and he was absolutely immersed in work. He had not allowed a minute for himself. I found it hard to keep the tears back as I realized I had wasted his time over the desk; that if I had understood my job, I would have had it ready before.

"I was awfully drowsy and had a habit anyway of dropping off beside him when he was working. I knew what he meant when he said 'punish' me by asking me to keep awake, although he only said it as a joke. But when I saw how he was working with all his heart and soul, without showing the least sign of wanting to sleep, and even looking at me from time to time with a cheerful smile, I felt terribly uneasy. I got up and went and fetched the water after a bit and poured some out to cool.

"Time enough to eat two meals passed before Chairman Mao stopped and stood up to stretch himself.

"'You have been with me several years now,' he said. 'How is it that you still don't understand what comes first? The first thing you have to do is find somewhere where the work can be done. Food and rest are quite secondary to that. You must realize that the work is the important thing under all circumstances.' He stopped a minute and then rubbed his hand over my head. 'You will have to get a bit of sleep,' he said. 'You can hardly keep your eyes open.' "[13]

[13] Wilson, *The Long March*, pp. 131–34.

By far the most hazardous, and critically important, of all exploits of the Long March was the taking of Luting Bridge over the Tatu River, and its successful crossing by the Red Army into North China.

Much history is concentrated here. For it was at this river that, nearly a century before, Prince Shih Ta-kai, a famous leader of the T'ai-p'ing Rebellion, met his final defeat by the armies of the tyrannical Manchu Emperor, and was slaughtered along with most of his troops. Chou and other Red Army leaders, like the common people of China, refer always to this popular uprising not as a rebellion, but as the T'ai-p'ing Revolution—the earliest effort by Chinese nationalism to throw off the imperialist yoke imposed by the Western powers after the Opium War (1840–42) first exposed China to foreign exploitation. It was also the era of such world-shaking events as the Communist Manifesto of Marx and Engels, Europe's revolutions of 1848, India's "mutiny" against British rule, and America's Civil War over slavery.

Ironically, the T'ai-p'ings were originally inspired by Christian teachings imported through Western missions. They took these teachings literally in a social as well as a personal sense. They attacked feudalism by dividing the land, emancipating women and outlawing slavery. Prostitution and the sale of opium were made crimes; tobacco and wine, forbidden. They outlawed footbinding, allowed remarriage of widows and permitted women to serve in the Army as well as compete in the examinations for government service. On Sunday mornings, in the early period of their fifteen-year dominance over South and Central China, they sang hymns, heard sermons, and repeated the Ten Commandments.

The T'ai-p'ing Revolution failed because it did not organize the peasants or train a revolutionary political party to lead it—errors which Chou and his colleagues, who had made a thorough study of the subject, were resolved not to repeat as they made the decision to force the Luting Bridge. Their meeting was held at Anshunchang, several miles downstream, and the Red Army set out at once along both banks of the Tatu. The scene is well-described by Edgar Snow:

> Sometimes the gorges between them closed so narrowly that the two lines of Reds could shout to each

other across the stream; sometimes that gulf between them measured their fear that the Tatu might separate them forever, and they stepped more swiftly. As they wound in long dragon files along the cliffs at night their 10,000 torches sent arrows of light slanting down the dark, inscrutable face of the imprisoning river. Day and night these vanguards moved at double-quick, pausing only for brief ten-minute rests and meals, when the soldiers listened to lectures by their weary political workers who over and over again explained the importance of this one action, exhorting each to give his last breath, his last urgent strength, for victory in the test ahead of them. There could be no slackening of pace, no halfheartedness, no fatigue.[14]

Arriving at the bridge, forged centuries before of sixteen enormous iron chains overlaid with planking, the south-bank Reds found many planks removed and the northern end of the bridge, a hundred yards away across the surging rapids, strongly held by Chiang Kai-shek's troops. The assault was to be in charge of Political Commissar Yang Cheng-wu (later acting Chief-of-Staff of the Army in Peking during the Cultural Revolution), who decided to attack the moment his men reached the southern bridgehead. Agnes Smedley pictures the assault:

Platoon Commander Ma Ta-chiu stepped out, grasped one of the chains, and began swinging, hand over hand, towards the north bank. The platoon political director followed, and after him the men. As they swung along, Red Army machine guns laid down a protecting screen of fire and the Engineering Corps began bringing up tree trunks and laying the bridge flooring.

The army watched breathlessly as the men swung along the bridge chains. Ma Ta-chiu was the first to be shot into the wild torrent below. Then another man and another. The others pushed along, but just before they reached the flooring at the north bridgehead they saw enemy soldiers dumping cans of kerosene on the planks

[14] *Red Star,* p. 197.

and setting them on fire. Watching the sheet of flame
spread, some men hesitated, but the platoon political
leader at last sprang down on the flooring before the
flames reached his feet, calling to the others to follow.
They came and crouched on the planks, releasing their
hand grenades and unbuckling their swords.

They ran through the flames and threw their hand
grenades into the midst of the enemy. More and more
men followed, the flames lapping at their clothing. Behind them sounded the roar of their comrades and, beneath the roar, the heavy THUD, THUD, THUD of the
last tree trunks falling into place. The bridge became a
mass of running men with rifles ready, tramping out the
flames as they ran. The enemy retreated to their second
line of defense.[15]

Next to the forcing of the Tatu River, the most precarious feat
of the March was the crossing of the Grasslands on the Tibetan
border by thirty thousand Red Army men in early autumn of
1935. The historian Jerome Ch'en has called it "undoubtedly the
most difficult episode in the history of logistics."[16] This mountain
plateau, nine thousand feet high, is in the main a gigantic bog
where it rains nine months of the year and the land is perpetually marshy.

"As far as the eye can reach," writes Smedley, who got her
facts from the participants, "day after day, the Red Army saw
nothing but an endless ocean of high wild grass growing in an
icy swamp of black muck and water many feet deep. Huge
clumps of grass grew on dead clumps beneath them and so it
had been for no man knows how many centuries. No tree or
shrub grew here; no bird ventured near, no insect sounded.
There was not even a stone. There was nothing, nothing but endless stretches of wild grass swept by torrential rains in summer
and fierce winds and snows in winter. Heavy black and gray
clouds drifted forever above, turning the earth into a dull,
sombre netherworld . . ."[17]

Chou En-lai became so ill during this ordeal that he was or-

[15] Smedley, Great Road, p. 321.
[16] Jerome Ch'en, Mao and the Chinese Revolution, p. 194.
[17] Smedley, op. cit., p. 337.

dered temporarily to relinquish his nightly military conferences. Teng Ying-ch'ao spoke of her being "deeply concerned because of the lack of proper medicine." Due to the surrounding bog, for much of the two weeks of the crossing the men had to stand all night leaning against each other. Many collapsed or had paralyzed legs. One of the youngsters, a "little devil" aged seventeen, began to give way the fourth day out. "I am a piece of iron politically," he explained, "but my legs fail me." They gave him extra rations and tied him on a horse, but he died the next day.

One marcher wrote that "the water under foot looked like horse's urine and gave off a smell that made me vomit." There were mosquitoes "the size of horse-leeches." Over five hundred succumbed to "black malaria" when, as another man put it, "our faces went as black as a Negro's, and our bodies became weaker and weaker, needing to rest after every few steps."[18] Even here, Chou would often add a touch of humor which helped maintain the spirits of the men. Once when literally nothing was available to eat, the marchers removed their leather belts, cooked them in water to make them soft, added a certain kind of wild herb, and served this concoction at the end of a tortuously grueling day. The brew, greeted with enthusiasm, was christened by Chou the "Soup of Three Delicacies."

The physical hazards were compounded by the hatred of the Mantzu tribesmen, a bitterly hostile non-Chinese minority who vacated the area, taking all food with them. Here, writes Snow, "the Reds for the first time faced a populace united in its hostility to them, and their sufferings on this part of the trek exceeded anything of the past. They had money but could buy no food. They had guns but their enemies were invisible. As they marched into the thick forests and jungles and crossed the headwaters of a dozen great rivers, the tribesmen withdrew from the vicinity of the March. They stripped their houses bare, carried off all edibles, drove their cattle and fowl to the plateau, and simply disinhabited the whole area.

"A few hundred yards on either side of the road, however, it was quite unsafe. Many a Red who ventured to forage for sheep, never returned. The mountaineers hid in the thick bush and

18 Wilson, *Long March*, p. 206.

sniped at the marching 'invaders.' They climbed the mountains, and when the Reds filed through the deep, narrow, rock passages, where sometimes only one or two could pass abreast, the Mantzu rolled huge boulders down to crush them and their animals. Here were no chances to explain 'Red policy toward national minorities,' no opportunities for friendly alliance! The Mantzu Queen had an implacable traditional hatred for Chinese of any variety, and recognized no distinctions between Red and White. She threatened to boil alive anyone who helped the travellers."[19]

Some students of the period are convinced that much of the severity of Communist China's actions in Tibet during the early years of Red rule was due to the memory of this experience of the Long March, when Tibetan antagonism had killed or maimed the comrades of many Chinese Army men who later held high rank in Peking.

The overall legacy of the Long March was of incalculable importance in shaping the philosophy of Chou and Mao and their colleagues in the years thereafter, and consequently the policies of the People's Republic following the final achievement of Communist power after 1949. That legacy has been well-described by the leading scholar[20] of the period under three general headings which may be briefly summarized here.

First is the tradition of voluntary self-discipline, which Soviet Russia never achieved but which has been a hallmark of Communist China's rulers over the past four decades. Chou and Mao, like the famous Greek Xenophon referred to earlier, held that "willing obedience always beats enforced obedience." Following his accession to power, at Chou's instigation, after the Tsunyi Conference in 1935, Mao gradually divested his security police of their arbitrary authority, preferring to preserve unity among his colleagues by private discussion rather than physical threats, imprisonment or liquidation. In fact, Mao formally pledged at a Central Committee meeting in Yenan in 1938 to achieve Party discipline "through indoctrination, study and intellectual-cum-emotional rectification," rather than by means of the traditional purges of Stalinist Russia.

[19] *Red Star*, pp. 192–93.
[20] Wilson, *Long March*, pp. 254–77.

8. Chou's house in Chungking in the 1940s. The sign at lower right indicates the entrance to an underground air-raid shelter.

9. Chou's living quarters, where he slept, worked and met with colleagues, is now restored as a museum.

10. Chou and Teng Ying-ch'iao at a Communist victory reception in 1946.

11. Chou greets Colonel Joseph Stilwell, Jr., at a 1943 Soviet Embassy reception in Chungking. Five years earlier Chou and young Stilwell's father, the famous "Vinegar Joe," often conferred in the author's Hankow home "over maps spread out on our dining-room table."

12. On December 15, 1945, Truman announced he was sending America's most respected public figure, General of the Army George C. Marshall, to tackle the problem of winning the peace in China. Here Marshall confers in Chungking in early 1946 with Communist China's chief negotiator, General Chou En-lai.

13. By late December 1946, General Marshall had given up on the negotiations and "packed his bags for home." Back in Yenan, the Communist Party's "Big Three" (Chou, Chu Teh, and Mao) prepared for two final years of civil war.

Second, the extraordinary voluntarism of Communist China was combined with a deep-seated idealization of simple peasant virtues. Once and for all, it became accepted that the basic conflict in the country was not between factory workers and industrialists, but between peasants and landlords. The prevailing urban culture became suspect, and the People's Communes—cooperatives of some fifty thousand each comprising all state, judicial, police and economic functions—were made the model for the entire country. These communes, based on "the guerrilla ethic," were described in 1958 by the Central Committee in Peking as "a new social organization" which has emerged "fresh as the morning sun above the broad horizon of East Asia."

A third legacy of the Long March was what might be described as the institutionalizing of independence from Russia. Breaking sharply with the close collaboration with Moscow which marked the era of Borodin and the Sino-Soviet honeymoon, Mao began, after the Shanghai massacre of 1927, to go his own way. The only leading Chinese Communist who until then had never been out of China, he was appreciative of early Comintern assistance—political and financial—but felt that Stalin did not understand China's unique problems and was chiefly interested in what the latter could contribute to Russia's own revolution. He resented Soviet preoccupation with China's practically nonexistent urban proletariat and the Russian leader's indifference to the peasantry, which Mao knew had to be the basis of his own country's revolution.

Stalin, for his part, contributed his full share to the estrangement. Incredible as it may seem, the Soviet dictator, as late as the eve of Mao's and Chou's final victory in 1949, had even suggested that the Red Armies halt at the Yangtze, leaving Southern China to Chiang Kai-shek. The Chinese leadership naturally paid no heed, and shortly thereafter were in control of the entire mainland.

To Stalin's credit, it must be added that he finally recognized the folly of his own views, admitting privately to the Yugoslav leadership in 1948 that "in the case of China, we admit we were wrong." Stalin's mistake had profound long-term results. The split between the two great Communist powers—not recognized by the world until over a decade later—not only decisively weakened Marxism's world appeal; it raised Chou and Mao to the top rank of world statesmen. Above all, it substituted for the conventional ideological division of Communist against Capitalist, the true issue of the last half of the twentieth century: the cultural-racial-economic chasm separating the U.S.-European industrial societies from the underdeveloped but far more numerous, and increasingly vocal, emerging rural peoples of Asia and Africa.

This issue is now becoming yearly more sharply defined. It is therefore small wonder that the Long March, perhaps the most stupendous military migration in history, should today be one of the principal events nourishing the pride and life-motive of nearly one quarter of mankind, with all that that implies for the future of the human race.

CHAPTER VI

AMBASSADOR FROM YENAN

The Long March, however, though a military epic, was only the beginning. It assured that the seeds of a new China would survive. The growth of that new society into unified nationhood, and its recognition by the world at large, still lay in the future. The eventual success of the first task was due primarily to the genius of Mao Tse-tung; that of the second, to Chou En-lai.

The end of the March thus marked the beginning of the creative period of what Edgar Snow called the symbiosis between the two men—a unique working relationship with each complementing the other—that until Chou's death forty years later remained the human cornerstone of the People's Republic.

On arrival in the loess[1] hills of Paoan and Yenan,[2] still weak from the March and her prolonged battle against tuberculosis, Teng Ying-ch'ao picked a cave for her husband and herself and started turning it into a home. It could hardly compare with

[1] Loess: a loamy deposit formed by wind, found chiefly bordering along river valleys or serving to form valley bluffs (e.g. the Mississippi River Valley) and extending over wide arid areas of the United States, central Europe and Asia. Ideal for cave dwellings like those that formed the Communist home base after the Long March.

[2] Communists' first base area in Shensi.

their rented house in Canton days, but it was sheer luxury compared to the grassland swamps they had just survived. There
was a table, spotlessly clean, a newly laundered coverlet on the
bed, and even a mosquito net.

Chou himself was seldom in, for on him fell the chief burden
of training the villagers in the new doctrines, and turning Yenan
gradually into a political Mecca for revolutionaries from all over
China and abroad. It was his task to welcome these visitors, arrange for interviews, and explain the Communist aims. Ed Snow
was among the first foreigners to arrive. Among the Chinese who
turned up was a young actress from Shanghai named Chiang
Ching, who caught the eye of Mao Tse-tung and later married
him.

Teng's days were filled with calling on the women, door to
door, to help with their family problems, teach them the elements of child care, and combat footbinding, the sale of young
girls, and other evils of the old society. She and her husband
rarely had time to share a meal, but when they did it was a
merry affair. He was surprised to come home one day to find his
wife preparing a cup of the popular American S&W brand
coffee. "Old Mao brought it over himself," she explained. "He
said a Western visitor had given it to Chu Teh, and it has passed
through the hands of many comrades, each taking a few spoon-
fuls, before reaching us."[3]

The Chou En-lais, however, had hardly settled into their new
cave home before China's civil war entered a new phase which
would profoundly affect their lives and prove the long-range
prelude to eventual Communist rule over the whole country.
Japan had begun her long-planned expansion onto the China
mainland. In search of new markets for her burgeoning industries, Tokyo assumed from the first that commercial expansion
would eventually have to be supported by military force. All that
was needed was a pretext for the invasion. In neighboring Manchuria pretexts were hardly needed, and it was generally
believed that Japan had plotted and carried out the assassi-

[3] This and some other quotations in this chapter are taken by permission
from Hsu Kai-yu, *Chou En-lai: China's Gray Eminence.* New York: Doubleday, 1968.

nation, in 1928 en route to Mukden, of the fabled Chinese warlord Marshal Chang Tso-lin. A more substantial incident, however, was needed for China proper, and Chou and Mao had no doubt that one would shortly be forthcoming. Meanwhile their response must be to submerge ideological differences for the time being with their opponents at home, and bend every effort to unite China's own competing factions against the common enemy.

Such a move would have for the Communists the added advantage of getting Chiang Kai-shek off their backs. And Japan obliged by furnishing a stream of provocations all over China. Tokyo sent more troops. Japanese police in Shanghai beat up and killed Chinese students. Japanese industrialists flooded China's markets with foreign goods smuggled in under armed protection.

All across the nation people were outraged, and the rise of anti-Japanese patriotism was expressed in the popular slogan: "Chinese don't fight Chinese! Look, who is our real enemy?"

The Central Committee of the CCP held out an olive branch with a proclamation stating that "our comrades must learn to work with higher-echelon and top leaders of all other political parties and factions who can influence the masses. Our Party must be prepared to negotiate and compromise . . . must remain active among all revolutionary segments, petite bourgeoisie and intellectuals as well as peasants, workers, and soldiers."

This was followed up on May 5, 1936, by a formal truce proposal to Chiang Kai-shek, jointly signed by Chou, Mao and Chu Teh. Faced by the specter of Japanese aggression, Chiang had reluctantly consented to assign the KMT's Security Chief Ch'en Li-fu to begin negotiations with Chou En-lai. Only five years earlier, Ch'en had been responsible for hunting down Chou's security guards in the Shanghai "underground." But times had changed, and Chou now prepared to face his deadly enemy and propose making common cause against the common foe. On behalf of the KMT Ch'en Li-fu laid down stiff terms, and under the pressure of events Chou accepted them. They included (1) replacing Communism with Sun Yat-sen's Three People's Principles; (2) integrating the Red Army into Chiang's KMT forces;

(3) converting the Chinese Soviet Government into a local government under Nanking's authority.

Chou, now moving between Shanghai and Nanking, took on himself the task of rallying support from the many unaligned liberal groups around the country who wanted to stop the civil war and resist Japan. Everywhere he found growing enthusiasm for the new united-front proposals; but Chiang himself delayed his acceptance, and the nation grew increasingly restive.

At this point fate intervened with an event of high drama. Chiang Kai-shek, who was inspecting his troops at Sian, was arrested on December 12, 1936, by members of his own command, under the leadership of Marshal Chang Tso-lin's son, the "Young Marshal", Chang Hsueh-liang.

This Sian coup had an interesting background. Young Chang hated the Japanese for murdering his father in Manchuria, and was growing resentful of Chiang Kai-shek's refusal to fight them. At the same time Chou and Mao, from Yenan, had been making astute overtures to him, sending winter rations for his troops from their own scanty supplies and providing women performers and entertainers who played on his men's homesickness for their native Manchuria and their hatred of the Japanese soldiers ravishing their homeland. In addition, following an earlier Communist victory over the Young Marshal's forces, many of the latter's officers and men were captured, and not released until they had received a rich diet of indoctrination. On returning to their units they proved able emissaries of their former captors, especially one brigadier who carried a personal letter from Chou to the Young Marshal pleading with him to turn his troops against their common enemy, the Japanese.

On one occasion the Young Marshal himself visited Yenan and invited the celebrated Communist commander, General Yeh Chien-ying, to go to Sian and advise him on the modernization of his northeastern army. A return visit by Chou to Sian followed. Then Mao himself wrote, offering to turn over command of the Red Army to the Young Marshal if he would only join in fighting the Japanese.

A further step in Chang Hsueh-liang's alienation from Chiang Kai-shek came when he was slighted in a National Day celebration in Nanking. Another was supplied when the Generalissimo, on arrival at Sian, unaccountably excluded the Young Marshal and his generals from a key military conference there, arousing their fear that their secret dealings with Yenan had been discovered. This was the last straw. Panic-stricken, the Young Marshal ordered his troops to surround the Generalissimo's villa. Chiang's bodyguards were attacked and disarmed, and Chiang fled out a back door and up into the hills in his underwear, where he was discovered by his pursuers hiding in a cave. Installed under duress in the Young Marshal's palace, China's titular chief of state was brought before his captor.

"How dare you?" shouted Chiang Kai-shek. "If you don't obey my orders you are a traitor!"

"If Your Excellency accepts my suggestions," replied Chang Hsueh-liang politely, "I will obey your orders."

"Which are you, my subordinate or my enemy? If my subordinate, you must obey my orders; if my enemy, you should execute me immediately. Choose either one, but say not another word, for I will not listen!"

"Generalissimo, you are the great man of this age. But why won't you stop carrying on civil war, accept the help of the Red Army, and lead them and all of us in the fight against Japan?"

The "kidnaping" of Chiang Kai-shek shocked the nation, threw Sian into confusion, and caught the CCP by surprise. Baffled by his chief's obstinacy, the Young Marshal in desperation turned to Chou En-lai for advice. The startling news brought Chou posthaste to Sian, where he lost no time in visiting the incarcerated Generalissimo.

What transpired between Chiang and Chou En-lai during this private interview has never been revealed, but in the weeks following, Chou, from whom one word would have spelled instant doom for the Generalissimo, worked single-mindedly to preserve not only his captive's life but also his dignity and prestige. He knew only too well that with Japan occupying key parts of Shantung, marching on Peking, and attacking in Manchuria, China could not afford any continuance of the civil war. The Generalissimo, while agreeing that many of Chou's proposals made sense, refused to bargain under duress.

Meanwhile the rest of the world—for two dramatic weeks—was in the dark as to what was going on. They knew only that the

Generalissimo had been "kidnaped" and that the deed was in some way linked with a "mutiny." Letters from my family in Hankow reflected some of the shock and dismay that had gripped millions across the country. Most people instinctively felt that whatever happened, the loss of Chiang—"the strong man of China"—at a time when Japan was invading the North, could mean only disaster for the entire nation.

The resulting impasse was broken dramatically on Christmas Day, 1936, when Mme. Chiang Kai-shek flew in from Nanking, and the Young Marshal, now contrite, escorted the Generalissimo back to Nanking, only to be detained in his turn for his pains. He never saw his Manchurian army again.

The Sian "incident," however, had left its mark on Chiang Kai-shek. And by July 7, 1937, when the Japanese used the celebrated Marco Polo Bridge encounter as a pretext for an all-out attack on China, the Generalissimo was ready to modify his policy. Chou rushed to see him at the mountain resort of Lu Shan, and found him now amenable to substantially the same proposals for KMT-CCP co-operation that he had refused only a few months before. My father and sister, who lunched with the Chiangs at their summer home in Lu Shan on July 14, reported that they found the Generalissimo alert, eager to mobilize the nation, and supremely confident.

As a result of the Lu Shan agreement, the Northern Shensi Border Soviet Area government was accorded the status of a provincial government under the Nanking regime, and the Red Army was renamed the Eighth Route Army. The Communist regime thus obtained for the first time legitimate status on a national basis in China, and Chou En-lai, the chief architect of this "United Front," after being for ten years a fugitive from the KMT, found himself once again, with Mao Tse-tung and their Communist associates, the ally of Chiang Kai-shek in a common cause.

During the formative year following the Long March, Chou had clearly emerged as Communist China's principal voice to the world. In mid-1936 the young American journalist Edgar Snow, led by an unerring instinct as to what would be the truly big news of the future, became the first foreign writer to pierce the hitherto impenetrable Red Army lines and interview Chou En-lai and Mao Tse-tung. His resulting book, *Red Star Over China,* is still the recognized world classic on the subject. Soon afterward Mao, by making Chou his chief spokesman and liaison with Chiang Kai-shek, symbolically installed him as the official voice of the CCP in dealing with other nations.

The KMT-Communist coalition now faced a full-scale Japanese invasion. Shanghai fell in November 1937, and soon after, Nanking was stormed and sacked. Chou, retreating with Chiang up the Yangtze, moved first to Hankow, where he set up temporary headquarters. Ten months later the wartime capital was moved still further west to Chungking.

When the Chous arrived in the tri-city of Wuhan during the winter of 1937–38 to head up the Communist delegation, the former envoy from the caves of Yenan was becoming a familiar figure in the press, but was largely unknown as a personality. Now he turned up at international parties and government functions smartly dressed in a KMT uniform as Deputy Director of the Political Department in the Generalissimo's Military Affairs Commission. For most of this period he kept his head clean-shaven and no longer wore a beard, though his ready smile was framed by an apparently permanent "five-o'clock shadow." Again, as in 1925–26, he found himself a member of Chiang's political staff, dividing his time between the office of the Military Commission, where KMT guards welcomed their chief with respectful salutes, and the offices of the Communist *New China Daily News*, where, as in the Tientsin days of 1919 when he directed the Student League paper, he again shaped the main editorial for the day.

The chief difference was that the united-front policy tempered his criticisms of the KMT. Indeed, he bent over backward to be complimentary. "The Generalissimo," Chou wrote, "is the rightful and only person to lead the entire nation to victory, because of his revolutionary experience and education."

Teng Ying-ch'ao, now largely recovered from the trauma of the Long March, moved into a comfortable house in the former "concession" quarter. Unlike today, when a new modern city has grown up all around it, the "concession" area was still incomparably the finest in that famous central Yangtze Valley river port. Teng mingled socially with the more affluent KMT ladies, even on occasion joining their mahjong games and having her dark hair treated to a permanent. Some of the most important united-front decisions were reached at her dinner and mahjong parties, when she brought to her home for intimate conferences the women leaders she had first befriended in Canton in 1925–26.

Like her husband, Teng spoke boldly in favor of the United Front. "Since the beginning of the war against Japan," she said, "the KMT and the national government under Generalissimo Chiang Kai-shek have had a fundamental policy change to cessation of civil war and alliance with the CCP. Chinese politics has begun to turn toward democracy, and toward a unified government to carry out the sacred duty of national defense. All Chinese must support the government against the aggressor."

As for Chou, the collaboration between him and his KMT nominal chief, Director of the Political Department General Ch'en Ch'eng (later Republic of China Vice-President on Taiwan), was so cordial that rumors began to circulate as to where the loyalties of the two men really lay. The rumors, of course, had no basis, but the cordiality was the more remarkable considering that it was General Ch'en who had been the architect of the "annihilation campaigns" in 1931–34 that drove Chou out of Kiangsi. A certain cordiality, in fact, survived even the eventual Communist conquest of the mainland. A few years before his death in 1965, Vice-President General Ch'en Ch'eng, though second in command of the rival Taiwan regime, spoke of Chou En-lai to the author with respect and warmth—and a touch of nostalgia. They had been schoolboys together at Nankai.

Historically these few months in Wuhan, when the Chou En-lais lived in Hankow and the Chiang Kai-sheks just across the Yangtze in Wuchang, were indeed the high-water mark of the United Front. Because it was the temporary wartime capital, the world converged on the tri-city of Wuhan for a firsthand look. A letter from my sister, written January 5, 1938, gives some of the flavor of these days:

> Father is right now in an adjoining room talking with Chou En-lai, Communist leader who has just been conferring with Chiang Kai-shek this afternoon. He is coming to supper with his wife here Saturday evening after another talk with Father. Colonel J. L. Huang, head of the government's New Life Movement, was in this afternoon. The Chiangs' Australian adviser, W. H.

Donald, came yesterday and the day before, and had a long talk with Father. Anna Louise Strong is here trying to get north to see the Eighth Route Army. Yesterday [while] entertaining Miss Strong during an air-raid, planes dropped [about] a hundred bombs during the meat course and antiaircraft kept up a nice little accompaniment to our conversation . . .

Others who joined the family circle included author John Gunther, poet W. H. Auden, the playwright Christopher Isherwood, Major ("Vinegar Joe") Stilwell, photographer Robert Capa (later of *Life* magazine), Dr. Leighton Stuart of Yenching University (to become the last American Ambassador on the mainland), and a varied assortment of visiting newsmen, diplomats, professors, students and social workers. A later letter fills in the picture:

Our luncheons swell from a planned six to an unexpected twelve. At teatime there are several parties going on at once. Dinner may find anyone here from Chou En-lai to Minister of Finance Dr. H. H. Kung, Chou's Secretary Ch'ang Tsz-hua, General Teddy Tu who supervised filming *The Good Earth,* English and Chinese newsmen, government officials including Mayor K. C. Wu, members of the diplomatic corps, Navy [British and American] and other types from missionaries to businessmen of all nationalities.

Agnes Smedley, the controversial American writer and biographer of General Chu Teh, arrived dressed in a soldier's uniform to stay four months in our home after a year with the Eighth Route "Red" Army. Dr. Norman Bethune was a guest for ten days before going north to serve in frontline hospitals and then die a hero's death.[4]

4 Dr. Bethune, who had joined the Communist Party in Canada some years before, was moved to volunteer his services to the Chinese Revolution and performed prodigies of front-line service with Mao and Chou's critically understaffed medical corps. His unremitting labors so impaired his health that he fell easy prey to infectious hepatitis, from which he died. Mao was much touched by his story. The Chairman's tribute to the Canadian (one of "his three most read speeches") is now known by virtually all Chinese, and his grave in North China has become a national shrine.

Family letters increasingly reflected the impact of the United Front:

> Father has seen a lot of Eighth Route Army leaders here. . . . We lunched at the Chiang Kai-sheks—a delightful informal family meal. Everyone in Hankow is talking about the Eighth Route Army. Even the Generalissimo tells the Kuomintang that they should have more of the spirit of self-sacrifice the Communists have, and then they might help their country more! Madame Chiang . . . laughed at all the silly women who were afraid to work with the Communist women.

It was symbolic of those days that when my father and sister left Wuhan in April 1938, they were given their two last farewell meals by the chief protagonists of the United Front—the Chou En-lais at Eighth Route Army Headquarters in Hankow, and the Chiang Kai-sheks at their home in Wuchang.

When the Japanese advance forced the government upriver to Chungking, swarms of international diplomats and journalists poured into that already crowded city. Chou, in his new position at the heart of the regime, used all his magnetic gifts to instruct these representatives of the outside world in the aims of the CCP and its plans for the future. It was all consistent with his part in the national coalition. It was discreet—and immensely effective.

An address he made one afternoon in Chungking in 1941 to an audience of students and reporters was typical. As usual he was immaculately dressed, but the audience noticed that he held his right arm stiffly, the result of a poorly mended fracture sustained in a fall from his horse in Yenan two years before. Finally, Chou spoke with barely restrained emotion: "My fellow students," he said softly, "this is *our* country. Whatever has happened to cause that fratricidal tragedy must be forgotten. From now on we must look ahead . . ."

New Year of 1941 in Chungking was the last to be celebrated in the exhilarating spirit of the United Front. After that, the mental reservations that had always existed in both the KMT and the CCP grew gradually into suspicion, mistrust, then retaliation, until finally only the framework remained to sustain the common effort against Japan.

Before the break came, however, an extraordinary meeting took place in this hinterland city of violent contradictions. It was Christmas 1940, and Chiang Kai-shek invited Chou En-lai to come to dinner. As the two old enemies conversed, the Generalissimo, his eyes moist, thanked his guest for saving his life in Sian. Taking Chou's hand in both his, the usually taciturn chief of state spoke with a rare tenderness of his gratitude. Sometime later Chou commented on the emotions they must both have felt: "Naturally I was moved; but unhappily human emotion, however sincere, cannot completely bridge ideological differences."[5]

Back again in Yenan on one of his frequent return trips, Chou in the spring and summer of 1942 joined Mao in a series of top-level sessions to correct the erroneous tendencies in Party ideology and discipline. At the end, in a final statement, he also revealed the progressive development of his own thinking on the relation of Communism to the national scene:

"The Party's 22-year history has proved that the views of Comrade Mao Tse-tung were formed and maintained with historical perspective . . . Through him, and after his effort to develop it and use it, Communism has gone beyond being a mere body of ideology suitable to China; it has become rather an ideology that is indigenous and has grown roots in the soil of China. Comrade Mao Tse-tung has integrated Communism with the movement of Chinese national liberation and the movement of improving the livelihood of the Chinese people . . . Because of his leadership, the strength of the Party has attained an unprecedented height."

This reassessment of Chinese Communism by Chou coincided with an epochal turn of events in the savage clash between Russia and Germany in Europe.

During the winter of 1942–43 Hitler's armies suffered a double reverse on their eastern front. They failed in their desperate attempt to take Moscow, while further south the defenders of

[5] The incident was revealed by then Marine Captain Evans Carlson of "Carlson's Raiders" in a biography of the World War II "Gung Ho" hero. Michael Blankfort, *The Big Yankee—The Life of Carlson of the Raiders*, p. 284.

Stalingrad turned defeat into victory as the cream of the Nazi forces were stopped in their tracks, decimated, and finally forced to surrender.

These decisive Soviet gains naturally put fresh heart into the beleaguered Chinese Communists. With the Chou-Mao team supreme within the CCP, Chou returned to Chungking with renewed confidence to present the Generalissimo with their enlarged demands: formal KMT recognition of the CCP as a legal party; expansion of the Red Army to twelve full-strength divisions; establishment of a northern Shansi border zone; postponement until after the war of removing the Red troops south of the Yellow River.

Meanwhile Chiang Kai-shek's position had also hardened. Chou made it clear that the CCP would reserve the right to withdraw their support from the KMT if the latter wavered in their allegiance to Sun Yat-sen's Three People's Principles, still officially accepted as gospel by both sides. The KMT, on the other hand, insisted that Chou's earlier commitment to their leadership and to national unity meant the Chou-Mao forces should obey Chiang Kai-shek's command at all times, *no matter what the circumstances*. Each side was determined to prove that they alone were in fact carrying out the kind of revolution the ambiguous Dr. Sun had called for—a dispute that persists even today.

Chou's house, while he stayed in Chungking, was in the heart of the city, its solid, windowless front facing directly on the street, its upper balcony high above an inner courtyard. Steps led from the paved court down to the inevitable air-raid shelter, for during the war years Chungking was subjected to remorseless bombings. On hot summer nights, Chou could look out from his rooftop onto scores of other rooftops descending in tiers down the side of the city's steep bluff. Beyond was the Kia-ling, emptying its brown waters into the great mainstream of the Yangtze. He was aware that the neighboring balconies and rooftops were manned by observers officially posted to keep an eye on the representative from Yenan, and that his every move was watched, analyzed and discussed in government negotiating circles.[6]

[6] Today Chou's house is a museum, restored apparently as it had been during those historic years, but the neighboring buildings are painted red on the Communist side and black on the sides occupied by the KMT.

A vivid portrait of Chou in Chungking during 1945–46 was painted by Jack Anderson in his syndicated column "Washington Merry-Go-Round" of January 20, 1976:

> Because I was the lowliest of the correspondents in postwar China, I was assigned to cover Chou En-lai. I found him at the end of a slime-covered, cobblestone alley. He occupied the lower floor of a dingy house, which served both as headquarters and living quarters for the Chinese Communist mission in Chungking.
>
> The windows were covered with greasy brown paper, which trapped stale cooking odors inside. To gain admittance, I would identify myself through a speakeasy-style peephole—a useless conspiratorial ritual, since Chiang's secret police occupied the room overhead.
>
> I dropped by regularly in search of news. I visited with Chou in the privacy of his living quarters. I talked with him over egg rolls and moo goo gai pan.

Meanwhile, as the war intensified, the KMT press in Chungking withheld all favorable news of the Eighth Route Army's record in combat, so that no one but Chou could supply information about the key guerrilla struggle going on furiously behind the enemy lines. His position in Chungking, which alone had news access to the outside world, became increasingly frustrating. On July 26, 1944, when the KMT propaganda chief informed the press that "progress has been made in the negotiations," Chou publicly contradicted him. "There has been absolutely *no* progress," he said. "The distance between the two sides on all concrete issues remains enormous!" Abandoning for once his usual suavity, he frankly accused the KMT spokesman of lying to the Chinese people.

The impasse was inevitable. Each side knew why the other would not budge—the KMT determined that unification could exist only under Chiang Kai-shek, the CCP refusing to yield either its hard-won territory or its army. By now the Communists were a lot stronger than before the days of the United Front. Chou felt he could afford to be truculent when, on returning to Yenan, he declared on October 10, 1944: "The orders we can obey are only the orders directed to strengthen our war effort, issued in a democratic manner. The orders we must oppose are those following the fascist line toward defeatism. We demand that the government and the army be reorganized to permit coalition government and joint control of the armed forces."

Now the demand for a coalition government was at least out in the open. It angered Chiang Kai-shek, both because it implicitly questioned his own absolute authority, and because he was well aware of the burgeoning Communist strength and knew it was growing week by week. Chou returned disenchanted to Yenan, and each side began openly to go its own way.

At this point a new American Ambassador, Patrick J. Hurley, appeared on the scene, flew to Yenan, and presently escorted Chou back to Chungking under his own guarantee of safe conduct. But it was of no use.

In January 1945, Chou traveled once more to Chungking as chief Communist delegate. It was the winter of Yalta in Europe. Roosevelt was a fast-dying man and everything, especially including the situation in China, was at a virtual impasse. Again Chou requested that a coalition government be formed immediately. "Why should the United States deliver arms only to Chiang Kai-shek's troops?" he asked the American mediator. When Ambassador Hurley replied that no United States arms could be handed over to the troops of a political party, Chou lost patience. "Isn't Chiang Kai-shek's army serving a political party?" Obviously nothing was to be gained by continuing such discussions, and by May all negotiations had broken down.

By this time, with Roosevelt dead and Chiang Kai-shek having announced his intention of convening a National Assembly on November 12 that same year, the Communists in the late spring of 1945 convened their own Seventh Congress in Yenan, with Mao Tse-tung delivering his historic report "On Coalition Government," proposing mass assemblies in all liberated areas to demand the formation of a national coalition regime.

Back in Chungking in July, the People's Political Council met and Chou En-lai, as a council member, explained once more why the Communists continued to demand that the formation of a coalition government be placed on the agenda. At mention of the word "coalition," the KMT members exploded. "What's the use of putting it on the agenda?" they said. "You Communists are fighting your way into the government anyway!"

A reluctantly admiring KMT official put it more succinctly: "The Communists are winning the mainland not through combat, but across the negotiating table, with Chou En-lai sitting on the other side!"

After a heated exchange, Chou and his delegates walked out—this time, it seemed, for good.

History, however, was surging forward, and the Japanese surrender of August 10, 1945, created a new situation. Both sides immediately rushed to recover as much territory as they could from the enemy. Chiang Kai-shek meanwhile sent three telegrams inviting Mao Tse-tung to a face-to-face talk, and a fortnight later the top Communist leadership arrived again in Chungking with Ambassador Hurley as escort.

Chou was, as usual, the chief figure in the forty days of talks that followed, and on one celebrated occasion Chiang Kai-shek and Mao Tse-tung exchanged elaborate toasts.

Chou's patience appeared inexhaustible as day after day he argued his case, never touching a cigarette and seldom even a drop of tea. His good-humored remarks at the end of one particularly argumentative session were typical of his attitude as a whole:

"I tell you what we'll do. Let's just get the men in the field to stop shooting and I'll be glad to lead a personal tour for you and your friends—anyone, including the Generalissimo and Madame Chiang—of the liberated area. We'll start from Yenan and go anywhere you like to go and see anything you wish to see. We'll go unannounced so that you can eavesdrop on the villagers' private conversations and listen to the farmers' songs from a distance, and you will know that they support Yenan not because we are Communists, but because of what we have done for them. And—forgive the illustration—if you catch a militiaman and a village girl together, I will stake my life that you will find that they may be committing adultery, but never, never rape! Then you can draw your own conclusions."[7]

Chou En-lai's appeal was striking an increasingly popular chord in a country now weary to death from nearly a century of

[7] Hsu, *Chou En-lai*, p. 168.

foreign imperialism topped by a quarter century of civil war. The
Communist side was winning the sympathy of all third parties in
the nation, including the Democratic League and even the left
wing of the Kuomintang.

America, following Germany's and Japan's surrender, and now
under the new but canny leadership of President Harry S. Truman, had one more card to play in an effort to settle the civil war
in China. This was the celebrated Marshall Mission.

On December 15, 1945, Truman announced he was sending
America's most respected public figure, General of the Army
George C. Marshall,[8] head of the vast military machine that had
just spearheaded the winning of history's greatest war, to tackle
the problem of winning the peace in China. Marshall, full of
years and honors, had just reached his home in Leesburg, Vir-
ginia, to begin a well-earned retirement, when the call came
from the White House. In her poignant biography of her husband, *Together*, Catherine Marshall tells how the General, with
a heavy heart but ever the soldier, descended from the peach
tree he was pruning, listened for a moment on the phone to his
Commander-in-Chief, and replied simply that he and his wife
would of course be ready to leave immediately.[9]

Marshall's arrival in the Far East injected a new element into
the China deadlock. Following four days of intensive talks, Chou
reported that Yenan, in deference to the people's will and world
opinion, had ordered all Communist troops to cease fire. "Personally," he said, "I have learned four lessons from these negotiations. Each side must approach the other with mutual recognition, not mutual enmity. They must bilaterally discuss, not
unilaterally dictate; they must give and take—more important,
they must give before taking; and they must compete only in
bringing about a prompt settlement of the difficulties."

Chou re-emphasized the importance of Sun Yat-sen's Three
People's Principles as the "right path" for China's revolution, and
added: "We recognize the national leadership of Generalissimo

[8] General Marshall told me once of the little-known controversy over his
military title. It appears that America's top military rank was "General of
the Armies" (held by Pershing) and the question arose whether the example
of other nations should not be followed and the supreme title of "Field
Marshal" should not be created for the U. S. Army as well. I have never
forgotten the General's dry remark: "I asked them how it would sound for
me to be addressed as 'Marshal Marshall.'" That ended the matter.

[9] Marshall, Catherine, *Together*.

Chiang Kai-shek. We did so during the past eight years of war, and shall continue to do so after victory. We accept the fact that the Nationalist Party is the Number One major party in the country—that is why we gladly agree to having the KMT and their supporters represented by twenty-five members in the proposed forty-member State Council, with the CCP and Democratic League sharing fourteen seats, or slightly over a third, and one going to an Independent."

Early in 1946 Chou flew to Yenan to report on the happy atmosphere that surrounded the talks. He went straight from the plane into a night session with the CCP Central Committee. Two days later he was back in Chungking to inform the country that Yenan was deeply gratified and that everything pointed at last toward success.

On February 28, a committee of three—Marshall, Chou and the KMT's General Chang Chih-chung—set out by plane to inspect the military lines in North China. In Yenan, en route, Mao toasted the American mediator and his colleagues: "All the people of China should be very grateful to Generals Marshall, Chang Chih-chung and Chou En-lai for their selfless dedication to the establishment of a peaceful, democratic and unified China. Let us cheer the lasting co-operation between America and China, between the Communist Party and the Nationalist Party."

Undoubtedly, the fact that Chou accompanied Marshall to Yenan made it possible for the American General to be received by all the Communist leaders, including Mao Tse-tung, with genuine warmth and enthusiasm—such was Chou's instinctive sense of fitness, tact and perspective in the presence of conflicting personalities. Yenan's welcome to the American envoy took the form of an unprecedented tribute, a specially composed song:

> Let us sing for you,
> For your clear clarion call to peace,
> And your magnificent influence
> Which extinguished the forest fire of war.
> Oh, General Marshall, let the Red Army
> Pay its supreme tribute to you.
> We of the Communist Party support you!

Taking leave of Marshall at the Yenan airport, Mao was asked when he would be prepared to go to Nanking. "Whenever Chairman of the National Government Chiang Kai-shek wants me to go," he replied, "I will go." At Hankow, Marshall, clearly moved, reported at a reception: "I can tell you in confidence, ladies and gentlemen, that I observed an atmosphere of optimism everywhere I went. I can tell you that an unprecedented era of progress awaits China."

Marshall made a flying trip to Washington on March 11, 1946, to report to a gratified President the promise of hope emerging from this first phase of his China Mission. Unhappily, the euphoria proved to be a passing phase. The universal longing for peace was of course wholly genuine, but behind the rhetoric each side had its own conflicting motives and plans, which quickly became apparent in the field.

The cease-fire order, supposedly issued jointly by Chiang and Mao on January 10, 1946, to take effect at midnight three days later, did not in fact take effect. Already on the sixteenth, a large-scale Nationalist attack took place in far-off Inner Mongolia, and the Communists duly counterattacked. No one has ever known for certain precisely what happened, only that the situation in Manchuria became explosive and remained so. Mao's local commanders were determined to hold on to their hard-won bases there, despite the cease-fire directive which officially, but with characteristic vagueness, agreed that "national" troops were to enter Manchuria to take over "the sovereignty." In addition, there were the Russians, who, having finally joined the war in the Far East and invaded Manchuria in hopes of regaining their former bases there, were only half-hearted in their evacuation and before leaving stripped the area of its key industrial installations.

Marshall pleaded with all sides, but to no effect. From Chungking, Chou En-lai continued to urge a peaceful settlement, but with growing discouragement. One April evening in 1946, after a grueling day, he accepted a ride home in his KMT colleague's car and remarked in a burst of candor: "I cannot say the position of our own side has always been rational. Perhaps we could have made a few more concessions. I really don't know . . . It is so perplexing." He sighed with frustration.

On May 19, 1946, a particularly unfortunate incident took place. With KMT troops armed with American equipment pouring into Manchuria, Marshall begged both sides to neutralize the major industrial center of Changchun—and both agreed. Three days later, the Generalissimo in Nanking asked for the loan of Marshall's plane to fly to Mukden, as he feared his invading troops might ignore the truce terms and march on Changchun. Marshall reluctantly agreed. Chiang reached Mukden the day his own troops had in fact entered Changchun, which the Communists, as agreed, had just evacuated.

Worse, Chiang's arrival in fact only accelerated the advance of his Nationalist forces beyond Changchun northeastward toward Harbin and beyond—a clear violation of the Generalissimo's earlier promise. Three protesting radiograms from Marshall urging an immediate cease-fire went unanswered. They were "lost" or "mistranslated," and in fact no cease-fire orders went out until three days after Chiang had returned to Nanking.

This incident, as it turned out, ended the practical usefulness of the Marshall Mission. Now that the American mediator's impartiality appeared compromised, Chou En-lai refused in the future to accept his vote in case of a tie. That summer arrests and murders in Kunming brought a protesting cable from President Truman to the Generalissimo on August 10, 1946: "I would be less than honest if I did not point out that latest developments have forced me to the conclusion that the selfish interests of extremist elements, both in the KMT and the CCP, are obstructing the aspirations of the people of China . . ."

With Chou in Shanghai, Mao in Yenan, Chiang in the summer resort of Lu Shan in Central China, and the American mediator in Nanking, Marshall persuaded the Mandarin-speaking and widely respected educator, former President of Yenching University Leighton Stuart, now U. S. Ambassador to China, to accompany him on the tedious journey by boat, auto and sedan chair up Lu Shan Mountain for a final plea to the Generalissimo. When Stuart brought Chiang's counterproposals back to Chou, the latter moved to the edge of his chair, listening intently, then bent his head for a long time in depressed silence. As Stuart later described the scene: "I took it this meant Chou might consider adjusting his position on the issues and waited, also in silence. But all that happened, at the end of the silence, was a tortured smile from Chou and a gentle shake of his head."

The last straw proved to be the sale of surplus U.S. war matériel to Chiang Kai-shek at bargain rates. Chou personally traveled from Shanghai to Nanking to protest to Marshall, and after the usual preliminaries got directly to the point.

"I suppose you know what I am here for this time."

"I think I do, but it is useless. The sale was strictly in accordance with the United States Government's policy of handling surplus matériel in the interest of a friendly nation, and China is one of America's friendly nations."

"But, my good friend," said Chou, "how about the policy statement of your President dated December 15, 1945, which says specifically, 'United States support will not extend to United States military intervention to influence the course of any Chinese internal strife'?"

"There is absolutely no United States military intervention in China!"

Chou demurred. "Are the United States Marines in North China and Manchuria not military? Are the United States trucks and jeeps and planes transporting Chiang Kai-shek's troops not military? Are most of the United States surplus and war matériel being transferred to Chiang Kai-shek not military?"

Marshall: "I know how you feel about Chiang Kai-shek, but in international practice it is the legal government, not the individual behind the government, that we have to deal with. The National Government of China is the only legal government with which we can formally conduct transactions."

"Aren't you being a bit mechanically formalistic?" insisted Chou. "Isn't there an element of hypocrisy when you know that anything you turn over to the National Government goes to the front facing the Communist troops? Aren't you . . ." Chou broke off as he observed a change of color on Marshall's face at the mention of "hypocrisy."

"I have indicated several times," replied the General wearily, "that I am ready to recommend that my government terminate its effort to mediate here. Your side has been particularly critical of me recently, saying that I am unfair and insincere. And yet, just a while ago, you insisted that I must stay on and keep trying this apparently futile job!"

The Communists, thoroughly incensed, now turned a full-scale propaganda barrage on Marshall, and on October 1, 1946, the General announced to Chiang:

"I am not in agreement either with the present course of the Government or with that of the Communist Party. I disagree with the evident Government policy of settling the fundamental decisions by force . . . On the part of the Communist Party, I deplore actions and statements which provide a basis for the contention on the part of many in the Government that the Communists' proposals cannot be accepted in good faith . . . Unless a basis of agreement is found to terminate the fighting without further delays, I will recommend to the President that I be recalled and that the United States government terminate its effort of mediation . . ."

Late in December, General Marshall packed his bags for home. Chou, after a sad farewell banquet in Nanking, also packed up and returned to Yenan.

On February 1, 1947, Mao released the Communist pamphlet "Greet the High Tide of Revolution." Finally on July 4, 1947, America's National Day, Chiang Kai-shek ordered "Mobilization for the Suppression of Revolution."

Strategically, the long-drawn-out peace maneuvers had worked to the Communists' advantage, giving them time to regroup and build up the Red Army. They were now prepared for the ensuing two final years of civil war.

Chiang scored an initial success when his troops, moving swiftly to the attack, marched on Yenan and forced the Communists to flee the capital they had held for eleven years. Chou and Mao assumed aliases and, protected by less than a regiment of security guards, fled westward. Chou's nose started to bleed and finally, at Mao's and Chiang Ching's insistence, he took turns with the less hardy women comrades in sharing the single litter. Rations were meager, as the villagers en route could spare only hard-baked barley cakes mixed with wild greens. As usual, Chou's sense of humor did not desert him. Taking a large bite, he grinned and remarked to Mao, "This isn't really too bad. I'd say even better than anything we had in the grasslands."

After finding refuge from their pursuers for several weeks at the Great Wall, Chou and Mao were finally cornered by the Nationalists at the Lu, a tributary of the Yellow River. The two men decided that, come what may, they would stick together. Crossing the stream during the night under a torrential downpour with the aid of a makeshift bridge, made of doors donated by nearby villagers, they eluded their enemies. But the Nationalists pressed them and Chou had to join the litter bearers to care for the wounded.

Finally reinforcements arrived, and gradually the tide of civil war began to turn in their favor. Chiang's outlawing of the Democratic League drove it and other "Third Party" elements to the Communist side, and on May 1, 1948, Mao announced the calling of an independent People's Political Conference, bringing together all parties and groups to form a "People's Republic of China."

Student riots flared across the country. The increasingly demoralized Nationalists lost battle after battle, ending at the turn of the year with a major defeat at Hsuchow in northern Kiangsu —not far from strategic Shanghai—in late 1948. This proved decisive.

On January 29, 1949, Chiang Kai-shek resigned. The stiff conditions offered to his successor were unacceptable, and eventually the Generalissimo evacuated some two million of his forces and adherents, and others fleeing Communist rule, to the 240-mile-long island province of Taiwan (Formosa), ninety miles from the mainland, which had been restored to China at the end of World War II following fifty years of Japanese rule. There, backed diplomatically and militarily by Washington, he maintained till his death at eighty-seven, a quarter century later, the firm but increasingly illusory belief that he would one day "return," again to rule the mainland.

CHAPTER VII

PEKING'S MAN FOR ALL SEASONS

The China mainland now belonged to the Communist Revolution. On October 1, 1949, Chou En-lai stood at Mao Tse-tung's elbow on the giant balcony of the Gate of Heavenly Peace facing Peking's vast T'ien An Men Square, as Mao announced in his harsh Hunanese: "The People's Republic of China is now established! The Chinese people have stood up!"

Before them stretched a sea of red flags waved with frantic enthusiasm by scores of thousands representing the hundreds of millions of the newly oriented nation. Chou and Mao exchanged glances while their thoughts must have gone racing back over the decades of their historic association.

Chou's beltless uniform was neatly pressed and buttoned to the collar, his slim figure erect, and despite cheeks hollowed by hardships and illness, his handsome face belied his fifty-one years. This moment marked a final farewell to noisome jails, hairline escapes, night marches, clandestine meetings and soup flavored with shoe leather. It marked the end of a long and stormy march from total obscurity only a quarter century before to leadership of the oldest and most populous nation on earth. And it marked the beginning of Chou's chance to fulfil a lifelong dream of a new China free from foreign domination without, and from monumental poverty, disease and despair within.

The first quarter century of Communist rule in Peking might fairly be called the joint era of Chairman Mao and Premier Chou. Edgar Snow, writing in 1971, not long before he died, caught their unique relationship in a vivid feature for *Life* magazine:

> Carefully avoiding any thrust for personal power, the Premier has been a zestful worker in pursuit of national and revolutionary power politics. His affable manner masks viscera of tough and supple alloys; he is a master of policy implementation with an infinite capacity for detail. His personal contacts are innumerable. He combines an administrative efficiency hard to reconcile with his ubiquity. His self-effacing dedication makes him Mao's indispensable alter ego. Symbiosis is perhaps the best word to describe their relationship. Very different in working style and personality, Mao and Chou complement each other as a tandem based on thirty-seven [eventually forty-two] years of trust and interdependence.

Indeed, from 1949 on it was Chou En-lai who more and more took the lead. Chou's absorbing interest and genius was always New China's international relations. He pursued them with tireless vigor. In 1958 he handed over the Foreign Office to his old associate of the Paris days and victor in the final battles of the civil war, Marshal Ch'en Yi. But even after that he continued to represent his country in all important negotiations at home and abroad.

Since 1949, and until Chou's death, the only other statesmen from Peking to appear even briefly in foreign capitals with any significant missions were Mao Tse-tung, on two trips to Moscow, and President of the People's Republic Liu Shao-ch'i, who earlier visited the Soviet capital several times. Liu Shao-ch'i also toured Burma, Cambodia and Indonesia in 1963. All the other important trips were made by Chou En-lai. Occasionally he was accompanied by Foreign Minister Ch'en Yi, but Chou's was the pace-setting personality.

His first preoccupation was naturally Russia, whose border with China runs in a great 5,500-mile arc from Vladivostok on the Pacific, to Afghanistan in the western Himalayas—the longest international boundary in the world.

In the first fifteen years of the People's Republic, Chou made seven trips to Moscow—these in addition to his many earlier visits. The alliances and treaties he brought back from the first three visits, assuring China of Russia's political and economic cooperation, were brilliant diplomatic achievements. By these agreements, Russia advanced massive loans to China, contributed technicians to assist in the building of railroads, dams and steel plants, and significantly renounced many long-held historical interests in the country.

By the mid-fifties, however, unknown to the outside world, the Moscow-Peking axis was revealing signs of stress.

Stalin's mass liquidations of his own Communist comrades had, of course, been known to Peking but had not been taken too seriously, since every revolution, including their own, had had its excesses. What did disturb the Chinese was that Khrushchev had not consulted them before taking far-reaching actions which affected the whole Communist world, such as having Lenin's successor, the great Stalin, denounced by the Kremlin as a common tyrant, since it raised obvious questions regarding their own leadership. After all, many felt that in Mao the People's Republic had its own legitimate "cult of personality."

China and Russia, however, were not yet ready for the great schism between them which was later to alter so completely the whole world-power picture. So when Moscow asked Chou and Mao to help them in their difficulties with Hungary, Poland and Czechoslovakia, the Chinese promptly accepted, and in January 1957, Chou flew to Moscow, and later to Poland, Hungary and Albania, in pursuit of his reconciling mission.

Moscow had been furnishing Chou and Mao with important commodity imports (machinery, equipment and complete plant installations) as well as much technical assistance. Between 1950 and 1960, altogether 10,800 Soviet and 1,500 East European specialists and technicians were sent to China. During this same period 8,000 Chinese engineers and skilled workers were trained in the U.S.S.R. while almost as many Chinese students were educated there. Chou's appreciation was unequivocal: "The experts from the Soviet Union have made an outstanding contribution to the building of socialism in China."[1]

But beneath all this surface collaboration trouble was brewing between the two Red giants. The immediate occasion was the fighting which broke out in March 1959 between the government of Tibet headed by the Dalai Lama, and Chinese Red Army troops who had been sent to implement a long-standing Chinese claim to that country.

There followed a major military clash with Indian troops along the high Himalayan border, which the Chinese won overwhelmingly. Then, with India's ill-equipped and poorly led forces in headlong flight, Chou dramatically withdrew his troops to await further negotiation.

Khrushchev, who had recently visited India and struck up a warm friendship with Nehru, protested the Chinese action—a move all the more galling to Peking in view of the vast expanse of former Chinese territory, extending from Vladivostok almost to Samarkand, which the Russians had been occupying for a century and a half.

When Khrushchev followed up his private objections by violent public denunciations of China's actions as "regrettable and stupid," it proved to be the last straw. Chou and Mao now decided to challenge Soviet Russia for the leadership of the Communist world, accusing Moscow of that greatest sin in the Communist lexicon—"revisionism."

The inevitable Sino-Soviet split then began, and rapidly developed both privately and publicly.

The Kremlin refused point-blank to provide assistance to Peking's nuclear industry. The mutual polemics were further escalated in a long complaint against China filed by Moscow at the Bucharest Communist Assembly in June 1960. The next month the Russians announced they planned to withdraw over thirteen hundred technical consultants and terminate several hundred industrial contracts. Initially it seems to have been a bluff, and soon afterward Moscow let it be known that if China would make certain border concessions, the technicians could stay.

[1] For further details, see Eckstein, Alexander, *Communist China's Economic Growth and Foreign Trade*, p. 169.

Chou, himself no mean bluffer, calmly replied that the Chinese had already made other arrangements.

Even after this body blow, Chou, when he faced the West, appeared undisturbed. When Edgar Snow questioned him pointedly on the rumored Moscow-Peking split, he admitted there might be some technical differences of opinion but claimed that this could in no way affect World Communism. "To be exactly identical would indeed be something strange and incomprehensible."

In any case, Chou indicated to Snow that whatever the quarrel between Peking and Moscow, the West would do well not to maximize it as a possible advantage.

Chou now turned to other nations, particularly the Third World nations which had so long been exploited under Western rule. He began actively to champion them in their struggle for freedom, inviting their representatives from many parts of the world as honored guests in Peking to study the People's Republic on the spot.

Following his exceedingly friendly sessions with Egypt's President Nasser during the Indonesian conference of the mid-fifties, Chou planned extensive trips to China for a long series of African delegates. His speech to the Congolese was typical: "Even though China and the Congo are separated by great oceans and thousands of miles," he said, "their common struggle against imperialism and colonialism has united our two peoples."

Chou personally expended prodigious efforts in overseeing every detail of hospitality for these overseas guests, and carefully acquainted himself with their special needs and views. During a North Vietnamese delegation visit to Peking, he joined Prime Minister Pham Van Dong in a vitriolic attack on American action in Indo-China. Then came representatives from Cuba, closely followed, between 1960 and 1962, by fifty different delegations from Latin America. To each of them Chou extended a personally tailored welcome.

One of the Premier's special guests was the famous and irrepressible British World War II veteran, Lord Montgomery of Alamein. Montgomery commented: "Chou is intellectual and very clever. He is a quick and clear thinker, extremely lucid in his speech with the most pleasing personality and a nice sense of humor. Altogether he is a very likable man with charming manners. He appealed to me so much that I invited him to come and stay with me in my home in England."[2]

Chou had already succeeded, some ten years before, in establishing diplomatic relations with twenty-five key countries, including in rapid succession Bulgaria, Rumania, Hungary, North Korea, Czechoslovakia, Poland, Outer Mongolia, East Germany, Albania, North Vietnam, Yugoslavia, Burma, India, Pakistan, Britain, Norway, Ceylon, Denmark, Israel, Afghanistan, Finland, Sweden, Switzerland, Holland and Indonesia. Then, after an interval, came Nepal in 1955 and Yemen in 1956. After longer intervals came France in 1964—the land of his early student days—which, with Canada in 1971, precipitated the bandwagon rush to eventual United Nations membership.

The startling early recognition by America's protégé, Israel, was due wholly to the personal conviction and initiative of Prime Minister David Ben-Gurion, a longtime student and admirer of China and the Chinese. "B.G." told me the story personally.

His action, it seems, was largely due to two factors. First, his profound knowledge of world history, including especially the vast European incursions into and dominance over Asia during the past four centuries. Second, his feelings, as a Jew, of empathy with the Chinese in that they had suffered, as had his own people, from the domineering arrogance of the European nations. When, on October 1, 1949, the Chinese people, in Mao's vivid phrase, "stood up" by declaring the establishment of the People's Republic, Ben-Gurion felt an instinctive rapport with them. He mentioned, a little wistfully, that China had not yet reciprocated by in turn recognizing Israel. But this did not in the least affect his conviction that Israel had done the morally right thing. Indeed, he expressed regret that the United States, which he so greatly admired in other respects, had not yet seen fit to face these international realities and exchange ambassadors with Peking.

Then, in the 1960s, began the current jockeying between the three great world powers—the United States, Russia and China. To Chou's dismay President Eisenhower, in May 1960, disregarding the Chinese, arranged a summit conference with Khrushchev in Paris with a view to developing peaceful coexistence in

2 *The Sunday Times* Magazine (London), June 12, 1960, p. 22.

Europe. But, to the relief of the Chinese, it all ended with the shooting down of an American U-2 spy plane and subsequent cancellation of the conference.

The Sino-Soviet relationship, however, continued to sour. As a precaution against further deterioration, Chou made a quick journey to Outer Mongolia to sign a treaty of mutual aid and nonaggression. Dressed in a Mongolian costume with a huge sheepskin robe, he joined in repeated toasts with Mongolian officials. His constant aim of winning friends for Peking against a possible attack by either the Soviet Union or the United States led him to work out similar treaties with Burma, Nepal, Indonesia, Cambodia and Ceylon.

Between 1954 and 1964, Chou En-lai executed a series of six joint statements with Burma—on nonaggression, mutual aid and peaceful coexistence. When he visited Rangoon in 1961, over four hundred Chinese delegates made it a gala affair. The festivities were highlighted by a Chinese loan to Burma of one hundred million U.S. dollars with no interest and no strings. Premier U Nu returned the gesture by defining, at long last, the Sino-Burmese borders—a perpetually irksome issue.

Following the 1954 Geneva Conference on Indo-China,[3] the International Conference of 1955 at Bandung, Indonesia,[4] marked the beginning of Chou En-lai's diplomatic debut on the world stage. He met for the first time President Nasser of Egypt and Prime Minister Nehru of India, and the three statesmen began a period of close collaboration.

With Indonesia Chou was less successful. He signed a treaty with President Sukarno dealing with the delicate problem of dual citizenship for Chinese who lived in that country. The Chinese in 1959 then loaned thirty million U.S. dollars to the Indonesian textile industry, and invited the Indonesian foreign minister to visit Peking. But certain elements in the Chinese Foreign Office opposed Chou's peace-building efforts, all attempts at

[3] Fairbank, *The United States and China*, p. 367. "At the Geneva Conference of April–July 1954, Chou En-lai joined the foreign ministers of the other powers in an effort to create stability in Indo-China as France withdrew."

[4] Latourette, *Short History*, p. 114. "Nehru was outstanding . . . but he was in part eclipsed by Chou En-lai who, speaking for the (Communist) Peoples' Republic of China, by his geniality and conciliatory attitude disarmed some of the criticism of his government."

conciliation failed, and the tenuous relationship was broken completely in 1965. On that occasion the Indonesian Army was surprised by a predawn Communist coup, and its senior Officer Corps came close to being wiped out. However, the Army rallied under General Suharto, later his country's president, and decimated the Communist Party in one of the most massive bloodbaths on record. Relations between Jakarta and Peking sank to their lowest point, and Chou's international diplomatic offensive suffered a severe blow.

As to America, in 1960 Chou declared that it would be impossible to achieve peace in Asia without diplomatic relations between China and the United States. This, of course, would depend on a compromise over Formosa, and Chou let it be known that, since the death of Dulles a year earlier, such a Formosan settlement might be a realistic possibility. It is interesting to speculate on the course of events, had Washington—a full decade before the history-making Nixon visit to Peking—taken Chou up on it.

The year 1961 marked the public break between Russia and China,[5] and it was without enthusiasm that Chou decided on one more journey to Moscow—this time for the Twenty-Second Soviet Party Congress. He knew China would be denounced by Khrushchev and had already prepared his counterstrategy.[6]

The climax came in the Kremlin on October 19 over the Albanian issue. Chou challenged Khrushchev by declaring that any public unilateral accusation against the recalcitrant little country "would neither contribute to the solidarity of world Communism nor help towards solution of the problem in point." He added that the accusation of Khrushchev would only "play into the hands of the enemy."

Khrushchev responded by persuading the Party Congress to issue a collective denunciation of Stalinism. Chou in his turn led his delegation from the Assembly to place a wreath on Stalin's tomb in Red Square. Defiantly, the wreath was inscribed to "the Great Marxist-Leninist."

In bitter riposte, Khrushchev rushed through a resolution to

[5] Privately, relations had been worsening for years. Indeed, as late as 1960, Chou felt obliged to assure a skeptical Edgar Snow that all was well.

[6] For a detailed account of the evolving Sino-Soviet estrangement see Clubb, *Twentieth Century China*, pp. 431–40.

remove Stalin's remains from the Lenin mausoleum to a lesser site in the shadow of the Kremlin wall.

To Chou this was the final insult. Quietly he rose in his seat, turned his back on the Congress delegates, and walked out, his face expressionless. On arrival at Peking airport he was personally greeted and congratulated by Mao Tse-tung.

With Moscow now an avowed antagonist, China had to make her own way abroad, and Chou lost no time.

In December 1963, he set out with Foreign Minister Ch'en Yi on a wide-ranging tour of Africa. For two months they visited ten African nations, hoping to stir up interest in a second Afro-Asian conference, and explaining Peking's case in the Sino-Indian dispute. He reminded his African hosts that much of modern Western civilization had been built on the blood and bones of cheap Afro-Asian labor. China's policy, Chou declared in Ghana on January 15, 1964, "is to support the African nations, to oppose imperialism and all forms of old and new colonialism." For Somaliland, on the strategic eastern border of the continent, he urged solidarity of the Afro-Asian bloc because "we Afro-Asian peoples share the same pulsation and are involved in the same revolution."

Statements like these, as Jomo Kenyatta pointed out to Chou, won little response in many African nations who felt they had already won their battle against imperialism by throwing out the British. It is to Chou's credit that he welcomed such criticism, and in later years—notably in Tanzania—used practical aid rather than slogans to find a responsive chord. The Tanzam Railway, connecting the rich Zambian copper mines with Tanzania's port of Dar-es-Salaam on the Indian Ocean, is one of China's major achievements abroad.

While passing through Pakistan, Chou reminded his enthusiastic hosts that the newly developed "Afro-Asian nations who have just struggled to their feet are exerting an increasingly positive influence in world affairs." He predicted doom for those neglecting the importance of the Afro-Asian bloc. Finally, on his return to Peking, he summed up Chinese policy before a festive reception for the Afro-Asian diplomatic corps in the gaily decorated Great Hall of the People:

"The Chinese Communists," he declared on March 24, 1964, "have shared with you the experience of imperialistic aggression,

and further are sharing with you the common mission of opposing both imperialism, and the old and new colonialism. Our
friendship has been tested through many an international storm.
It is indestructible."

Eastern Europe, being mostly in the Russian orbit, had had
only limited contact with the New China. But when Chou En-lai
visited Budapest and Warsaw in January 1957, he was accorded
a warm welcome by Hungary's Kadar and Poland's Gomulka,
who counted on the visit to help offset their own recent anti-
Moscow outbreaks.

In Albania everyone remembered how Chou had stood by
them against Khrushchev in 1961, and gave a tumultuous reception to the Chinese Premier when he arrived there on New
Year's Eve, 1963. He was feted and honored continuously for
eight days by leaders of all circles in Albanian life, and formal
documents were signed pledging eternal friendship with Peking.

By the mid- and late-sixties Peking had more or less reg-
ularized its relations with the leading countries of the Western
world, including Britain and particularly France, with whom,
under Charles de Gaulle, Chou and Mao had developed a special relationship. Indeed, by 1970 the French Foreign Minister,
Maurice Couve de Murville, was already in Peking preparing for
the General's personal visit. Death decreed otherwise, but the
cordial sentiments between the two capitals have largely remained. Mao, always sparing in his personal messages, sent a
warm cable of condolence to Mme. de Gaulle—the only one to
any foreigner other than to Lois Snow when her husband Ed
died in early 1972.

French Ambassador Etienne Manac'h had enjoyed one of the
longest tenures in the capital of any diplomat of the period, and
conversing with him showed clearly how close he was personally,
and the nation he represented, to the Chinese leadership.

With her closest neighbor, relationships in the early years of
the People's Republic were not easy, because of bitter war memories and Tokyo's dependence on Washington. Indeed, when I
was in Peking during the two months just before the Nixon visit
(winter of 1971–72), I found the Chinese attitude toward Japan
frigid, to say the least, and was shown a series of highly pro-
vocative anti-Japanese propaganda films. As everyone knows, this
attitude changed dramatically in the next few years. Peking has

felt the need for further support against Moscow. But Chou insisted with Tokyo, as with other capitals, that the price of normalizing Sino-Japanese relations included the severance of Japan's ties with Taiwan. Painful as this was—emotionally as well as politically, since Japan had ruled Taiwan for half a century and trade was booming—continued estrangement from Peking was still more painful. Chou demanded the withdrawal of Japan's ambassador from Taipei before admitting one to Peking. But he proved willing to permit *de facto* continuance of Taiwan-Japanese trade, and on this basis a deal was struck and Premier Tanaka was cordially welcomed to the mainland to sign a new accord. Sino-Japanese relations became virtually normal, with travel and trade between the two countries, as nearly normal as with any other country.

Internationally, China by that time had formal diplomatic relations with one hundred countries, and trade links with some one hundred and fifty, while most of Southeast Asia—both Vietnams, Laos, Cambodia, followed by Thailand and the Philippines —was already in the mainland orbit.

Chou insisted all along that China's chief aim in Vietnam and Southeast Asia was not to annex these countries but to form a neutral buffer along China's southern border. The situation may be compared to American sensibilities regarding border states like Mexico and Canada—or even, under the Monroe Doctrine, to all countries of the Hemisphere. The most recent test of Washington's sensitivity on this point was President Kennedy's preparation to invade Cuba (ninety miles from the Florida coast) during the famous "missile crisis."

There remained, of course, Chou's major diplomatic problems —China's relations with the super powers of Russia and the United States.

From his youth, America had always held a special place in Chou's affections. He had been keenly disappointed at missing out on visiting the United States on a Boxer Indemnity scholarship in 1913. Later he decided to study in France instead, and spent those formative years in Paris and Europe, already referred to. But America had always been his first choice, and Chou took every occasion to maintain contact with former friends across the Pacific, even during the unhappy period of mutual ostracism. With my own family, the Premier, on three separate occasions during those difficult years, went out of his way to send personal messages. One was during the 1955 Peking visit of Dag Hammarskjöld, then Secretary-General of the United Nations, inquiring about my sister's marriage and sending condolences on my father's death. He seemed to know which part of the world we were in, and his New Year's cards reached us from time to time.

In the end, Washington, not Peking, made the first move, when President Nixon, shortly after his inauguration in January 1969, intimated to President de Gaulle in Paris that America wished to initiate relations with Peking. It was de Gaulle's private relaying of this information, by sending Ambassador Manac'h on a special mission to Peking, that first alerted the Chinese to the fact that there might be a change of policy in the offing in Washington.

Not long after, when Edgar Snow, on his notable last visit to China, had his usual long talks with Chou En-lai, the latter indicated that Peking had not quite made its choice as between Moscow and Washington. Then at the great national celebrations on October 1 of that year, Mao summoned Snow and his wife to stand with him on the Gate of Heavenly Peace, jointly to review to cheering throngs marching past. "Such an honor," wrote Snow, "was a clear signal."

Later that autumn, in a talk with Snow, Mao indicated that the decision had been made in favor of America, and immediately began his first private response to the overtures from the White House. The momentous Washington-Peking courtship was under way.

The story of China's "ping-pong" diplomacy, beginning in the spring of 1971, created a spate of world publicity unrivaled, except possibly by the first moon shot, in the history of world communications. As for the Nixons' week-long Peking visit itself, the size of the international television audience is a record likely to stand for many years.

Indeed, the U.S. media, long conditioned to an automatic hostility toward Chinese Communism,[7] made a major policy shift, competing in a furor of acclaim toward the previously vilified Peking regime.

Snow, for instance, had for years eked out a meager subsist-

[7] See Theodore H. White's television script, *China: The Roots of Madness.*

ence by marketing his factual China stories to various obscure European journals, having been turned down regularly by the New York *Times* and by the Luce and other American publishing empires. Now he suddenly found himself popular. American editors competed in offering him princely sums. "God Almighty!" breathed one of them to me with awe, "I never dreamed I'd see the day!"

Tragically, Edgar Snow was stricken with cancer on the eve of his greatest vindication—a commission to cover the Nixon visit for Time-Life, Inc. He died only a week before the President arrived in Peking. Author Theodore H. White, whose own wartime *Thunder Out of China* was a best-seller thirty years earlier, commented: "Ed's discovery and description of Chinese Communism was a staggering achievement, like Columbus discovering America."

The triumphant Nixon visit was carried out almost exclusively by Chou En-lai. He was the President's host from his arrival at Peking airport to his departure from Shanghai. He chaired the banquets, represented China at all discussions, and finally cosigned with Nixon the celebrated Shanghai communiqué, frankly stating the issues regarding Taiwan and Vietnam that still divided the two countries, but also stressing the vital points on which agreement had been reached, including a pledge of future collaboration. For Chou it was the climax of over half a century of top leadership in the Communist Party of China—a tenure of high Party office longer than that of Lenin or even Mao—and of over a quarter century of continuous national power as Premier of the People's Republic.

For much of this time Chou was Foreign Minister as well as Premier, heading thirty different ministries. But no title can convey the multiplicity of his functions or the all-pervasiveness of his influence on Chinese affairs. Former French Premier Maurice Couve de Murville, when I last saw him in Paris, summed it up: "He *is* the government."

Along with pursuing his dominant interest in foreign affairs, Chou as Premier also exerted a controlling influence on domestic policy. Even before the new state was proclaimed on October 1, 1949, he had been hard at work preparing a "Common Program" for a "People's Democratic Dictatorship." Though based on

Marxism-Leninism, the program was distinctively Chinese. A 2,500-year-old Confucian classic states: "When the Great Way prevails, the world belongs to the public . . . Since one hates to see goods wasted, one does not hoard them for oneself, and since one hates to keep his talents unused, one does not work just for oneself. . . . Thus no robbery or chaos need arise and no door need be locked. This is the society of Great Harmony."

As Chou defined it in his "Common Program," the People's Democratic Dictatorship was not yet a proletarian dictatorship, but a "people's democratic United Front composed of the Chinese peasantry, petite bourgeoisie, national bourgeoisie and other patriotic elements, based on an alliance of workers and peasants and led by the working class."

"We use," says Chou, "the combined approach of old methods and modern methods of production, whichever is the most efficient at a given time."

During 1956–57, Chou with Mao sought to release the pent-up energy of the intellectuals with the "Hundred Flowers" movement[8] and later with "The Great Leap Forward."[9] Up until December 1964, Mao was still repeating: "We must continue to implement the policy of 'Let one hundred flowers bloom together, and let one hundred schools of thought contend.'" In this attempt to encourage individual self-expression, the admitted risk eventually proved too great, matters became chaotic, and the whole campaign was eventually dropped.

"The Great Leap Forward" (1958–59), aimed to spur agriculture and industry for the new Communist state in keeping with the collectivist incentives of the Revolution.

In preparing the "Great Proletarian Cultural Revolution" of 1964–69, Chou as usual worked in closest co-operation with Mao—this time with far greater effect. Indeed, the finally successful outcome of the Cultural Revolution was due, in a major degree, to the Premier's tact, resourcefulness and personal courage.

[8] ". . . so that through such healthy competition and mutual vigilance the Chinese people can live forever together in prosperity." (From Mao's original directive of February 27, 1957: "How to Handle Properly the Internal Conflicts of the Nation.")

[9] For a fuller presentation of both the "Hundred Flowers" movement and "The Great Leap Forward" see Fairbank, *United States and China*, pp. 362–64 and 370–75.

At the height of the turmoil, Chou was the only senior leader on hand in Peking when half a million Red Guards[10] virtually imprisoned him in the Great Hall of the People. Mao and the then Defense Minister Marshal Lin Piao, with his Red Army forces, happened—presumably by accident—to be away from the capital.

Chou, with immense *sangfroid*, suggested a series of private conferences with the youth leaders to discuss their grievances and explore solutions. The Premier, as already explained, had always been trusted by China's young people, and as the hours dragged by, the vast throng grew less and less threatening. After three days and two nights of virtual nonstop discussion, the Red Guard leaders declared themselves fully satisfied and agreed to return to their homes throughout the country. When Marshal Lin finally arrived with his troops, the crisis was over.

Though unswervingly loyal to Mao from January 1934 on, as early as the 1920s Chou was nevertheless against timid yes-men in the party. "It is natural to have divergent views," he warned, "but our comrades are afraid of argument, afraid of any heated debate they think might cause a schism . . . afraid of offending friends, they therefore avoid discussion and tend to gloss over differences . . . But so long as we keep our political discussion impersonal, the more intensely we argue, the closer we can come to the truth!"

Chou, as an intellectual himself, felt strongly the need for "remolding" them. "The way the bourgeois intellectuals can learn proletarian thought," he once reflected, "is not just by spending a few days in a factory or farm. They must participate in collective productive labor in order to overcome their tendency toward becoming bureaucrats, and to convert themselves into true laborers who can share the life of the masses with all its sweetness and bitterness."

When a young college girl asked him, "How can we become proletarian intellectuals?" Chou replied, "It is not by studying for an examination or being judged by the leaders. It comes only when your thought and philosophy are in accord with those of the working masses, when you yourself know you are whole-

[10] The Red Guards, a select teen-age force of Chinese youth, were created by Mao and Chou in the mid-sixties to counteract the lack of revolutionary zeal in the privileged but increasingly sterile senior Communist Party bureaucracy.

heartedly serving them, and when they know it too. There are still many who imagine that simply having been in the country-side for several months, makes them automatically proletarian intellectuals. This is like the old days when a man thought of himself as educated simply because he had just graduated from college with a mortarboard on his head. It is sheer formalism, and downright bourgeois!"

The girl had graduated from the chemistry department of the University of Nanking, and was then engaged in agricultural production in a commune outside Shanghai, along with a group of co-eds. They all greeted Chou En-lai with great excitement. They had already spent three months in manual labor. The girls were not quite sure what to say about the amount of time de-voted to reading, as they were supposed to be "learning from the proletariat": some thought they should continue to read when-ever they had time to; others held that they should steer clear of all books during their period of learning from labor.

Chou put them at their ease. "You are not yet used to working with your hands," he said. "Once you get used to it, you will know how to budget your time."

"Practice should be constant," he said. "After you have finished a period of manual work here, go back to your office and laboratory and think it over for a while, then come back here to work physically for another period of time. When the farmers are busy, you should try to come and help them."

He turned and addressed the secretary of the Shanghai branch of the CCP. "How are these girls doing here?"

"Oh, they are just like professional farmers," was the reply.

"No," said the Premier, shaking his head, "they can't be. They have been here only three months. They can't be exactly the same as regular farmers. If you say that, you are inflating their ego."

The secretary hesitated and said: "They are much more like regular farmers now than when they first came."

"That sounds more like it," said Chou.

With real personal solicitude the Premier inquired about life on the commune. He noticed they were covered with mud.

"Did you cry when you first arrived at the farm?"

"No," they answered.

"It wouldn't have mattered if you had. It is only human to cry when you are not used to something," he said.

He wanted to know about the self-criticism program.

"How has it been going?" he asked.

"Everybody progresses from backward to forward. Take me, for instance. Once I was much more backward than you girls. In my young days I had a pigtail on my head which was so full of the old, old stuff, that there was no room even for capitalism—which got in there later. And it was a long time before I found Marxism-Leninism . . . Once I had two brothers. One of them rotted away along with the old society and died a decadent, never awakened. I helped the other join the revolution, but after working with us for some time he also fell by the wayside . . . The road to revolution is not easy; it takes constant self-awakening to stay on it."[11]

That constant "self-awakening" was the chief hallmark of Chou himself throughout a revolutionary career of some sixty years.

In early 1975, at the age of seventy-seven, in one of the highlights of his long life, he presided over the first meeting in a decade of the National People's Congress. Furthermore, he had the satisfaction of announcing a Politburo containing a strong contingent of veteran Party moderates, who for a time collectively gave the nation an unprecedented degree of unity at the top.

To a unique degree Chou En-lai embodied in his personal life style the Party ideal of a "greater-than-self world outlook." At an age at which few American leaders, and no Presidents, have ever continued in high office, China's Premier was once again chosen Chief of Government, and from his hospital bed continued on major issues, until shortly before his death, his unique and indispensable role in shaping China's future.

All this was during a period of failing health and in the teeth of a campaign of personal defamation by the radicals of the Party. Chou grew tense and gaunt, but he never lost heart or perspective.

Domestically, Chou also saw to it that the new and streamlined Constitution confirmed the Maoist theory of "permanent revolution," while permitting a limited degree of private labor

11 Hsu, *Chou En-lai*, pp. 220–22.

and private plots of land, and allowing "freedom of religious worship" along with "freedom of speech, correspondence, the press, assembly, association, procession, demonstration, and freedom to strike."

The hallmark of the era of Chou and Mao—co-founders of the People's Republic—might be described paradoxically as "continuity of social change." Mao often predicted several centuries of alternating tranquillity and transformation. Chou, in an interview in his later years, put the matter still more clearly.

"The original Cultural Revolution," he emphasized, "could not possibly solve all the problems at once; such a revolution must be conducted again and again, each time to a more advanced stage, and each going deeper than the one before."[12]

In accordance with the Chairman's own wishes, the "cult of Mao" was drastically de-emphasized, the formerly omnipresent Mao buttons began to disappear, and the numbers and prominence of Mao statues were greatly reduced.

On the other hand, such staples of the Revolution as the May 7 schools for the rehabilitation and training of Party members were increased in number, some two million young "barefoot doctors"[13] were at work in the countryside, as were ten million city youths, mostly high school graduates, who were required to work at least two years on the land before a limited number would be picked by their fellow workers for enrollment in a university. Largely thanks to Chou's quiet insistence, the tumultuous "Red Guard" upheavals were not allowed to touch the key scientists of the country's atomic program, and the nation's art treasures were again put on exhibit.

Westerners, with our liberal traditions, often are concerned about the seeming lack of personal freedoms in China's homogeneous society. Indeed, an impression is often current abroad that artistic and scholarly activity has come to an end in the People's Republic. Michael Sullivan, Professor of Oriental Art at Stanford University, poses the question: "Has not the improvement in the

[12] Felix Greene, "The Further Thoughts of Premier Chou: Why China Must Revolt, Revolt and Revolt Again," *The Sunday Times* (London), April 30, 1972.

[13] A barefoot doctor is a young person who has had basic first-aid and medical training and gives treatment without leaving his or her area of productive work. In parts of China peasant medics work barefoot in rice paddies, hence the name.

lot of the masses been bought at too great a cost? Does not the playing down of individual creative achievement in the arts lead to the stifling of the human spirit, and so to the death of art itself?"

In reply, Sullivan declares: "To these questions, the new China answers a resounding 'no.' Indeed, there is a deep creative satisfaction to be got from serving and helping to educate one's fellow men, from writing poems and painting pictures that move them, a sense of being wanted by society which some Western artists, driven to exploit a personal idiosyncrasy to gain any attention at all, may well envy."

Sullivan concludes: "Unless, as seems extremely unlikely, 're-visionism' once more gains the upper hand, and Chairman Mao's philosophy is repudiated, the guiding principle for creative artists and craftsmen must surely continue to be to 'serve the people'" —the Chinese ideograph motto which was invariably the sole insignia on Chou En-lai's lapel.[14]

The Premier won his many battles, as one foreign observer shrewdly noted, by "refusing to meet the opposition on their own grounds of bitter personal and doctrinal contention."

Through a career of unprecedented duration and achievement, Chou usually contrived to exercise immense power without giving the impression of desiring it. Furthermore, those who knew him best affirm his sincerity in not desiring it.

This quality of self-effacement, possessed only rarely by world leaders but distinctively by Chou, probably explains better than anything else why, till his death, he was regarded as a truly irreplaceable pillar of the state.

[14] Sullivan, Michael, *The Arts of China*, Berkeley: University of California Press, 1973.

CHAPTER VIII

CHOU'S CHINA: THE MYTH

It is now necessary to take an objective look at the "myths" regarding Communist China which were part of the normal thinking of most Americans for over a generation. It must be added parenthetically that during this same period Peking's conception of Washington was almost, if not quite, as mythical.

The seven days following the Chou-Nixon handshake that midwinter morning at Peking airport in late February 1972 transformed all that. They have been described by Mr. Nixon as "the week that changed the world."

But with equal truth it might be called "the week that changed America."

Consider, for example, the "myth" of Chou's China during the first half of the century, corresponding almost exactly with the first half century of Chou's life—from America's "Open Door Policy" of 1899 to the founding of the People's Republic in 1949.

During the first two decades of the century, as already noted, Westerners enjoyed through the "Unequal Treaties" unparalleled opportunities in commerce, residence, missionary activity, and military and naval dominance.[1] The United States was not a

[1] See John K. Fairbank, *Chinese-American Interactions: A Historical Summary*, Chapter III.

signatory to these treaties, but through the Open Door concept we claimed all privileges accorded the treaty powers. "Hitch-hiking imperialism" it was called by one discerning correspondent. For millions of Americans at home it was the era of Dr. Fu Manchu, described by Hollywood publicists as possessing a "menace in every twitch of his eyebrows, terror in each split-second of his slanted eyes."

As for the twenties and thirties, one Anglo-American writer describes them disarmingly: "Not many of the thousands of Americans living in China during this (to them) golden period . . . because they liked the way of life and liked the Chinese—not many of those ever paused to speculate whether their affection was reciprocated." Except for a few foreigners—and my father was one—the truth of course was that the white man's presence was regarded by most patriotic Chinese with resentment, bitterness and—more often than even fair-minded Westerners would admit—with hate. Only when Mao announced, on October 1, 1949, that China at last had "stood up," did the hate begin to ebb.

In America, people generally had no inkling of the fact that Chou and Mao had made persistent efforts to journey to Washington and personally negotiate a U.S.–China accord.[2] The prevailing hard-line anti-Communism of the following years, personified in Secretaries of State Acheson and Dulles, combined with a general sympathy for the exiled Chiang Kai-shek to produce an almost universal hostility to Peking. Diplomatic relations were maintained with the Republic of China, now based on Taiwan. The new People's Republic in Peking was wholly ignored and all contact severed.

Lack of contact naturally produced, on both sides, abysmal ignorance and some of the wildest reporting on record.

Consider also the pre-Nixon U.S. reportage of mainland China, including the most responsible journals of opinion and our top national leadership. This fell into several broad categories. There were the "Blue Ant" and "Slave State" theory, the "Soviet Satellite" theme, the "Mass Starvation," "Bloodbath," "Yellow Peril," "Faceless Hordes," "Roots of Madness" and "World Domination" syndromes.

[2] See Barbara Tuchman, *Notes From China,* and its reprint of her article in *Foreign Affairs,* "If Mao Had Come to Washington in 1945."

Knowing what we do today about China—modest as our knowledge still is—it seems hardly credible that such capsule characterizations were the basic intellectual diet of America's millions hardly five years ago.

Take the "Blue Ant" image. "The Chinese," stated Secretary of State Dulles in a Seattle speech in 1958, are "imposing mass slavery on six hundred and fifty million people." They have "degraded the dignity of the human individual" and "created a vast slave state."

Mr. Dulles that same year was almost universally supported in these views by the American press. "Nightmarish" was the editorial description of Peking by the respected *Christian Science Monitor*, whose able Washington correspondent, Joseph Harsch, accused Communist China of the "greatest mass sacrifice of human heritage, human comfort and human effort in all time."

Not to be outdone, the nation's leading newspaper, the New York *Times*, referred to "the countless crimes of the Red regime of Mao." UPI reported "open revolt" which the Chinese Communists "obviously are putting down with force right now." The *Herald Tribune*'s Marguerite Higgins accused mainland China of putting "gun worship over ancestor worship," asserting that "what Mao Tse-tung has done . . . makes Stalin look like a piker."

Time magazine declared that "Mao has herded more than 90 per cent of mainland China's 500 million peasants into vast human poultry yards," claiming that when "the old folks" die "their bodies are dropped into a chemically treated pool and converted to fertilizer."

In a Scripps-Howard newspaper series entitled "Chain Gang Empire," R. H. Shackford asserted that "abolition of the family is an avowed, primary sociological objective of Red China's commune system," flatly predicting there would be "no more individuals in China if Mao has his way." An accompanying drawing shows rows of skulls on a blood-spattered wall, upon which is written in blood-red characters "family destruction," "bestiality," "slave labor."

Then there was the "Soviet Satellite" image, largely responsible for Washington's original refusal to recognize Mao's regime, for our involvement in the Korean War, and for the long subsequent estrangement from Peking. This was given official credence by U. S. Secretary of State Dean Acheson in an address to the National Press Club as early as January 12, 1950. Mr. Acheson claimed that "the Soviet Union is detaching the northern provinces of China (Outer Mongolia, Inner Mongolia, Manchuria and Sinkiang) from China and is attaching them to the Soviet Union."

Amplification of this State Department theme occupied the U.S. press for several years following the founding of the People's Republic. "The Chinese Revolution," warned Henry Lieberman of the New York *Times*, "has been hijacked by Russia"—a "hijacking" which the *Herald Tribune* denounced as "lethal." C. L. Sulzberger, the able New York *Times* foreign-policy analyst, revealed that the Chinese Communists had "sold Manchuria and Sinkiang to Russia, completing a Soviet-controlled land bridge between Vladivostok and Alma Ata." Meanwhile, across the continent, China expert Professor Ivar Spector claimed in the Seattle *Times* that "the Chinese are going to adopt a Russian alphabet."

Pursuing this Soviet takeover line, the liberal *New Republic* made the astonishing claim that "Chinese Communist troops probably were ordered into Korea by Soviet officials without the consent of Mao Tse-tung." Much of the American press quoted Nationalist China's T. F. Tsiang[3] as claiming in the United States that "the Chinese Communists have 'sold' Manchuria and Sinkiang to Russia," the New York *Times* speculated editorially on "secret agreements" which "would admit Soviet forces to Chinese bases athwart our own Pacific lines of communications," and UPI stated categorically that "Mao has swapped huge areas to Russia in exchange for Chinese Communist domination over Southeast Asia."

Reports such as these, actively spread while Washington was pondering recognition of Communist China, weighed heavily, if not decisively, in the final United States decision to remain diplomatically with Chiang Kai-shek.

A classic expression of this rationale was that of Dean Rusk, then, in 1951, Assistant Secretary of State for Far Eastern Affairs. In an address on May 18, Mr. Rusk announced to Americans

[3] United Nations Representative.

"Russian annexation of one-third of China," and concluded: "The Peiping regime is a colonial Russian government, a Slavonic Manchukuo on a huge scale. It is not the government of China. It does not pass the first test. It is not Chinese." Five years later (May 19, 1956) the *Saturday Evening Post* was still pursuing this analogy, reporting that "it looks as though the men in Peking have stopped even trying to remain Asian."

Another stock image—"The Starving Chinese"—spiced U.S. reporting for more than a decade, especially in the first years when Americans could not believe that hunger was beginning to be systematically eradicated in that vast country. "Famine in China Catastrophic" (New York *Times*, March 26, 1950); "Shanghai, City of Hungry Millions" (UPI, June 23, 1953); "Red China in Grip of Spring Famine" (New York *Times*, April 24, 1955); "Famished Red China Slaves Steal Pigs' Slop" (New York *World-Telegram and Sun*, June 25, 1959); "Soy Sauce made of Human Hair" (*Time*, December 1, 1960).

Most potent of all the China images at the back of the American mind has been that of the "Yellow Peril"—or the "Genghis Khan Syndrome." Dormant during the colonial and warlord eras, when China was a prey to imperialist powers and the Chinese soldier was regarded by the West as inept, easygoing, playing at battle (an old saw had it that the only absolutely safe moment in the interminable civil wars was when a Chinese aimed directly at one), the image was revived with a vengeance for Americans by our rude awakening during the Korean conflict. In the autumn of 1950 a massed Chinese army poured across the Yalu and swept General MacArthur's astonished troops out of North Korea and almost into the Pacific. "Now," reflected Harold Isaacs,[4] "the men who couldn't handle machines or shoot straight were flying jets and proved 'better artillery-men than the Germans ever were.'"

In the anger, humiliation and bewilderment over our defeat in Korea, forgotten memories from Boxer days revived of the Chinese as brutal and savage, "faceless masses" with no regard for human life—a modern reincarnation of Genghis Khan's "Mongol hordes." Typical phrases from the U.S. press of that period: "war-lovers," "terrifying," "implacable," "psychotic," "fanatical,"

4 *Scratches on Our Minds*, p. 226.

14. In the first fifteen years of the People's Republic, Chou made seven trips to Moscow. Here, in the Kremlin on September 13, 1952, he signs a treaty gradually abolishing Soviet controls in Manchuria. Flanking him is almost the entire Soviet Politburo, including Stalin, Malenkov, Beria, Mikoyan, Preobrajensky and Bulganin.

15. Foreign Minister Anthony Eden of Britain calls at Chou's villa during the Geneva Conference on Vietnam in 1954. It was then that Eden successfully transmitted United States Secretary of State Dulles' proposal that Chou persuade Ho Chi-minh to agree to a strict two-year division of Vietnam. Ho reluctantly agreed—and Chou later called it "the greatest mistake" of his life. "We were 'had' at Geneva," he told Western diplomats in Peking. "We thought the Americans would support the decisions of the Conference. We were wrong."

16. Prince (later King) Feisal of Saudi Arabia meets Chou at the Bandung Conference in Indonesia (April 1955). This began Communist China's concerted diplomatic activity throughout Asia, Africa and the Middle East.

17. China's Chou and Vietnam's Ho Chi-minh, the two most widely traveled leaders of the Communist world, renew their friendship in Peking after Bandung.

18. After the Sino-Indian border war of 1959–60, precipitated by the Dalai Lama's flight from Tibet, Chou and his new Foreign Minister Ch'en Yi (extreme right) conferred seven times with Nehru in New Delhi. This time the two friends failed to agree and shortly afterward Nehru died, a bitter enemy of Peking.

19. Following Stalin's death, relations between Peking and Moscow rapidly deteriorated. The climax came with Chou's 1961 Moscow visit when Peking openly challenged the Kremlin for leadership of the Communist world. On his return, Chou was given a hero's welcome by Mao.

20. A historic handshake: Premier Chou En-lai welcomes Nixon's emissary, Henry Kissinger, on July 9, 1971, at the Government Guest House, Peking. Their secret meeting was the first contact between Chou and an American official since the Dulles episode at Geneva thirteen years before.

21. February 26, 1972. Premier Chou, President Nixon, Secretary of State Rogers and Dr. Kissinger (arm showing on left) en route in a Chinese government plane from the historic Chou-Nixon talks in Peking to a final two days, in Hangchow and Shanghai, of "the week that changed the world."

"smoldering belligerence," "obsessive hatred," "impervious to reason," "intransigent," "dread apparition," "evil portent."

This new obsession with Peking as the fount of all evil was reinforced in due course by a sensational news flash from Yugoslavia. Marshal Tito, then engaged in a feud with Peking, was quoted in the New York *Times* of June 16, 1958, to the effect that "the Chinese liked to boast that their population of 600,000,000 was a guarantee of victory in war . . . that 'even if 300,000,000 were killed there would still remain 300,000,000 Chinese.'"

Next day the *Times* commented editorially: "We knew from the past bloody history of the establishment of Chinese Communism—a process that cost countless lives—that the present Peking rulers regarded human life cheaply; but even their most bitter Western opponent would have hesitated to believe Tito's revelation that they regarded 300,000,000 lives as of little import."

A month later, Joseph P. Lash seized on the Tito report in a sensational piece for the New York *Post* of July 28. He described Stalinist Russia and Orwell's apocalyptic *1984* as "benevolent" compared to what was happening in Red China. "Mao," wrote Lash, "is said to have remarked that another world war might well mean the death of 1,500,000,000 people; but of the 600,000,000 who would survive, half would be Chinese and they would rule the world."

By September 23 that same year, the *Herald Tribune*, in an editorial on Chinese population increase headed "Red China's New Weapon," commented: "The Chinese program of seeking more people for cannon fodder is almost terrifying in its audacity . . . could soon make of China the greatest power the world has ever seen . . . the first nation to adopt a population explosion as an instrument of state policy. It is a mark of the implacability of leaders who have turned a face of unrelenting hatred toward the West and all its ways."

Columnist Drew Pearson (October 28, 1959) expressed the general American reaction: "[Mao] doesn't worry about atomic war because [China] could afford to lose half its population." Four years later Lucius Beebe of the San Francisco *Chronicle* (January 28, 1963) stated categorically: "The Chinese Government approves war, agitates for war, and predicates its entire existence on war . . ." And another *Herald Tribune* front-page feature (October 17, 1962) summarized the outlook: "A vast and grisly wasteland, offering only a future of nonexistence to a massive but starving population, is Red China's bleak prospect for 1980 . . ."

The effects of this type of reporting were of course contagious. The respected *China Quarterly*, in a 1962 article by Michael Lindsay, son of the noted former Master of Balliol College, Oxford, reported that China was ruled by people "near the borderline of actual insanity," and that relations with the People's Republic "are not a problem that can be handled within the categories of traditional diplomacy but only within the new categories of applied international psychiatry."

A similar view was popularized by Theodore H. White in his television special "China: The Roots of Madness," and further amplified by Stewart Alsop in the *Saturday Evening Post*. Writing in the issue of October 26, 1963, Alsop assured his readers that "Mao is mad. The madness is a fact of world significance. The Chinese leaders have 'gone crazy.' To permit these men to get their hands on even a limited nuclear capacity would be an act of supreme folly."

Other equally mystifying speculations about Mao's general health, mental powers and political status filled much of the American press for nearly a quarter century. The well-known columnist Robert S. Allen led off in the New York *Post* shortly after formation of the new Peking regime with the ritual "Where is Mao?" (December 16, 1950), speculating that he was a virtual prisoner of a Russian-controlled government. Allen was followed by Stewart Alsop in the *Herald Tribune* (March 18, 1951): "Mao is actually very ill, or has been marked for liquidation. Mao has tuberculosis, and has also had several severe heart attacks."

Three years later *Time* (March 15, 1954) led off a spate of Western rumor that Peking was concealing reports of Mao's death following a cancer operation. During the Mao-Khrushchev battle for control, the New York *Times'* Tillman Durdin (May 27, 1962) wrote that "Mao Tse-tung is known to be in failing health with his mental powers faltering," while other U.S. correspondents reported him as alternately "deposed," "shorn of power," or "dying of cancer."

The skepticism of the American news media regarding Mao's

physical and mental well-being was paralleled by its insistence that his regime itself was a transient affair and bound to die. This attitude recalled the U.S. press attitude toward Russia's revolution over forty years before, when the New York *Times*, during the two years immediately following Lenin's access to power, asserted a total of ninety-one times that the Soviets were nearing their rope's end, or actually had reached it. Then came the abortive U.S. military intervention in Siberia. But even by 1925, with the Bolsheviks already eight full years in the saddle, the Chicago *Tribune* embarked on a two-year series of calamity headline reports ranging from "Claim Starving Poor Threaten Doom of Soviet" (June 15, 1925) to "Russia Calls Soldiers Home as Revolt Rises" (April 21, 1927). Not until Franklin Roosevelt became President, sixteen years after the Russian Revolution, did Washington formally acknowledge the reality of Soviet rule.

With the Peking regime, though U.S. military intervention had been limited to the border states of Korea and Indo-China, Washington still, over a quarter century after the accession of Mao and Chou to power, refused to recognize the People's Republic. For the first twenty years, indeed, the American attitude was succinctly expressed in a memorandum from Secretary John Foster Dulles (August 11, 1958) to all eighty-four U.S. missions around the world: "The United States holds the view that Communism's rule in China is not permanent and that it one day will pass. By withholding diplomatic recognition from Peiping [Peking] it seeks to hasten that passing."

Another popular U.S. myth—there is no other word for it—cultivated by our government and press during Communist China's early years, was that the Mao-Chou regime was bankrupt. These people, stated *U.S. News and World Report* (August 29, 1952), "have used up their reserves of foreign exchange. Cash, jewels, everything that could be converted into money for trade has been squeezed out of the Chinese people . . . China is out of cash and out of credit." Similar themes blossomed regularly in our news media until well into the sixties.

Nations in actual contact with Peking, however, saw things differently. For the first dozen years of Communist rule, with calamity reports from China filling the U.S. press, international trade journals blossomed with accounts of profitable European commercial deals with the mainland. The great river port of

Shanghai was full of ships, with turnaround times at record lows. Chinese exports and foreign exchange reserves were up. The prestigious *Far Eastern Economic Review* of Hong Kong (April 11, 1963) noted that branches of the People's Bank of China outnumbered even postal and telegraph offices, and that the communes had already many social amenities, including universal education, medical services and old-age security.

Westerners with firsthand knowledge of mainland conditions, from the British Colonial Office to officials of the United Nations, tried to set Americans straight. A noted Swiss scholar, Professor Gilbert Etienne of the Graduate Institute of International Studies in Geneva, wrote that "conditions are far from the mass starvation China has known in the past." Malcolm MacDonald, son of the former Prime Minister and himself British High Commissioner in India, noted "the first effective organization for the distribution of food in China's history."

But most such reports shared the fate of a letter sent in October, 1961, to the New York *Times* by a British scientist, Dr. J. S. Horn, FRCS, protesting one of that normally reliable paper's accounts of Chinese deprivation. Like a 1958 report by James Muir, President of the Royal Bank of Canada,[5] it was never printed. For Americans, China was still "starving," with a break-up of the Communist regime perennially "imminent."

In 1961–62 Peking's foreign trade briefly declined and there were serious agricultural shortages. Then, confounding the skeptics who continued to report the country bankrupt, China began to buy grain abroad in huge amounts. Canada, Australia, France and Argentina were among the suppliers. These facts staggered U.S. observers, who wanted to know where Peking got the needed foreign exchange, and speculated that it must come from Russia. But since Moscow was already withdrawing her technical experts from China, this line of thinking could not last.

By late 1962, leading American news organs had begun, sporadically, to report the facts. "Australia," commented *U.S. News and World Report* (December 3), "is to go on sending Red China about a million tons of wheat a year." *The Christian Science Monitor* agreed, on December 18, that "Canada's grain

[5] "The growth in industry, the change in living standards, the modernization of everything and anything, the feats of human effort and colossal impact of human labor are not within our power to describe."

sales to Communist China, which have raised some criticism in the U.S., will continue in the largest possible volume . . ." and added the clincher: "Communist China guarantees payment in convertible sterling within 273 days . . . 'There has been no default in payment,' the government told Parliament."

Two widely publicized episodes—China's "invasion" of India and "rape" of Tibet—for years stoked the fires of anti-Peking hatred in the West.

Let us consider first the "invasion" of India. For years it had been regarded by the American public as axiomatic that an "aggressive" and "expansionist" China was pressing a "peace-loving" India for territorial concessions along their lengthy common border. "The [Kennedy] Administration," explained the *Wall Street Journal* (July 9, 1962), "is defending its request for a boost in economic assistance to India on grounds that India is a bulwark against Red Chinese encroachments in the Far East." During this same year India, in fact, headed the list of recipients of U.S. aid, with grants from Washington totaling close to one billion dollars.

In October came the border war itself, generally pictured in the U.S. press as wholly caused by Chinese aggression. Indian forces were overwhelmed and driven pell-mell onto the plains of Assam. India herself lay helpless before China's Red Army.

Then, to the stupefaction of the West, Peking suddenly declared a unilateral cease-fire and withdrew behind her borders. By next spring the Chairman of the U. S. Joint Chiefs of Staff, General Maxwell D. Taylor, was reported by the New York *Times* (April 19, 1963) to have indicated in secret Congressional testimony that, after all, "India might have started the border fight." But at this point his testimony was censored out of the public transcript. Not till seven years later, in his scholarly study entitled *India's China War*, did British author and Reuters correspondent Neville Maxwell, using mainly Indian sources, make clear that responsibility for the fighting had in fact rested almost exclusively with India and Prime Minister Jawaharlal Nehru.

Again, there is the "rape" of Tibet. Contrary to romantic legends current in the West, the facts are that the old Tibetan way of life, except for the ruling few, was dismal indeed. During centuries, hundreds of thousands of peasants and herdsmen had been born into serfdom as oppressive as anything out of the West's Middle Ages. This feudal state of affairs ceased with the advent of Chinese Communist rule. A social revolution, initiated from Peking, did indeed take place. The often barbaric punishments of the past were outlawed. Secular schools and hospitals, hitherto unknown, were introduced by Peking. The land, most of which had been held by the monasteries, was divided among the serfs.

To the Buddhist theocracy and landlords, integration into the People's Republic brought the end of age-old privileges. For them, certainly, the revolution was a tragedy. But for the vast majority whom they had previously ruled it was clearly, in the context of their own long-suffering history, a genuine liberation.

Though somewhat modified by the early 1970s, this was the general situation and climate of opinion facing Richard Nixon when he made his decision to reverse course on China. In such an atmosphere no Democrat, of course, could have seriously considered a move toward Peking. Harry Truman, John Kennedy, Lyndon Johnson all thought about it fleetingly and put the thought aside. They knew that, for any of them, political massacre would have followed swift and sure. Even a liberal Republican folk hero like Dwight Eisenhower felt himself vulnerable and shrank from the carnage.

Only Richard Nixon could have risked it. Nixon—the ideological heir of Joe McCarthy, nemesis of Alger Hiss, conqueror of "pro-Communist" Jerry Voorhis and Helen Gahagan Douglas in California—was the original hard-liner who never, even by his own worst enemies, could possibly be tagged with the lethal label "soft on Communism." Only a Nixon in the White House could have made the move and survived. Only a Nixon could have gone to Peking and carried the country—including even the Barry Goldwaters and Ronald Reagans of life—triumphantly with him.

No one knows for sure when the decision was made. It is probable—such was the ideological turmoil of the times—that Mr. Nixon himself could not pinpoint the moment. But somewhere between his disastrous defeat by Pat Brown for Governor of California in 1962 and his successful bid for the presidency in 1968, there began a metamorphosis in the Nixon concept of the world.

Some of his closest former right-wing colleagues are convinced it was during those half-dozen years, when he took up residence in New York as a Wall Street lawyer, that their man was seduced —or at least compromised—by the eastern liberal establishment.[6] In any case, there is no doubt that from the hour of his victory over Hubert Humphrey, the tenacious Nixon mind became riveted almost exclusively on the foreign-policy field, and that at the heart of it all was China.

Nixon might very well have read one of the scholarly and informed opinions then increasingly seeping into the consciousness of the nation. As a longtime legislator on Capitol Hill, he would have studied reports such as that on *Mainland China in the World Economy* from Hearings Before the Joint Economic Committee of Congress in 1967, given by Professor John G. Gurley:

> "So, there it is—a picture of an economy richly endowed in natural resources, but whose people are still very poor, making substantial gains in industrialization, moving ahead much more slowly in agriculture—but, nevertheless, moving ahead—raising education and health levels dramatically, turning out increasing numbers of scientists and engineers, expanding the volume of foreign trade and the variety of products traded, and making startling progress in the development of nuclear weapons.
>
> "But I do not think that China's economic growth can be properly understood only in terms of investment in material things without reference to the gains she has made in investment in human beings through education, medicine and public health, and scientific research.
>
> "To begin with, there has been a major breakthrough

[6] It is an intriguing fact that the second spot on the 1960 Republican ticket came very close to being offered, not to Henry Cabot Lodge, but to the veteran Minnesota Congressman and former China medical missionary, Dr. Walter H. Judd. It seems that President Eisenhower, who felt politically indebted to Lodge, tipped the scales in favor of the former Massachusetts Senator. But if Judd (a persuasive orator with a wide following in the Midwest) had been the choice, and Nixon had then gone on to win the critically close race against John F. Kennedy, as many feel he might then have done, his China initiative might never have come at all, since Judd, a firm Chiang Kai-shek supporter, was vehemently opposed to any dealings with Peking.

in education. Today, the number of children and young
adults in full-time educational institutions is five to
seven times the school enrollment in 1949. . . .

"In addition to this full-time education, there is much
part-time, part-study education going on, where students spend half of their time in school and half at work.
There is also spare-time education, which allows workers to take classes in a wide range of subjects after working hours. Indeed, if 'school' is extended in meaning to
include these as well as study groups, organized by communes, factories, street organizations, the army—then
there are schools everywhere in China: then China may
be said to be just one great big school."[7]

The veteran French Ambassador to Peking, Etienne Manac'h,
recalls his own involvement with the Nixon initiative. It was during the new U.S. President's European tour shortly after he took
office in January 1969. Nixon, following a formal welcome at
Orly airport by President de Gaulle, had replied in terms that
had touched and warmed the old General, who then hosted a
series of intimate talks at the Élysée Palace. During these talks
Nixon confided to his host that he intended to (1) withdraw
from Indo-China and (2) make up with Peking.

Impressed by this news, de Gaulle had promptly summoned
Manac'h to Colombey-les-deux-Eglises, privately told him of
Nixon's China secret and dispatched him on an early plane to
Peking with instructions to brief Chou and Mao in strictest
confidence regarding the American President's intention.

It had taken the Chinese leadership, well versed in Nixon's
arch-cold-warrior past, another two years before the steady U.S.
withdrawal from Indo-China convinced them he was sincere,
and the threatening Soviet presence on their borders moved
them to act. But act they finally did, and as everyone knows,
there followed the now familiar scenario of the ping-pong episode, the Kissinger missions, and finally the Presidential journey
to Peking. That Presidential journey impressed the Chinese and

---

[7] *Mainland China in the World Economy; Hearings Before the Joint Eco-
nomic Committee, Congress of the United States*, Ninetieth Congress, First
Session, April 5, 10, 11 and 12, 1967. U. S. Government Printing Office,
Washington, D.C., 1967, pp. 187–88.

burst on America with explosive force, scattering the illusions of twenty years like chaff before a whirlwind.

Even the normally tranquil "Scotty" Reston of the New York *Times,* then in China himself,[8] was as staggered by news of the first Chou-Kissinger handshake as the *Life* magazine editor, a protégé of the late Henry Luce, who was on the phone to me in New York within minutes of the announcement. "Jesus Christ," he breathed in bemused excitement while confiding the record sum being offered Edgar Snow for an exclusive profile of Chou and Mao. "We've been billing those guys as the original sonsabitches for so long it gives you the bends to describe them as humans without going through a bit of decompression first."

Among U.S. opinion-makers the *volte face* has been dramatically illustrated by one of our most celebrated anti-Communist reporters, Joseph Alsop.

Throughout the first two decades of the People's Republic, the Peking regime had no more vitriolic critic. During the Eisenhower, Kennedy, Johnson and early Nixon eras, Alsop's thrice-weekly column, "Matter of Fact," portrayed the rulers of Peking to millions of Americans as the prime evil geniuses of mankind, and their Communist state as the quintessence of social degradation and political infamy.

Some random Alsop quotes: "Chinese reduced to dining on afterbirths . . . the drilled, intimidated people . . . series of slave farms without any modern parallel . . . Communist massacres will pass a hundred million human beings . . . likelihood that the U.S. will end by having to fight an atomic war for Formosa's off-shore islands." And in a notable *Saturday Evening Post* peroration: "Mao might order half of China's 600 million people to the slaughterhouses, and compost the 300 million corpses for fertilizer. . . ."

Alsop had made no effort to see China for himself, and following the Nixon visit assumed with good reason that he would be permanently barred. He reckoned, however, without the Chou-Mao propensity for turning enemies into friends, and in the late autumn of 1972 was astonished to hear through a mutual ac-

[8] Though naturally eager to fly from Canton to the capital, he was mysteriously kept cooling his heels on a train to Peking, wholly unaware that at that precise moment Henry Kissinger was in the midst of his first and totally secret talks with Chou En-lai.

quaintance just back from Peking that the Chinese had expressed surprise that he had not applied for a visa.

In mid-December of 1972, just before reaching the Hong Kong border with his wife after a kaleidoscopic month on the mainland, Joe Alsop summarized his firsthand impressions of the regime he had so long, so venomously and so persuasively abused: "Both my wife and I found this long, unprecedented Chinese journey neither suffocating nor depressing. Indeed—the fact may as well be faced—we found the journey fascinating and exhilarating. Rather than thanking God to be crossing the border, we wished we could have had several months more. So why? The best answer, so far as we could figure it out, is that this new Chinese society *works*, in Chinese terms . . . whether in agriculture or in industry you find eye-popping achievements. Everywhere you see the strong foundations for a better future being boldly, laboriously, intelligently laid."

As for Chou En-lai himself, who typically turned the other cheek by receiving his former arch-critic for a frank and intimate three-hour *tour d'horizon*, Alsop noted: "In a sadly long experience I cannot recall any leader of a great country who more strongly conveyed extreme intelligence and total *sang-froid* than China's present Premier."

The Alsop episode was vintage Chou: total belief in the worth of the Peking experiment, along with a serene confidence in the reaction of any fair-minded critic, friend or foe, willing to face the facts.

This belief and this confidence also bred in Chou a distaste, amounting almost to contempt, of the rhapsodies of some sentimental Westerners. To him the myth of the "Communist Paradise" was as absurd as that of the "Faceless Hordes." Many American and other foreign correspondents besides me have heard him speak with asperity and vehemence along this line.

"No! No! No!" he would reprove a well-meaning visitor. "This is no paradise we've got over here. This is the largest and certainly one of the poorest countries on earth. It is true we have made a good start in getting China back on her feet. But never forget, it is only the smallest beginning, and that by far the greatest tasks remain."

At one point he quoted Chairman Mao: "It will take China a matter of centuries to become a truly modern state." Again and

again he emphasized that the true friends of China were those
who saw both her weaknesses and her enormous potential, and
gave their best to put the country on her feet. Ever the realist,
Chou saw his own nation as he saw other nations, in strictly realistic terms.

Realists in the American academic community are now in-
clined to greater optimism regarding China than the ever-
cautious Chou. Stanford economist John G. Gurley, writing in
1976, the year of Chou's death, states forthrightly his view of
the People's Republic today:

> "The basic, overriding economic fact about China is
> that for twenty years it has fed, clothed, and housed
> everyone, has kept them healthy, and has educated
> most. . . .
> "China has outperformed every underdeveloped
> country in the world; and, even with respect to the rich-
> est one, it would not be far-fetched to claim that there
> has been less malnutrition due to maldistribution of
> food in China over the past twenty years than there has
> been in the United States. . . ."[9]
> "Communist China is certainly not a paradise, but it
> is now engaged in perhaps the most interesting eco-
> nomic and social experiment ever attempted, in which
> tremendous efforts are being made to achieve an egali-
> tarian development, and industrial development with-
> out dehumanization, one that involves everyone and af-
> fects everyone. . . ."[10]

Gurley chides his fellow economists of the West for their assumption of capitalist superiority. "China," he claims in his recent book, "has been dealt with as though it were simply an
underdeveloped United States—an economy that 'should' develop
along capitalist lines and 'should' forget all that foolishness about
Marxism, Mao's thought, great leaps, and cultural revolutions,
and get on with the job of investing its savings efficiently." This
"unthinking acceptance" by Americans that there is no develop-

[9] John G. Gurley, *China's Economy and the Maoist Strategy*, Monthly
Review Press, New York, 1976, p. 13.
[10] Ibid., p. 16.

ment like capitalist development "has resulted," Gurley concludes, in studies of China that "lack insight."[11]

Chou En-lai, master builder of the People's Republic, would surely agree. Then, ever conscious of the enormity of the tasks ahead, he would as surely add, as he once remarked to me: "It will be a long time before a classless society can truly be established worldwide. Until that day arrives a socialist country will constantly have to continue the revolution within itself. Even when all humanity enters such a society, there will still be the difference between the advanced and the backward, the progressive and the conservative. The necessity for continuing the revolution remains."

[11] Ibid., p. 1.

CHAPTER IX

CHOU'S CHINA: THE REALITY

As already indicated, Premier Chou En-lai always exercised, in conjunction with Chairman Mao, a dual responsibility. He was Chief of Government, and as such supervised overall the vast machinery of China's internal affairs. He was also, either *de jure* or *de facto*, the nation's Foreign Minister, and thus had the final word on all issues of foreign policy.

It is in his capacity as controller of domestic affairs that we now turn to a more detailed examination of Chou's stewardship. For one who, like me, knew the old China during her days of international vassalage, the internal state of the country today represents an even more spectacular transformation than her independence from foreign rule.

The nation's multiplying hundreds of millions have come a very long way since the episode in Chapter One that opened this book—about the child on his roller skates, the coolie in the gutter and the foreigner with his cane.

We will, of course, have to select. China is vast, and her accomplishments, despite Chou's modest disclaimers, are also vast. By now a flood of books is being written on many phases of the country's life. It would manifestly be impossible to cover in a single chapter even a fraction of what one observed during a seven-week visit. But the samples chosen are representative, and should convey a general idea of what is going on.

On the last day of 1971, I crossed the China border. Soon afterward, through the courtesy of Chou En-lai, whose memory rarely fails regarding the early days of those foreign friends who were born and raised in his country, I was en route to my birthplace, Hankow on the Yangtze.

Searching frantically for our old home in the former British "Concession," I found the sidewalk sadly shrunken from the broad expanse of childhood memory. But the distinctively V-shaped gutter across which the coolie had collapsed was unmistakably the same. And after a diligent search in the now massively built-up area nearby, I found the handsome, high-ceilinged, red-brick house where I was born. Ironically, my father's cathedral next door had been demolished by American bombs during the wartime Japanese occupation. But the Bishop's residence was intact.

Once the center of Hankow's international society, it had dispensed a welcome to China's leaders and visitors from abroad since the turn of the century. It had also provided sanctuary for fugitive revolutionaries, from the time of the anti-Manchu uprising of 1911 which erupted within a mile of our home, to that of Chiang Kai-shek's 1927 break with the Communists which began the mutual slaughter of the civil war.

Throughout the united-front period of 1938, with the Japanese advancing upriver and Chiang's government centered at Hankow, our old house was a crossroads for the foreign correspondents and personalities swarming through the Yangtze Valley. John Gunther, Peter Fleming, Edgar Snow, Robert Capa and A. T. Steele shared its hospitality with poet W. H. Auden, playwright Christopher Isherwood, explorer Sven Hedin and the Canadian doctor Norman Bethune—immortalized in Mao's famous eulogy—whose medical supplies were piled high on our front veranda for shipment to Yenan. Chou En-lai himself, then beginning his long career as Communist China's foreign-policy spokesman, would often come to sip tea, and test my father's fluent Mandarin well into the night.

Now, not unfittingly, the place serves as headquarters of the Department of City Planning for the Wuhan district's three mil-

lion people. In the central hallway where the Bishop received his
guests, as in the old parlor where an American family once decorated their Christmas tree, I was greeted—as if to underline the
coming of a new era—by two impressive color portraits of Chairman Mao.

Other changes abound in Hankow and her neighbors, Hanyang and Wuchang, which form the tri-city metropolis. Long
vanished are the turbaned Sikh policemen who gave the Concession its reputation for law and order. Gone is the English Church
where, on Sunday mornings, children of the foreign community
would stare wide-eyed at the American and British sailors as
they marched, bands blaring, to their pews from the warships in
the river.

The fragrant garden of the British Commissioner of Customs,
who supervised the city's trade, once the monopoly of Anglo-
Saxon babies in their prams, is now a Chinese children's park.
No foreign naval vessels ride the Yangtze waters, and since the
bridging of the river, hardly a sampan. Instead, one is shown the
spots on either bank between which Mao, already over seventy,
made his celebrated hour's swim which signaled the coming of
the Cultural Revolution.

Then there are the trees.

In the old days most of the hills and valleys of China had for
centuries been bare, any new growth being regularly cut down
for firewood by the poor. Only the rich and the foreigners could
afford the luxury of trees for shade or beauty. Tree planting has
now become a government subsidy; it was introduced among the
earliest official measures of the regime to encourage public
health and morale, and everyone in the land knows the importance of planting trees and maintaining them.

An environmental scholar, Yi-Fu Tuan, comments on China as
follows:

> Besides such large projects as shelterbelts along the
> semi-arid edges of the North, forest brigades of the in-
> dividual communes have planted billions of trees
> around villages, in cities, along roads and riverbanks,
> and on the hillsides. A visitor from New Zealand re-
> ported in 1960 that, as seen from the air, the new

growths spread a mist of green over the once-bare hills of South China.[1]

For one familiar with the old regime, a tree-covered China is a sensation, especially for residents of the three Yangtze River ports known popularly as "The Three Ovens"—Chungking, Nanking and Wuhan. Here temperatures of over 107 degrees, combined with a paralyzing humidity, affect every living thing. Every summer we privileged foreign families went to the hills, largely because of the devastating Yangtze Valley climate.

En route to Hanyang, where a cotton mill has replaced the ancient arsenal, you drive down the fifteen-mile Liberation Avenue (twice the length of Peking's famous T'sang An), passing the beflagged Opera House, Chung Shan Park (formerly the Anglo-American Race Course), the Hankow Radio tower, Communist Party Headquarters, Industrial Exhibition Center and the lively new Hsin Hua Bookstore. The area used to be a vast warren of mat huts which regularly went up in flames, leaving tens of thousands homeless.[2]

Across the broad, mile-long rail and highway bridge which spans the mighty Yangtze, pedestrians and bicycles are thronging, and trains during the Vietnam war would pass at ten-minute intervals. The massive structure had been rushed to completion between 1955 and 1957 with the help of a score of Soviet engineers, and despite Russia's later withdrawal of her technicians, the head of the Revolutionary Committee is generous in acknowledging the debt. "For this," he said firmly, "we should be grateful to the Soviet people."

Approaching Wuchang on the southern bank, a gigantic sign in red characters high on Serpent Hill—THE GREAT ENEMY IS U.S. IMPERIALISM!—reminded a visitor that the bridge was Peking's chief supply link with wartime Hanoi. Wuchang itself now boasts, deep in the countryside, the second largest iron and steel works in the nation, and along with Hankow, hundreds of new housing developments, department stores, small-scale industries,

[1] John A. Day, Frederic F. Fost and Peter Rose, *Dimensions of the Environmental Crisis,* p. 44.
[2] We children, when the fire siren wailed, would rush up to our attic windows and gaze, awestruck, at the long line of flames that swept from hut to hut on the outskirts of the foreign concessions.

hospitals and schools in suburbs which are exploding in all directions.

The physical transformation of this intercity complex—already over three times the size of old Wuhan—seems symbolic of the Communist impact on China as a whole, where a formerly privileged social, economic and intellectual elite has lost its privileges in the spectacular upgrading of the people's common lot. The riverfront Concession quarter of my youth, with its stately promenade, the Bund, from which all Chinese were once barred, used to be an oasis of safety and comfort for the prosperous few. But only a few yards across the Concession boundary was the squalor and filth of the teeming native city, part of that poverty-stricken China whose staggering mortality rate from famine, flood and disease was largely accepted as inevitable until the regime of Mao and Chou effectively ended it.

Today, positions are reversed. The former "Concessions" (British, Russian, French, German and Japanese) are the least-favored part of town. The once-proud commercial houses of the foreigner, though still utilized, stand dilapidated and forlorn while beyond them the new city, with its broad boulevards and burgeoning apartment buildings, has been swallowing up the hovels of the past. Still, they do exist—the old, worn-out shacks of the poor lining narrow, muddy streets—but as I try not to notice them, my guide quickly explains that soon they will all be replaced by new apartment buildings.

The cultural transformation in Wuhan is pronounced. Education, formerly severely limited, is now on a mass basis. One in three of the total population are students: 520,000 in 600 primary schools; 400,000 in 180 secondary schools; 50,000–60,000 in 25 colleges and universities (up from a low during the Cultural Revolution).[3]

Wuhan, like every major city, has its training centers for music, dance and the theater; Hankow's is called "The Wuhan Song and Dance Troupe." Even the youngsters start performing

[3] In the China of my youth the illiteracy percentage was astronomical—well over 95 per cent nationwide. Now there is virtually no illiteracy among those aged thirty-five or under, and little among the thirty-five to forty-five age group. Above the age of fifty, of course, the former conditions prevail, but it can be only a question of time before literacy is as widespread as illiteracy was before.

early. One evening in Hankow I saw a ballet performance by primary school children (seven to eleven years old), who sang and danced in professional style. "Chairman Mao's Little Red Soldiers," they called themselves. In their piping voices they sang about the need for helping farmers with their crops, helping peasants and Army men to assist and learn from each other, understanding the problems of minority groups in Mongolia and Tibet, and practicing the "greater-than-self world outlook," Mao and Chou's widely heralded ideal for every Chinese.

I had asked the administrator of the Yangtze Bridge how his twelve hundred workers, many of whom had never seen a steel bridge before, managed to complete it in half the scheduled time, and later accomplish without Soviet aid a far more formidable job at Nanking. "Chairman Mao," he replied simply, "teaches us that our greatest asset is people and their potential; that if we can arouse and mobilize the people we can work miracles."

The following morning I spent a day at the Wuchang General Hospital, now expanded to half a dozen times its previous size. A forty-year-old woman, fully conscious and obviously pain-free during removal of an ovarian cyst, paid a cheerful tribute to Mao as nurses, seated at her ankles, manipulated the needles for acupuncture anesthesia.

Later the chief surgeon, a woman, explained: "The attitude of that patient is routine here. But what is more remarkable has been the effect of the Cultural Revolution on our staff. Before, we would take the easy way. We stayed in the hospital, refused house calls, let patients come to us. Now we get out among the people. Our ninety-eight doctors, besides their regular work, including emergency operations, often make four hundred house calls a day, in factories, apartment buildings, hotels, railway yards, homes. We organize traveling medical teams to visit the countryside. We train relays of young 'barefoot doctors.' We try to cultivate the attitude and purpose of 'serving the people.' If we get slack, a visit to a May 7 school recharges our batteries. We have a new spirit here—everyone—doctors, nurses, cooks."

The one hundred and fifty new hospitals and health centers built by the Communist regime in the Wuhan area reflect China's astonishingly successful war on disease. In Wuchang's No. 3 hospital, cholera, malaria and smallpox are now so rare that young doctors, lacking clinical experience, must try to understand them from their medical texts. Most impressive of all is the virtual elimination of venereal disease and prostitution. The superintendent of the largest hospital in the Wuhan area is a middle-aged woman doctor whose answer to my question on the status of V.D. was brief and pungent.

"For three years now," she said, "the disease has been nonexistent in this area. The fact is gratifying, of course, but it has created a problem for our young interns. We are unable now to provide a single case for them to diagnose! They can only read about it in their medical texts."

A distinctive feature of the Cultural Revolution was the "May 7 School." These institutions, now universal throughout China, were originated in a memorandum issued by Chairman Mao on May 7, 1966—hence the name. In his original directive Mao stated: "Going into the countryside to do manual labor gives vast numbers of cadres an excellent opportunity to study once again; and this should be done by all cadres except those who are old, weak, ill or disabled." There were soon hundreds of May 7 schools throughout the People's Republic, including one in each of Peking's eighteen districts.

One January morning in 1972 I had my first chance to visit a May 7 school—"The East is Red Cadre School"—in the Tsungwen district of Peking. Established October 30, 1968, the institution had had eighteen hundred students in the previous three years. Of these, fully a thousand had already returned to their former posts, leaving eight hundred students still in session.

The "students" from this May 7 school are all from administrative offices in the capital, including many primary and middle-school teachers; they are all adult. Membership of the school rotates every six months, though in most schools it is possible for students to remain for a year or more. Every three to five years all the official and managerial personnel of the district would be returning to the school for re-education. The purpose is to "change the political orientation of the students, to help them to learn better how wholeheartedly to serve the people."

The curriculum is organized under three headings: 1) serious study of the theory of Marxism, Leninism and Mao's thought; 2) one to three hours of theoretical instruction each day (twenty hours a week) during the busy farm period; 3) during the not-so-busy farm period, half of each day is given over to theoretical instruction.

Group discussions, based on this self-education, occur daily. The students write papers which are then used for further study. Students also attend classes in the district. They practice the "Four Togethers"—eating together, rooming together, studying together, working together. Great emphasis is also given to learning from the poor and lower-middle peasants.

There is strong emphasis on: 1) a clear and firm proletarian stand; 2) frugality and self-reliance; 3) tilling the land for revolution; and 4) a knowledge of production. The peasant farmers are invited to come and instruct the students. This utilizes the experience of the older farmers who know firsthand the bitterness of the old society. Most of these senior farmers have had three or more years' experience working on the land prior to liberation, and before the 1950 land reform.

The same thing is done with industrial workers from the factories of each district. Here, too, a worker's experience of the pre-Liberation society can be invaluable.

From all reports, the attitude of the students does change dramatically at these schools: 1) They lose their sense of officialdom and learn to be ordinary people; 2) they learn to be workers themselves and to overcome their distaste of physical work; 3) they learn to acquire the spirit of "fearing neither hardship nor death."

In the "East is Red" Commune, the students racked up some solid achievements. They had reclaimed over 1,200 *mou*[4] of formerly barren land. They had planted 600 *mou* with rice . . . 200 *mou* with peanuts. There were side occupations such as raising vegetables, pigs and ducks (fattened up for "Peking Duck" in the restaurants).

Students constructed their own buildings. They also made their own iron and wooden tools, dyes and loudspeakers. There is a women's dormitory of ten beds—Spartan conditions, neat, one chair or one stool for each bed; also a men's dormitory of twelve bunks in tiers. In the dormitory are tea mugs, thermos flasks, small radios, calendars.

My Party guide, whose husband worked in the European and

[4] A *mou* is one third of an acre.

American Departments of the Foreign Ministry, added a vivid commentary on the *raison d'être* of the May 7 school:

"It should," she said, "serve as a place where we Party members and officials will be re-educated. At the Cadre School there is none of the depersonalization which is the curse of government offices. At the school we sometimes get closer to our colleagues than to our families. Sometimes we feel we would like to stay there forever."

Then, with great feeling, she spoke of China's two leaders:

"Taken together, the writings of Chairman Mao and the blameless personal character of Premier Chou En-lai are the greatest single influence in this country."

Certainly the importance of character and its impact on a whole area were nowhere more apparent than in the construction of New China's most celebrated public-works achievement—the Red Flag Canal at Linhsien. This visit was a highlight of my entire China trip.

Overnight by train from Peking to Anyuan brings us considerably south of the capital's bitter January weather. Trains are the standard mode of transport in China and bring back to any older American a nostalgia for the great days of American railroading. As I watch the North China fields turn from brown to green, and sense the mildness of the air, the huge red-wheeled steam engine suggests younger days punctuated with the rhythmic click of the rails and whistles that wail in the night.[5]

Anyuan is teeming with life. There are three girls running along in colorful coats as they push a cart of logs and firewood. A gaggle of small fry are trying vigorously to fly a green paper kite.

Everywhere are women wearing bright kerchiefs. Many are carrying babies resplendent in long, vividly hued outer garments —bright red, yellow, green and blue silk (made long so as to completely cover them) with matching bonnets. Underneath, because of the brisk weather, is so much padding as to make each child resemble a round ball. The adults in China, as everyone knows, wear the universal blue Mao jacket and pants, and all the

[5] Plane transport, using mostly British and Soviet models, is still primitive but adequate. Recent purchases of American jets will soon change China's long-range international transport, and before long the internal picture as well.

artistry, love of color, and human warmth of the people seem to be lavished on the very young.

As our jeep jogged along toward Linhsien, down roads lined with long rows of newly planted poplars, we drove through fields covered with the green sprouts of winter wheat. We passed the Anyuan Iron and Steel Works built in 1958 during the Great Leap Forward, and a machine-tool factory, tractor factory and fertilizer plant. None of these existed before the days of the People's Republic.

A feature of our drive from Anyuan to Linhsien was a series of flat white stone markers set up, like the old Burma-Shave signs along U.S. highways, every fifty or one hundred yards down the road.

Each marker was engraved in Chinese characters with various slogans and Mao quotes, such as:

"We can do what our forefathers have never done before."

"We must care for the national health."

"When a people are happy, the counter-Revolutionaries are unhappy."

"The PLA [People's Liberation Army] and the people are one."

"Plan, but be ready for the unexpected."

"Intelligence, self-reliance and initiative."

"Without a people's army that belongs to the people, we don't have anything."

"Unite to win still greater victories."

"If you make a mistake, you must admit and correct it."

Later we began passing in the darkening dusk hundreds of small donkey carts returning to Anyuan with a load of iron ore from the Linhsien mine to be processed at the Anyuan Iron and Steel Works. By then it was night, with no street lights and the road in deep shadow, but the donkeys trotted along in the dark, nose to tail, reins tied to the driver's seat, and reclining in the back, head pillowed on the ore, was the driver peacefully sleeping.

To my startled question as to how the animals could keep such perfect formation without even a moon to guide them, my interpreter smilingly replied: "Oh, these donkeys can see better in the dark."

Liberation came to Linhsien in 1944, earlier than most areas.

Before that, this part of Shansi Province was among the most depressed sections of the country. Here are some pre-Liberation facts:

1) Four big landlord families owned 60 per cent of the land;

2) Another 20 per cent was owned by small landlords and "rich peasants;"

3) The remaining 20 per cent was shared, owned or used in varying degrees by the 70 per cent of the population classed as "poor or lower-middle-class peasants" (lacking practically anything that could be called their own).

Over three hundred of Linhsien's five hundred villages lacked water, and people often had to walk ten or twenty li (about three to seven miles) to get it. Besides all this, the area suffered from drought nine years out of ten. So most of the time water was more valuable than oil.

For example, in Tu Men district, people had to trudge ten li for water from the landlord. The landlord owned the only two ponds in the village, and the villagers had to pay him for every bucketful of water. So they had to work for him to pay for the water.

Consequently, every few years, most people would move to other areas. They would sell their children and go begging. Indeed, a large part of their lives had been spent fleeing from one famine or another, with many of the family dying along the way.

Typical was one man I talked to who was nine years old during the great famine of 1941–42. He remembered vividly losing a grandfather, father and younger sister at that time.

Another recalled a poignant incident of pre-Liberation days. A father-in-law had walked four miles to fetch a pail of water to make possible, for the first and only time that year, the cooking of dumplings as a New Year treat. His daughter-in-law, becoming anxious, went after him, running to meet him halfway to help carry the pail. In the process, the water was spilled.

The girl was so overcome with shame that she hanged herself. Following this tragedy, the father-in-law left the area in despair.

Now, with the Canal, he is back, spending a delighted old age in the newly irrigated and smiling valley with its three hundred reservoirs for excess water, so different from the desolation and poverty of his former years.

Linhsien eventually was transformed by the Revolution. Fol-

lowing the advent of the People's Republic, agricultural cooperatives were set up and ditches dug to catch rainwater and
increase the supply. When this experiment failed, three reservoirs were built. But in 1959 came a severe drought and the
reservoirs dried up.

When people finally saw the futility of depending on rain,
they began to think seriously about the water problem. It was
the poor and lower-middle-class peasants who first proposed the
Canal. I was told they were discouraged by agents of President
Liu Shao-ch'i and others who claimed it was far too big a job.
But following a struggle between the Liu line (cautious conser-
vatism) and the Mao line (bold experimentation), the Mao line
finally won, the Canal was planned and construction began.

The Red Flag Canal was built in ten years—1960–69. One hundred and ninety thousand men and women took part. Thirty-six
thousand actually started the job. Total overall involvement was
twenty-two million man-days, including evening work. The task
involved immense physical labor, imagination and engineering
skill with only the most primitive hand tools available. In nego-
tiating the mountain range, when valleys intervened, bridges or
aqueducts would be built over them for the canal; when a mountain came between, they would tunnel through it.

The main canal is 26 feet wide and 14 feet deep, with a water
flow of 81 cubic feet per second. It includes 134 tunnels with a
total length of 14 miles, and 150 aqueducts with a combined
length of 4 miles.

The canal's total length is 900 miles, with 500 channels and
branch canals flowing from it into the valley to water the whole
area. Often it had to skirt a bare overhanging cliff face at 500–
600 feet above the riverbed, and the same distance from the top.
In such cases workers did their drilling, blasting and construction suspended by ropes from the summit.

The Chinese have named their handiwork the "Man-Made
Heavenly River" because it winds high up around the mountains. And with good reason, for results have been sensational.
Formerly twenty thousand tons of grain had to come from the
government to support starving Linhsien. Now forty thousand
tons are sold by the county to the government.

As elsewhere in the new China, one sees tree farms all over
the countryside, especially young aspens. Some 30 per cent of

22. Chou visits the Tachai Production Brigade in Shansi Province, southwest of Peking, in May 1965. The villagers have transformed their barren eroded hills into some of the most fertile farmland in China. Chou's lifelong and consuming interest in the people often took him to similar villages all over the country.

23. Tanzania's President Julius Nyerere embraces Chou En-lai during his last visit to Peking before Chou's death. Nyerere, black Africa's most respected Chief of State, with Kenneth Kaunda of Zambia, represented his continent during the 1976 Kissinger negotiations with white Africa. A longtime friend of the United States, he reluctantly turned to China some years ago when Washington rejected his repeated requests for aid.

24. The question of how to change the motives of man was often discussed by Chou and the author's father in the Roots Hankow home early in 1938. They are shown here at Chou's farewell reception to him during that last spring in China.

25. Following a dinner given by the Premier for the author's sister and her husband, Frances Hadden points out to Chou some of the pictures taken during days spent together in Hankow thirty-four years before.

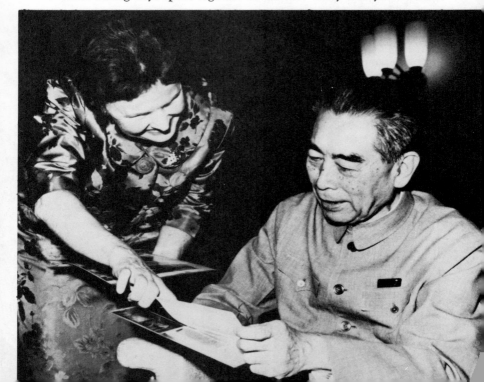

26. A warm greeting by an old family friend: The Premier says good-bye to the author following their midnight-to-3:00 A.M. visit in Peking shortly before President Nixon's historic trip to China in 1972.

27. "Mrs. Mansfield and I may well have been the last Americans to see the late Premier. We visited him in his hospital room in late December 1974, and spent over an hour with him . . . He accompanied us as we prepared to say farewell, and then spoke these final words: 'The door between our two countries should never have been closed.'"

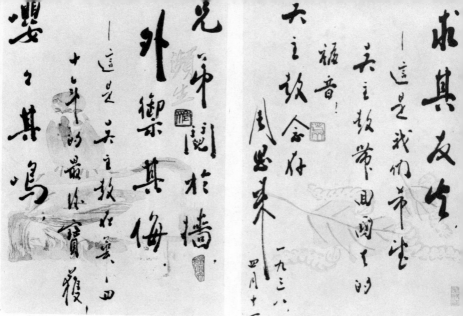

28. Chou En-lai's autograph, dated April 11, 1938: A double page of messages for the author's father, Logan Herbert Roots, was contributed by Chou En-lai to the farewell memorial volume of autographs presented to the Bishop by his friends, including most of China's leadership, after his forty-two years in China. The writing is done in Chou's own hand with the traditional scholar's brush and black ink on specially designed thin rice paper, folded double to take the ink. The seals are the seals of the artist and of the firm that made the paper. These, together with the paintings of a bird perched on a stump and caterpillars feeding on leaves, appear as a faint background to the bold brush strokes of the Premier. A strict translation of the writing (reading vertically from top to bottom and from right to left) is as follows:

> Brothers battle out their differences within the walls,
> Outside they resist the attacks of the enemy . . .

>> Our beloved Bishop Roots finds this is the
>> situation after spending over forty years in China!

> "Just as the birds, with deep instinct of choice,
> Seek the echo of a friend's well-known voice . . .
> (May it not be true that man, banishing strife,
> Will in true friendship find the fuller life,
> Then God—all the gods—will lend a listening ear
> And send to man the gift of peace so dear.)"

(Signed and Dated)

The six lines in quotes above are extracted from *The Book of Songs*—the classic book of odes from the Chou Dynasty (1112 B.C.–249 B.C.), known to all traditional scholars. Although Chou actually wrote out only the first two lines on the page, it is customary among knowledgeable Chinese to infer that the following lines in context are also meant in the inscription.

the households in the rural areas own a bicycle. Many new stone houses are being built. An old man walks along the road, cleaning it of fresh manure dropped by draft animals and later used as fertilizer.

My local guide at Linhsien, Chin Yuen-tsang, aged thirty, had an interesting life story. He told of the past suffering of his mother who had come from a poor peasant family. In that family a total of fourteen or fifteen died from drought, starvation or disease, including two uncles, an older sister, a grandfather and an aunt.

One was reminded of the Jews in Israel who tell you what happened to their families in the European pogroms, and of the Russians killed in the Hitler war.

The young guide said with great conviction: "Virtually everyone among the people I knew had lost members of their families before 1944 simply through starvation."

Linhsien has in fact been transformed by the Canal into one of the great exporting centers of the area. Back at Anyuan the Chairman of the County Revolutionary Committee ticked off some of the items: apples, pears, walnuts, chestnuts, persimmons, beets, crabapples—most delivered to the state, and the rest sold at county markets.

Before reluctantly leaving the Red Flag Canal, I inspected the Dawn Tunnel, used to divert the Canal water across the countryside. The main shaft runs nearly half a mile through the mountain and was completed in one year and eight months—breaking all records for speed by drilling thirty-four shafts from the hill surface down to the tunnel and then working from each side of each pair of shafts. This meant that the tunnel workers were operating on seventy worksites simultaneously, instead of only two.

Foreign visitors, especially from Africa, Asia and Latin America, swarm over the area. Said our interpreter: "It gives us a chance to disseminate Mao's thought while we act as guides. This is an ordinary job," he emphasized, "but I regard it as a vital part of the world revolution."

The training of youth is a key, if not *the* key, long-term objective of the government.

In 1973, one hundred and twenty-seven million boys and girls were attending primary (the first five grades) school—ten times the number before 1949. Thirty-five million were attending middle school (grades six–ten)—thirty times the number before Liberation.[6]

Following middle school, every student is required to join the work force for two years either in agriculture, in industry, in the Army, on a hotel staff or in some other specialized job in the country.

Communist China is determined to avoid the difficulties created in Western countries of turning out too many school and college graduates for whom employment is unavailable and who are unwilling to settle for manual labor. Chinese assert the equal merit of work and study, and my own observation on the spot was that they are achieving a more homogeneous society as a result.

Take, for instance, primary school education as observed in five schools by a group of American psychologists and sociologists in 1973. Reporting on this, William Kessen states that what most struck their delegation about China's primary school children was "the high level of concentration, orderliness and competence of the children. We were impressed by the sight of fifty children in a primary classroom quiet until addressed and chanting their lessons in enthusiastic unison when called upon; even more impressed by the apparent absence of disruptive, hyperactive and noisy children. The same quiet orderliness, the same concentration on tasks, the same absence of disruptive behavior was to be seen in all the classrooms we visited, down to the children barely able to walk. The docility did not seem to us to be the docility of surrender and apathy; the Chinese children we saw were emotionally expressive, socially gracious, and adept."[7]

Take again middle school education, which I had a chance to observe for myself in 1972 at Peking's Middle School No. 260. Students (ages thirteen to sixteen) numbered 2,784; staff, 154.

The curriculum included twelve main subjects:

    1. Politics
    2. The Chinese language
    3. A foreign language (for a long time Russian; now exclusively English)

[6] William Kessen, ed., *Childhood in China*, p. ix.
[7] Ibid., pp. 216–17.

4. Mathematics
5. Physics
6. Chemistry
7. Agriculture
8. Health, hygiene, sanitation
9. Physical training
10. Revolutionary art and culture
11. General history and geography
12. History and philosophy of the class struggle.

Supplementing the regular curriculum were specialized classes in extracurricular activities such as sewing group, barber shop, shoe repair shop (where students learn to repair the shoes of their fellow students, using waste materials and extra leather bits from the factories), electronics shop and radio shop.

Ideological training is also stressed, and each student is required to summarize and appraise his own actions: 1) how he personally studies Mao's thought; 2) how he integrates theory and practice; 3) how he behaves himself.

Following the required post-school two years' manual work as part of the country's labor force, a small percentage of the students, chosen by their peers, go on to university. The preferred choice of many is the famous Peking University, where I met with the Vice President, Harvard-graduate Dr. Tso Pei-yuan, and the Faculty Student Council, and learned from them of the pioneer role this institution played in the Cultural Revolution as a whole.

Founded in 1898, Peking University is now seventy-nine years old. Mao Tse-tung worked in its library in 1918–19, and it was there that the famous May Fourth Movement began. In 1958 Mao's "big-character poster," insisting that "Education must serve proletarian politics and must be combined with productive labor," was displayed on the university walls, initiating the "Great Leap Forward" and foreshadowing the later Cultural Revolution. The Chairman's still more famous poster of June 1, 1966, at the same spot, formally began the Cultural Revolution itself.

The then President of the University, Lu Pin, criticized the Cultural Revolution and was deposed, and soon afterward selected workers and PLA men joined the professors and students on the University Council. When I spent a morning with the Council, all four elements were present, with a PLA man presiding.

In September 1970, the University had been reopened after being shut down for three years, with 2,667 students in attendance. But the student body now included not only intellectual youth, but also workers, peasants and soldiers, all of them chosen by their workmates in city or countryside before being finally approved by the faculty in Peking. Age requirements were elastic, and all expenses—tuition, board and medical care—were borne by the state.

The Vice President summed up this revolution in policy: "In the past," he told me, "we used to train spiritual aristocrats divorced from the masses. We produced 'ivory tower intellectuals.' Now our policy aims to enable the students to develop morally, intellectually and physically, and to become revolutionary fighters with socialist consciousness and culture."

Then followed a tour of the production units on the campus— alcohol distillery, antibiotic and insulin production, radio and plastics manufacture. "At the University," remarked my faculty guide, "we have a factory, and in our factories a university."

A striking innovation at Peking University is that students and teachers both have a part in the instruction. The teacher will give his notes to the students before the lecture, and use the lecture hour to discuss student questions on them. "Thus," commented Dr. Tso, "we help to guarantee the quality of the teaching, for the teacher will be on the spot. Thus, both teachers and students participate, and everyone learns.

"Of course," he pointed out, "we are still in an experimental stage. But I know Western education pretty well, and everything considered, I feel we are farther ahead in pioneering the learning of the future than any other country I know."

My day at Peking University ended with an inspection of the library; its 2,700,000 volumes, mostly in open stacks, make it the second largest in China. I knew that Chinese invention of woodblock printing in 940 A.D. was the earliest in the world, while their invention of movable type in 1040 antedated the Gutenberg Bible by some four centuries. "Even so," said Dr. Tso as I reluctantly took my leave, "what we are trying out here is only the first step in the long march of our revolution in education."

One of the distinctive features of Chou's China was the excitement, color and extensive mobilization of resources, manpower and artistic imagination that went into receiving various state guests from abroad.

I had the privilege of being the last American correspondent on the mainland before President Nixon arrived, and was a personal witness to the preparations in Peking.

In a dispatch for the Associated Press at the time, I wrote:

> This capital of China is ready to welcome President Nixon. Shop fronts are newly painted. Signs denouncing "U.S. imperialism and its running dogs" have come down. Peking Union Medical College, renamed by the Communists Anti-Imperialist Hospital, had its name changed around the first of the year to the Capital Hospital.
>
> The tastefully appointed government guest house in a quiet suburban area of west Peking has been readied for the Nixons. It recently housed Emperor Haile Selassie of Ethiopia and later President Zulfikar Ali Bhutto of Pakistan.
>
> As for security, it is generally conceded that in this homogeneous and highly disciplined society, the President may be considerably safer than in the United States. . . .
>
> What do Chairman Mao Tse-tung and Chou expect from the actual talks?
>
> On the basis of a fortnight's conversations with government officials and the most knowledgeable diplomats from Europe, Asia and Africa, a fairly clear consensus emerges.
>
> —They expect neither too much nor too little from the visit. Both Mao and Chou have said publicly that either success or failure would be acceptable.
>
> "This is the carefulness of a country that for over a century has been buffeted and humiliated by the West and doesn't wish to expose itself by being too optimistic," observed a highly regarded ambassador.
>
> —No principle will be sacrificed. Taiwan, the island of the Chinese Nationalists, is as much a part of China

as Alsace-Lorraine was of France—that's the evaluation
of a French diplomat.

As for Indochina, the view is that U.S. forces must be
withdrawn and that what are regarded as artificial divisions within Vietnam, Laos and Cambodia must be
ended.

Chou, when he talked with this reporter a few days
ago, was categorical that if the President insisted on his
eight points for a Vietnam settlement, no solution was
possible.

—While there is not the faintest hint of compromise,
there also is none of belligerence. "Your President is
coming," mused Chou philosophically. "Who knows if
he may change his mind?"

The sense of quiet confidence pervading this stately
capital is rooted in the conviction that in championing
the developing two thirds of the human race, China is
championing mighty historical forces which will prove
irresistible.[8]

The reality of Chou's China is rooted in a passion so to practice the beliefs governing the policies of the nation that they will
appeal irresistibly to the underdeveloped world—and perhaps
elsewhere as well.

[8] Sunday, February 20, 1972, from Peking (AP).

CHAPTER X

CHOU THE MAN

"The greatest statesman of our era," was the verdict of Secretary of State Kissinger.[1]

However sweeping such an evaluation may seem, my own belief is that it could be substantiated, for Chou En-lai did in fact possess an array of personal qualities seldom combined in a single government leader of any age. He had a unique status within the Communist Party and a long, intimate working relationship with Mao Tse-tung; a close rapport with the military; an extensive knowledge of the world; the confidence of the intellectuals; a rare affinity with the young; a capacity for friendship which for years put him on excellent personal terms with friend and foe alike; and, finally, a lifelong preoccupation with transforming the nature of man.

Chou's unique status within international Communist ranks was based first of all on sheer durability. His tenure of high Party posts was longer than Lenin's, Stalin's or even Mao's. Mao, indeed, joined the Party in 1921 in China, at roughly the same time as Chou joined it in France. But Mao never rose to top rank

[1] *Time*, January 19, 1976.

until shortly before the Long March, while Chou's rise began over a decade before.

The Chou-Mao partnership was unexampled in Party annals as to length, intimacy and historical importance. It lasted forty years, was frank but creative, and was surely the most vital single factor in the birth and survival of the People's Republic.

When Chou returned to Canton from France in late 1924 to offer his services as Political Instructor at Whampoa Military Academy, he first began to work with Mao, who was then absorbed in founding his pioneer Peasants' Institute. The close comradeship between the two men, however, may be said to have begun only at the famous Tsunyi Conference ten years later, in January 1935, during the first phase of the Long March. At this time, Chou was senior to Mao in Party leadership. But he saw quite clearly that Mao possessed qualities that he, Chou, did not possess—among them an instinctive understanding of China's peasantry, and an uncanny ability to communicate with them in their vernacular.

Chou recognized his own unique gifts of organization and negotiation, and in fact knew he probably could have maintained his senior position had he wished. But he recognized Mao as possessing a natural appeal to the masses of China. When, therefore, he took the initiative at Tsunyi in proposing to the assembled leadership that Mao be formally elected Permanent Chairman of the Party, he was well aware that, though he himself would nominally be functioning in second place, theirs was in fact an equal partnership.[2]

Chou and Mao complemented each other in character. They also symbolized the two elements in the national life which united in the Red tide that swept China—the peasant oppressed for centuries by government and landlord, and the frustrated Confucius-trained intellectual radicalized by the massive inequi-

[2] Foreign newsmen were slow to realize that the top Party leaders would seldom act without consulting each other, especially in those early years. Gunther Stein of the Manchester *Guardian* and *Christian Science Monitor* (one of the many correspondents to visit our family home in Hankow) was waiting for his notes to be returned to him after a 1944 interview with the Chairman in Yenan. He writes: "When I happened to meet Mao Tse-tung during those days he apologized for the delay and said, 'I had to consult Comrades Chu Teh and Chou En-lai about all I told you. They approved.'" (*The Challenge of Red China*, p. 108.)

ties of the imperial establishment and its helplessness before a foreign invader.

Chou was always an expert at balancing (earning the occasional description of "the elastic Bolshevik" and similar phrases), as any man would have to be who succeeded in retaining Moscow's trust, although privately agreeing with Mao's opinion in the early days when Mao's policies were anathema to the Comintern.

Some felt in him, in former times, an element of opportunism. To most, however, his capacity to adjust to changed circumstances or a fresh "Party line" appealed strongly as "pragmatic realism and a refusal to be doctrinaire."

Chou's status was thus chiefly due to his inner stature as a man. Free to an extraordinary degree from self-seeking, he won the confidence and friendship of his comrades because they instinctively trusted the purity of his motives. This rarest of qualities enabled him to engage in the give and take of Party controversy without exciting personal rancor.

This selflessness in Chou received its ultimate test in his relationship with Mao. As Party leader, with power to bestow or withhold position or privilege, the Chairman might expect to be the object of intense competition for his favor among those around him. It seems he did not feel such competition from Chou, who would rather yield to some ambitious associate than contest with him.

Mao instinctively felt and responded to this self-effacing quality in Chou, and over the years the latter almost imperceptibly became the Chairman's one truly indispensable associate.

Besides his pre-eminent Party status, Chou was universally acknowledged, along with Commander-in-Chief Chu Teh, as having founded China's Red Army. His martial record began as Political Adviser to Chiang Kai-shek at the Whampoa Military Academy near Canton in 1925. A year later (when I first met him) he was acting in the same capacity with Chiang's joint Kuomintang-Communist forces at the start of the famous Northern Expedition. Then, following the 1927 Kuomintang-Communist split, Chou ordered the so-called Nanchang Uprising on August 1, and along with Chu Teh held the area for the Communists against the Kuomintang during a brief but critical period. At Army Day celebrations on the anniversary of the uprising, Chou, until just before his death, always assumed a key role.

Chou and Mao were from the beginning in advance of their colleagues in grasping the central importance of the military arm in any political movement. Thus Chou, who virtually held the rank of General-for-Life, kept closely in touch with the top Whampoa graduates, led the earliest insurrections, and with Mao and Chu Teh directed the fighting in Kiangsi, the final breakout, and the daily operations of the Long March, where his Whampoa student Lin Piao served under him. The most respected leaders in the Red Army have not necessarily been only combat heroes, but also political strategists and military tacticians. Such a combination, to a consummate degree, was Chou En-lai, who remained a respected general and guiding spirit in the Party's Military Committee, even with no troops under his direct command.

This synthesis of qualities enabled Chou to play a key part in creating unity between Party and Military, thus constructively preparing for the emergence of the young Red Guards, as well as for their later dispersal after having served their purpose during the Cultural Revolution.

Another unique factor in Chou En-lai's leadership was his extensive knowledge of the outside world. Ho Chi Minh of Vietnam was the only Asian Communist leader with any international experience remotely comparable. Certainly no Chinese Communist can begin to rival Chou's record abroad. It is doubtful whether even the famous Lenin, who spent many years in European exile, could have matched it.

That delightfully sophisticated French diplomat, former Foreign Minister Maurice Couve de Murville, once discoursed to me with restrained eloquence about Chou: "He is wise, immensely well-informed, prudent." The French statesman expressed particular astonishment at his Chinese colleague's intimate knowledge of Berlin (from his European days) and of every detail of European diplomacy. "Chou," he added, "insists that hard work and long hours are the way to stay young!"

Chou acquired his profound knowledge of foreign affairs "the hard way." At lunch one day at the French Embassy in Peking, the veteran French Ambassador Etienne Manac'h explained how it began in 1954 at the Geneva Conference on Indo-China. "Chou told me at least a dozen times," he remarked, "that they had been 'had' at Geneva. 'We were inexperienced. We thought the

Americans would support the decision of the Conference. But we were wrong.'"

Not long afterward, as recorded earlier, Chou made a series of major excursions through Africa. Here he met with unexpected rebuffs. Here, too, he demonstrated his unique capacity to learn from error, and China, accordingly, soon began to match the influence of the Western super-powers on that continent. Indeed, given her greater capacity for identification with the needs of underprivileged peoples, she may eventually surpass them.

As for the United States, Chou probably knew more Americans than any other top Communist leader, East or West.

He had been in the business of charming Americans for some forty years—ever since he first captivated Edgar Snow in Paoan in 1936 during the KMT-CCP civil war and set up for him the Yenan dates that resulted in Snow's classic *Red Star Over China*—the first detailed portraits of Mao and Chou to reach the West, and still unrivaled in its field.

During the wartime United Front days in Chungking, 1938 to 1945, Western diplomats, officers and correspondents beat a path to Chou's door. They agreed that from a public-relations angle he put on a virtuoso performance. The soon-to-be U. S. Secretary of State, George C. Marshall, formally referred to him "with friendship and esteem." Even the strongly anti-Communist General Albert C. Wedemeyer, to whom Mao and Chou had offered command of their Red Army, at one time came under his spell. "Chou," he told me, "is unfailingly courteous, frank, scrupulously honest, and very human."

Even after the war, when the United Front yielded to U.S. support of Chiang Kai-shek, and most correspondents failed to take Chou En-lai seriously, a now-celebrated columnist paid a remarkable tribute to Chou's prescience in predicting U.S. collaboration with the Chinese Communists as a key to the future. Following Chou's death, Jack Anderson devoted an installment of his "Washington Merry-Go-Round" to the man he had interviewed regularly in Chungking during the civil war.

No one would listen to Chou En-lai thirty years ago.

In those critical days following World War II, most Americans were listening to Chiang Kai-shek. The U.S. embassy in Chungking saw him as China's man of the

future. The correspondents thronged to his press conferences.

It was the political wisdom of those days that the Russian and Chinese Communists were inseparable. But
Chou insisted that Russia, because of its proximity, was
a menace to China. He kept repeating that China, if it
should come under Communist rule, would want to cultivate friendship with America.[3]

The Communist conquest of power and Chiang's flight to Taiwan in 1949 moved Washington, under Secretary of State Dulles,
to continue to regard Chiang's regime as the Government of
China, and to end official relations with Peking. Chou was not de-
terred. Soon after the Dulles back-turning episode, he was let-
ting it be known that he would like to sit down with the U.S.
representatives. When U.N. Secretary-General Dag Hammarskjöld brought a young American assistant (reportedly a plain-
clothesman) with him on his Peking visit, Chou showed the aide
special courtesy.

"We need not be afraid of American secret agents," he said.
"On the contrary, we should work on them."[4]

Chou was also the moving spirit in the creation of the distinctive exhibit of Chinese art which toured Europe and America
in 1973–75. He allocated substantial sums to rediscovering, re-
storing, and preserving these treasures of China's past, and took
vigorous steps to guard them from the excesses of the Cultural
Revolution. The universal acclaim accorded in the West to the
traveling exhibitions of these treasures must have afforded the
Premier keen satisfaction in his last years.

Chou had a special feeling for China's intellectuals. Schooled
in the Confucian classics, and with his Mandarin family background, the Premier, more than other leading Communists, always had an instinctive understanding of the nation's troubled
academics and was trusted by them over any other government
leader.

Linguistically he was a cultivated man, with a fair command

[3] January 20, 1976.
[4] Hsu, *Chou En-lai*, p. 205.

of French and a working knowledge of English, German (learned in Germany by reading *Das Kapital* in the original), Japanese and Russian. There was a revealing scene in Moscow in 1957 when Chou, tired of the continuing stream of Russian, upbraided Khrushchev for "never having taken the trouble ever to study our language."

"But Chinese is so difficult," pleaded Khrushchev.

"It's no harder for you than Russian was for me," shot back the indignant Chou.

By contrast, Chou was delighted by the youthful Professor Ross Terrill's command of Chinese, and when told that Harvard's Australian scholar-journalist had learned it "in America," smiled broadly. "That is a fine thing," he beamed, "to learn Chinese in America."[5]

The Chinese Premier's acute mind was constantly probing for new facts. Once a Turkish journalist spent a conventional half hour questioning him. Chou then spent a vigorous hour and a half probing his visitor for the latest European developments.

The years 1956–65 were years of turmoil in the entire international Communist movement. In Russia, Khrushchev denounced Stalin. In China, Mao announced his epochal plan to utilize the criticisms of non-Communist Chinese to enrich and broaden the Party program.

Of the hundreds of thousands of non-Party citizens—many of them highly trained senior intellectuals and scientists—fully 90 per cent had stayed on in China after 1949 to help with the Revolution. Chou, an intellectual himself, was specially trusted by them, and when in 1956 it was publicly proposed to "Let a hundred flowers bloom and a hundred schools of thought contend," many of them responded.

By 1957 the flood of criticism of the Government by the academics had grown so violent it had to be curbed. But characteristically, in no instance did Chou involve himself in the hairsplitting, often ridiculously demagogic vilifications waged by Party-line defenders to knock down an author by finding fault with one of his novels or poems. Among all the leaders in Peking, he always showed a wholesome respect for the integrity of a

[5] Ross Terrill, *800,000,000—The Real China*, p. 132.

true intellectual. Uniquely, he retained to the last the unwavering respect of the intelligentsia.

Chou was one of the world's rare intellectuals who was also a man of conviction and action—a "scholar turned insurrectionist." Nevertheless, there has never been any "personality cult" about him—though anyone who knows his unique revolutionary record must fervently wish he had committed more of his best thinking to print.

The late Premier was also a poet. In a 1957 anthology published by the Chinese Writers' Union—an "extensive anthology of the finest poems written in the preceding year"—a poem by Chou En-lai is included. His metrical pattern was chosen from the ancient *Book of Songs* (first half of the first millenium B.C.)— apparently a favorite collection.[6]

Chou's appeal to the young had begun with his own early years. As we have seen, he was not yet out of his teens when he assumed a natural leadership of China's pioneer youth in Tientsin. By then it was 1919, the May Fourth Movement was in full swing, and Chou and his colleagues brought the students of North China swarming out of their classrooms to parade down the streets of Peking shouting "Down with the warlords!" They had exchanged their books for rifles, raced to the mobilization points, marched on Japanese stores and smashed them. In 1920 young Chou left for his decisive four years in Europe, where his main objective was enlisting for the Party young Chinese studying abroad.

After Europe, Chou's involvement with youth was transferred to the young officer trainees at Whampoa Military Academy. It continued during the Long March when he had charge of hundreds of teen-age fighters. Later he worked with the youth at Yenan, visiting their classes, counselling, encouraging and providing for them a benevolent discipline. Even in wartime Chungking he made a point of advising and training the young who worked under him.

The Red Guards, who adored Chou and Mao, felt a special affinity for Chou, who saw them more often, had a lifelong record of leading student demonstrations, and maintained a special

---

[6] It is from these classical verses the Premier chose the lines he wrote for my father's farewell memorial volume. See photo of the double page of Chou's calligraphy.

interest in their future. In the summer of 1966 Mao, eager to pu-
rify his senior Communist leadership and avoid the problems
Lenin had so clearly predicted for Russia many years before, had
turned his young Red Guards loose on China's own increasingly
inflexible bureaucracy. These teen-agers would drag out selected
"anti-Maoists" and parade them in dunce hats through Peking
streets. Now, after a year "on the road," they were streaming
into the capital from all over the country, had finally gotten out
of hand, and we have already seen how Chou, with Mao and Lin
Piao out of the capital, had single-handedly dealt with half a
million of them in the Great Hall. After a couple of nights and
days Chou had completely won them over.

Following the Cultural Revolution, Chou took a year out to
visit the youngsters in their home villages all over China, getting
to know their parents and friends, and making sure they were
still pursuing the revolutionary path.

It was a lifetime preoccupation. Not long before he died,
when my sister was showing him some photos of a college-age
American and his young friends, the Premier's face lit up as he
said, very slowly and emphatically:

"We must never—*never*—pour cold water on the young!"[7]

Chou En-lai ("En-lai" means "coming of grace") was a man
of immense charm and poise. To those who knew him well,
he gave an appearance of complete self-possession, thorough
awareness of every move made or word spoken and intense
interest in those around him. He was a man who laughed easily
and often uproariously—a man who knew his own charm and
magnetism and had no scruples about using them—though never,
to our knowledge, simply to draw people personally to himself.
He was totally dedicated to the goals that had governed his life
and was willing to use or justify the use of anything that would
advance those goals. He was a cosmopolitan, a man of the world,

[7] David and Nancy Milton in *The Wind Will Not Subside: Years in Revolutionary China—1964–1969*, p. 108, pay a moving tribute to this compassionate side of Chou En-lai's nature: "Millions of Chinese believed that he
personally was the only man in that enormous country capable of solving
the problems in which they all found themselves entangled. His long-tested
skills as a negotiator and his capacity for political survival were put to daily
tests, but what many people looked to him for was his understanding of
their personal difficulties, his answers to their anguished letters, or quilts
for their Red Guard children wandering through the cold of North China."

yet not worldly. He was willing to be "all things to all men" if that would serve to advance his purposes.

Chou's wide-spaced, penetrating eyes looked out from under bushy black brows—only after his illness did they show signs of graying. His habit of looking directly at a person conveyed an appealing forthrightness. His erect, easy stance lent force to an urbane personality, while a gently pitched, cultured voice and suave manner revealed nothing of his turbulent revolutionary background.

Writers, newsmen and statesmen alike, drawn by Chou's undeniable charisma, have always delighted in broadcasting their impressions of this slight, tough, magnetic Chinese statesman. To Professor Ross Terrill he was a "small man but he seemed to dominate any roomful of people; his eyes steely except when lit up with laughter; the mouth set low in the face and the lips set forward in a taut way. Among the sharply sculptured features there are signs of strain. The black hair is now half silver."[8]

To Helen Foster Snow, Edgar Snow's first wife, a longtime close friend of the Chous and author of many books under the pen name Nym Wales, the Premier was a man "very much alive, alert, quick and on tension, like a tight-wound steel spring. . . . He was very masculine."[9]

To Snow himself, who knew him earliest and best,[10] "Chou still retains traces of 'boyishness' . . . a man of the world yet not of this world . . . a true intellectual." Snow's earliest impressions are of "a slender figure of soldierly bearing who brought his heels together, touched his faded red-starred cap in salute and examined me with large dark eyes under heavy eyebrows. Then his face, half-covered with a beard of heavy growth for a Chinese, parted to show even white teeth and a friendly smile. 'Hello,' he said, 'are you looking for somebody? I am in command here.' He had spoken in *English*. 'My name,' he added, 'is Chou En-lai.' "[11]

[8] Terrill, from memorial address at Harvard University following Chou's death.

[9] Helen Foster Snow (Nym Wales), in personal correspondence with the author.

[10] His widow, Lois Wheeler Snow, tells in her poignant book *A Death With Dignity* of the unprecedented tribute paid to her husband by the Chinese Government and people.

[11] Edgar Snow, *Journey to the Beginning*, p. 157.

Snow adds a further description: "Boyish in appearance when I met him, despite his thirty-eight years and the beard, he was a person of charm and intelligence, and I thought that in earlier times he would have been a fastidious mandarin. Beneath his outer urbanity he had a tough, supple mind . . ."[12] Minus the beard, that is also not a bad capsule profile of the man in his final years.

Noteworthy, too, is the exemplary standard of personal rectitude—amounting almost to a puritan emphasis—regarding Chou's personal life, remarked on by most writers both Chinese and foreign.

Helen Foster Snow speaks of the "Chinese characteristics" in his personality, especially "the ability never to 'break the surface'—the old Chinese absolute rule in human and political relations. Chou was always self-controlled, reasonable, rational and flexible." She refers to one of the few times Chou is known to have lost his temper—when the Red Guards attacked and burned the British Liaison Office in Peking. He had personally gone there in a towering rage and commanded them to leave. Her comment: "This type of action—which he would consider not even civilized—was the kind of thing Chou En-lai always tried to prevent during his long years as a revolutionary."[13]

On another occasion an English journalist was finishing a long, serious interview with Chou.

"'Why are you so worried?' the Premier commented, smiling. 'All your questions are worried questions. . . . How old are you?'

"'Fifty-one' was the reply. 'Well,' said the Premier, 'I'm much older than that and I'm not worried. So why should you be?' "[14]

Chou could manage his enormous physical workload, including early rising and inhuman hours, because of a Spartan personal regime. Unlike the chain-smoking and wine-loving Mao, he avoided tobacco, proposed mostly nonalcoholic toasts at diplomatic dinners, and in his later years gave up drinking entirely.

No spellbinder on the public platform, Chou was a master of personal contact. This was strikingly evident during the celebrated visit of the U.S. table-tennis team to Peking in early 1971.

[12] Ibid., p. 159.
[13] Helen Foster Snow, personal to the author.
[14] Felix Greene, *The Wall Has Two Sides*, p. 366.

"Chou was a lot of fun," said Graham Steenhoven, the Chrysler executive who led the young Americans. "He was a good sport, a guy with a terrific sense of humor . . ."

Chou's sense of humor was subtle, but to many nonetheless appealing. The British correspondent James Cameron relates a delightful anecdote. While Chou was hosting the mercurial Jawaharlal Nehru at a mammoth Peking party, the Cambridge-educated Indian Prime Minister, clearly exasperated by an over-dose of Chinese small talk, took Chou by the arm as they moved among the celebrities. "A little English now, Mr. Prime Minister?" Chou grinned, raised his glass and said: "Ah! yes—How do you do?"—and continued as before in Mandarin.

China's Premier, as mentioned earlier, had one of the rarest and most potent qualities of leadership—the ability to learn from error. Says a former associate: "Chou regards anyone's mistakes, and especially his own, as incentives to do better. He has a highly developed capacity for analyzing and applying the lessons of history."

An example would be his African tours. The lesson of course was that high-pressure methods, no matter how sincere and well-intentioned, are usually counterproductive.

One leading African put it succinctly: "Most of us on this continent felt we had gone through our revolutions when we took over from the usurping white man. But the Chinese acted at first as if no basic revolution at all had occurred. There may well have been truth in this, but it was hardly for foreigners to point it out. Now they say frankly: 'We were wrong. Today we come simply as friends to help where we can.' It has made all the difference."

The Premier's magnetism and charm were of course legendary. A passionate nationalist from the beginning, and a dedicated Marxist from the early 1920s, Chou was an inflexible opponent of foreign rule in Asia. At the same time, he held what must be the all-Asian record for beguiling Western leaders. It is hard indeed to find an American or European statesman or officer who, exposed to his charm, failed to succumb to it. Even Chiang Kai-shek, kidnaped during the famous Sian incident of 1936 and saved by Chou's personal intervention, called his benefactor the most reasonable Communist he knew, and U. S. Marine Colonel Evans Carlson has described for us the anniversary dinner when the Generalissimo thanked Chou with deep emotion for "what you did for me."[15]

Chou's charm and shrewd manipulation of language had historical repercussions before and during World War II, when he undoubtedly contributed to a Washington illusion that China's Communists were only "social reformers" or, in the words of a wartime British ambassador, "agrarian reformers."

To those who know her, Chou En-lai's wife of fifty years—the soft-spoken, motherly-looking Teng Ying-ch'ao, emphatically contradicts the usual assumption that a mild-mannered person is incapable of supreme revolutionary dedication. They met during the early student demonstrations in Tientsin, when she was seventeen and he twenty. During his years abroad in Paris they "fell in love by post" (as she describes it), were married in Canton in 1925. It proved to be a model political partnership as well as a genuine love match. There seems never to have been, since their marriage, any other woman in his life.

Ying-ch'ao's career paralleled her husband's at all points, and she eventually headed up the women's federations of China. Her father had died when she was a baby, and her widowed mother had a hard struggle to earn a living as a teacher and governess in the male-dominated China of those days. The daughter grew up resentful of the inferior status of women, and determined to alter it—a dream certainly fulfilled in overflowing measure in the People's Republic of today.

From the Communist takeover of power in Peking until his last fatal illness, the Chous lived in a small but attractive apartment inside the red walls of the old Forbidden City. The dining room, where the couple usually ate alone, overlooked a courtyard with beds of flaming peonies. A piano was set against one wall, beside a hi-fi radio and a television set. A large bust of Chairman Mao dominated the room.[16]

What was Chou En-lai's global aim?

Curious Westerners will make what they will of this extraordinarily gifted human being. But a true evaluation of him, as of his country, is surely one of the most difficult journalistic and scholarly tasks of our times.

[15] See Chapter VI, p. 89.
[16] Richard Hughes, in the New York *Times* Magazine, October 4, 1964.

The Honorable Mike Mansfield, formerly Majority Leader of the United States Senate and its most informed student of the Far East, in a letter to the author soon after Chou's death and not long before the Senator's own retirement, wrote this personal appraisal:

> I had great respect for the late Premier Chou En-lai, admiration for his intellectual and political traits, and appreciation for the efforts he made to bring about a reconciliation between our two countries.
>
> Mrs. Mansfield and I may well have been the last Americans to see him. We visited him in his Peking hospital room in late December of 1974 and spent over an hour with him. He recalled that we were both in Chungking in late 1944—I was there on a special mission for Franklin D. Roosevelt—and he remembered other incidents in his relationship with former President Nixon and Chairman Mao. He stated at that time that the motivating factor in the People's Republic of China for the Nixon meeting in Peking was the fact that Mao Tse-tung had read an article written by Mr. Nixon before he became President and appearing, I believe, in *Foreign Affairs Quarterly*. Chou En-lai said that no one in the government had been aware of that article but that Chairman Mao was so impressed by it that he helped to set the wheels in motion for the meeting which occurred in Peking in 1972.
>
> At my first, private breakfast meeting with former President Nixon in January 1969, the first topic he brought up was the need to bring about a normalization of relations between the People's Republic of China and the United States. He outlined a series of proposals such as lifting the secondary boycott which had been in effect since the Korean War; an increased emphasis on the meetings between the United States and Chinese Ambassadors in Poland; and the possibility of more travels by groups to China from this country and from China to the United States. He also expressed a personal de-

sire to visit Peking, but he did not expect that he would be given that opportunity.

As my wife and I prepared to say a final farewell to Chou En-lai, he accompanied us to the door of his room and said these last words to us—"The door between our two countries should never have been closed."

He was the survivor who maintained his position through all the conflicts, the differences and the difficulties which confronted his country during its period of re-emergence. His steadying hand and moderating influence will be deeply missed but long remembered.

He was indeed, as you have stated, "a man for all seasons."

As everyone knows, the West, and especially the United States, abounds with those, many of them high-minded and intelligent citizens, who continue, as China-haters, to execrate the Peking regime because, like the Soviet Union or Yugoslavia, it is called Communist.

There also exists a far smaller but equally vociferous minority of what we might call "China-worshipers"—scholars, journalists, businessmen—who having been officially invited to spend a few weeks in the "new China," return to express, in books and lectures, paeans of praise of the human "Utopia" which they judge the People's Republic to represent.

My own experience here may be useful to the reader. Knowing the "old China" firsthand from my youth, I was understandably overwhelmed by the manifest transformation of the poverty-stricken, disease-ridden, chaotic, foreign-dominated, demoralized land I once knew so intimately, into the vibrant, teeming, purposeful, hard-working, intensely patriotic and apparently happy society one sees on every hand now.

In my first interview with Chou En-lai (shortly before the Nixon visit) I was routinely asked by him, as one born in China, my impressions of the country today. Naturally, but as it turned out rashly, I ventured an enthusiastic commentary on the present as contrasted with what I had known in the past. Chou's reply, while courteous, was frank in its rebuke at what he implied was my naïveté in stressing the positives of Modern China as against its still relative backwardness compared to America and Western countries generally. "You seem to forget these things, my friend, and we must never forget them. It is true China has made some progress—indeed, great progress when we consider conditions as you and I once knew them. But we still have a long, long way to go even to approach the material standards of your country. It will certainly never happen in our lifetime—nor, in all likelihood, for several centuries."

Chou's frank verdict was echoed some three years later, as the Premier lay dying in Peking, by his longtime comrade Mao Tsetung, who addressed to him one of his final poems:

> Loyal parents who sacrificed so much for the nation
>   never feared the ultimate fate.
> Now that the country has become Red,
>   who will be its guardian?
> Our mission, unfinished, may take a thousand years.
> The struggle tires us, and our hair is gray.
> You and I, old friend, can we just watch our efforts
>   being washed away?

Will they be washed away? Let us try, in a final chapter, to consider some of the elements involved in an answer.

CHAPTER XI

REMOTIVATING SOCIETY

Not long before he died in 1924, Russia's revolutionary hero
V. I. Lenin, paralyzed from the stroke which eventually killed
him, evading his doctors and aided by his wife Krupskaya, pain-
fully dictated "a last testament." The candid self-criticism, both
expressed and implied, of Lenin's testament was to have a profound effect nearly half a century later on China's revolutionary
leadership. In this extraordinary and still little-known document,
the founder of the Soviet state declared: "I am, it seems, strongly
guilty before the workers of Russia, for the many deficiencies
of the Soviet government."[1]

Everyone knew that Russia desperately needed the social, economic and political overturn that was achieved in late 1917. But
what the Revolution did not achieve, he seemed to sense, was
any basic change in the motivation of society. The result was
that five years later, as Lenin lay dying, there had developed a
burgeoning Soviet bureaucracy staffed for the most part with men
largely absorbed by personal ambition, jealousy and rivalry—in

[1] Isaac Deutscher, "The Moral Dilemmas of Lenin," *The Listener*, London, BBC, February 5, 1959.

short, by much the same human desires that dominated the old Tsarist bureaucracy.

For this betrayal of their common revolutionary ideals, Lenin felt himself to be chiefly responsible, and he enjoined his successors, for the sake of the cause to which all had dedicated their lives, to deal firmly with the situation before it was too late. Evidently Russia's great revolutionary, in his last days, was reaching for the concept that China's Communists would later explore, and bring to power: the changing of human motive.

For thirty-three years Lenin's message was to be concealed by Stalin from the Soviet people. Only in the past two decades, through the pioneer work of Isaac Deutscher and other scholars, has it been brought to light. But the passage of time had dulled its impact and it created little stir in the West.

Nikita Khrushchev, it is true, in his celebrated de-Stalinization speech, began to explore its implications. But only China's Chou and Mao, after the Long March, had the insight and temporary leisure to develop a campaign to create a selfless man, giving it eventually not only the highest official priority from cradle to grave, but enshrining it as a full-fledged state doctrine.

In this respect China holds an enormous advantage over Soviet Russia. Isaac Deutscher, in his book *The Ironies of History*, points out that the Chinese Communists were able to experiment with their theories of transforming human nature and test them out long before they came to power. "Although the material resources of the Chinese Revolution were so much poorer than those of the Russian," he writes, "its moral resources were larger; and in revolution as in war the Napoleonic rule holds good that the moral factors are to the material as three is to one." He speaks of the suffering and privation during two decades of battling for survival as an experience "no other ruling group has gone through," and claims that it "may have left its imprint on their character and in some measure shielded them from the worst corruption of power."[2]

It was during these two decades before the founding of the People's Republic in 1949 that the philosophical and ethical principles of China's new society were formulated and put into practice. Brought to birth in the rugged mountains of South China,

[2] Isaac Deutscher, *The Ironies of History: Essays on Contemporary Communism*, pp. 114–16.

weaned on the Long March and nurtured among the barren hills of Yenan, the new ethic grew to adolescence in the ranks of the foot soldier who lived on the land and courted the goodwill of its people. It was soon to find expression in a Red Army song—now a hit all over China. Its title: "The Three Main Rules of Discipline and the Eight Points for Attention."

When I revisited the mainland in the winter of 1971–72, I heard this jaunty, catchy tune again and again, its eight verses a Marxist "Ten Commandments" for the revolutionary life: 1) respect people, don't be arrogant; 2) buy fair, sell fair, be reasonable; 3) return everything borrowed; 4) pay full price for anything damaged; 5) don't swear at or hit people; 6) don't damage people's crops or property; 7) take no liberties with women, and don't indulge in decadent habits; 8) don't ill-treat prisoners. Its initial "Three Main Rules" were the key to success on the historic Long March, winning the trust and support of the common people en route: 1) absolute obedience; 2) absolute honesty— no stealing; 3) serve the people—restore what is theirs.[3]

From such guileless beginnings evolved a highly developed national ethic which, in its maturity, found repercussions as far afield as the United States Marines and their wartime slogan, "Gung Ho!"[4]

During the early stages of Japan's invasion of China, General Chou En-lai (he held, but seldom used, General's rank through most of his public career) became a good friend of the U. S. Marine Captain Evans Carlson, one of the ablest and least-known U.S. officers of World War II, founder of the celebrated "Carlson's Raiders." The two men often met in our Hankow home.

[3] My sister remembers hearing this song as early as 1938 when she visited Red Army Headquarters in Shansi. She compares its precepts with the earlier Kuomintang attempts at social reform known as "The New Life Movement." Western journalists of that day delighted in poking fun at Nationalist efforts to get people to stop spitting and button up their jackets ("cleanliness and good manners"). Even the more serious campaign which eventually developed against official as well as private corruption, extravagance, stealing and dishonesty failed to achieve its goal. It foundered on the ancient rocks of not practicing what it preached. The program of the Red Army, on the other hand, was to succeed because, in the example set by officers and men alike, they managed to inspire a genuine popular response. They prided themselves on "obeying the rules" to the letter.

[4] "Gung Ho!" or "Pull together!" (literally "Work together!"—colloquially "Let's go!").

Sometimes the American military attaché, the then Major Joseph
Stilwell, would join them over maps spread out on our dining-
room table. Together they would discuss the question that
has fascinated every commander from the days of Alexander
the Great, Caesar and Hannibal, through Washington, Robert E.
Lee and Ulysses S. Grant, and the World War II campaigns of
MacArthur and Patton, Rommel and Montgomery: How remotivate the military man?

As told by his biographer,[5] the heart of the famous "Gung
Ho!" philosophy, which later spelled countless victories for Carlson's Raiders, lay in the story of this dynamic American officer
who served in China. It runs, in part, as follows:

> It was morning and he was with the Eighth Route
> Army—about 600 of them on a forced march in Shansi
> Province, with orders to head off a Japanese column.
> The terrain was the roughest he had ever seen: deep
> gorges, thick forests, swift and bitterly cold rivers. The
> days were blasphemous with cold. And through it they
> had marched steadily for twenty-four hours without
> rest, and had covered fifty-eight miles. Most of the way
> the Chinese soldiers had been singing but now the col-
> umn was silent. Only the sounds of panting men and
> the ceaseless shuffle of sandals or bare feet against the
> rock and the earth could be heard. Every face in the
> morning light was marked with the stigmata of exhaus-
> tion—bulging eyes, slack jaws, cracked and dried lips.
>
> To Carlson who marched with them, the fifty miles
> had been an accumulation of miracles. Not merely had
> men endured an enormous trial of strength, but of the
> 600 who had started, not one had fallen by the way and
> dropped out. In his own country on maneuvers, he had
> led men on marches of similar duration and intensity; in
> Nicaragua he had marched against the "bandits" and
> the going had been almost as strenuous. But there, as
> always, some few men had given up, had deserted or
> had surrendered to fatigue.
>
> He looked at the Chinese soldier next to him,

[5] Blankfort, The Big Yankee.

watched his face, listened to him pant, and wondered what it was that made him endure.

Far ahead in the column they were beginning to sing again. The song moved down slowly like ripples on a mill pond.

The soldier next to Carlson noticed that he was being studied—and smiled.

"A long march," he said in his own language.

Carlson nodded. "Tired?" he asked, his breath hurting.

"Tsan Tsan,"[6] the soldier said slowly between gasps. "If . . . a . . . man . . . has . . . only . . . legs . . . he gets tired . . ."

Some years later, Carlson would address his audience of young trainees—marines carefully selected for the elite corps of "Raiders."

"That day in China," Carlson said, "I saw in practice the secret of the Chinese Eighth Route Army. Two words—'ethical indoctrination.'

"Those are big words, boys, but let me tell you simply what they mean. The reason those 600 men were able to endure such hardship was because they knew *why* it was necessary for them to complete that march. But more than that, they knew *why* that march was important to the whole series of battles they were fighting; and they also knew *why* those battles were important to the whole war against the Japs. And the war against the Japs was one they understood and believed in. In short, they understood why the effort of every single one of them was necessary for the victory of the whole Chinese people. That's ethical indoctrination. That's what you've got to have besides 'legs.' That's why 600 average Chinese men did what 600 average Americans might not have been able to do—march fifty-eight miles in twenty-four hours without rest and without one man falling by the wayside."

From the military, China's prodigious experiment in remotivation moved concurrently to embrace every phase of national life.

[6] "Tsan Tsan" meaning "All the time!"

Robert Lifton, the noted scholar-psychiatrist who has studied and researched the process of character remotivation, calls the Chinese experiment "the most ambitious version of 'the new man in the socialist era.'"

This new man, writes Lifton, is "expected to embody the original bourgeois virtues—diligence, frugality, self-discipline, honesty, belief in the moral value of work, and unselfishness."[7]

As for the Cultural Revolution—that great upsurge in society which broke over China in the late 1960s and after—it is clear that it was not so much cultural as motivational: i.e. beyond the cultural phase, its key objective was nothing less than a gigantic attempt to transform the basic motives of man.

The true character of China's Cultural Revolution can better be grasped if we contrast this objective with some of the drives which, to the non-Westerner, appear to dominate our Western society today: personal gain, personal status and personal success. As a matter of actual practice, these motives taken together supply much of the impetus behind what is generally described as our "free-enterprise system."

Actress Shirley MacLaine, for example, describes her visit to a luxury shop catering to Westerners visiting Canton:

> "Are you interested in jewelry like this?" I asked the Chinese guides.
> "No," replied one. "Such trinkets prevent us from working well. They get in the way when we move about . . ."

---

[7] *Revolutionary Immortality: Mao Tse-tung and the Chinese Cultural Revolution*, pp. 41 and 46. Lifton claims further that the Chinese Communists have always felt that the human mind was infinitely malleable, "capable of being reformed and rectified without limit . . . the will all-powerful . . . man's capacity for both undergoing change and changing his environment unlimited, once he makes the decision for change." He says, "One could also view it as a method of purification which by means of detailed self-examination, provides benefits akin to those of psychotherapy and spiritual enlightenment." His comments on purity and power in this connection are revealing. He says "purity includes such things as self-denial (or even self-surrender) on behalf of a higher cause . . . Purity and power are in fact psychologically inseparable . . . Power becomes the harnessing of purity for an immortal quest." (pp. 70, 45–46 and 50)

MacLaine then comments:

> It was as simple as that. I did not sense any doubt,
> regret, or hypocrisy in Chang's voice. All around her,
> we were oohing and aahing over the jewelry, as if we
> had walked into Tiffany's. Even when Chang said,
> "Women from the outside world are always interested
> in beautiful jewelry and silks and brocades, and men
> want new technological inventions that can make work
> and money and profit go much faster," she did not seem
> dogmatic or sarcastic. It was as though she was sum-
> ming up the differences between her world and ours.[8]

Historically, of course, such self-interested motives which so
dominate the thinking of contemporary Western society today,
did not apply in anything like the same degree to the Spartan,
and often sacrificial, nature of the communities established by
the Pilgrim Fathers during the *Mayflower* era. My own ancestor,
the pioneer Thomas Hooker, only sixteen years after the land-
ing at Plymouth Rock, marched west cross country from Cambridge at the head of a party of men, women and children, driv-
ing their cattle before them and carrying much on their backs
through the wilderness, to found Hartford, Connecticut. Once in
the New World, a man stood on his own two feet with a joy of
living that welcomed hardships as the ultimate test.

Even at the time of the Declaration of Independence, the ideals
of the pioneers[9] still retained a strong hold on the popular imagination. They were tenaciously held, too. Thomas Paine wrote in
1777: "'Tis the business of little minds to shrink; but he whose
heart is firm, and whose conscience approves his conduct, will
pursue his principles unto death."

However, no one can deny that in the twentieth century, basically self-oriented motives pervade the life style of the vast majority of both governors and governed. Such motives are not only
widely accepted, but widely assumed to be inevitable and even
desirable.

[8] Shirley MacLaine, *You Can Get There from Here*, p. 137.
[9] Samuel Eliot Morison, *The Oxford History of the American People*,
p. 67.

James Reston of the New York *Times,* on his return from
China in late 1971, remarked: "At a time when we are losing the
old doctrine of work hard, work outside yourself for larger goals,
be cooperative, be modest, along comes a society which is picking up these very ideas which we are tending to forget." He
spoke of the curious kinship with Scottish Calvinism he had
sensed there. "Here are these people," he wrote, "actually trying
to . . . bring about a moral reformation of a quarter of the
human race. It sounded to me as if I was back in the Wee Kirk
listening to the old exhortations to be modest and to be self-
critical and helpful to others. The 'little red book'[10] is just
McGuffey's Reader updated . . ."[11]

It is the scope of this endeavor which overwhelms. Suddenly
and unexpectedly one is confronted by a Communist country
seriously grappling with the whole spectrum of human virtue
and needs on a national scale—a task which the West traditionally has long considered to be its own special prerogative.

Even the Vatican went so far as to make "a public overture
for a 'dialogue' with Peking on the basis of Roman Catholic recognition that the thoughts of Chairman Mao also reflected Christian values . . . devoted to a mystique of disinterested work for
others." The Vatican's missionary bulletin asserted "that Maoist
doctrine 'contains some directives that are in keeping with the
great moral principles of the millenary Chinese civilization and
[that] find authentic and completed expression in modern social Christian teaching.'"[12]

All this, of course, was quite alien to my own young life when
making my foreign correspondent debut in Canton in the mid-
twenties. As a typical young Harvard graduate—ambitious, mate-
rialistic, cynical, but still tinged with idealism—to my mind
"Christian values" were largely represented by a missionary father whom I had comfortably and conveniently pigeonholed as a
conventional prelate who need never disturb my world. For him,
I represented a life style he deplored, and could not begin to

[10] The "little red book": *Quotations from Chairman Mao Tse-tung,* until
recently prominently displayed on all public occasions and intensively
studied.

[11] Horace Sutton, "Scotty Reston of the *Times:* The One, The Only—The
Last?" *Saturday Review,* January 29, 1972, p. 15.

[12] The New York *Times,* April 19, 1973.

understand. Neither of us had a clue as to how to bridge the widening gulf between our generations.

Borodin—little though he knew it—had been the first to span that gulf.[13]

All across the vastness of the Soviet Union, the wheels of the Trans-Siberian railway seemed to be grinding out the words he had flung at me in Canton: "That man Paul . . . He was a real revolutionary . . . A *real* revolutionary . . . But where do you find him today? . . . *Where* find him today? . . . Answer me!"

Much as I loved and respected my father, after Canton I knew he did not have—any more than I did—and would not have understood, what Borodin was talking about.

On arrival at Moscow's Alexandrovsky Station during this first visit to the Soviet Union, my passport had been stolen—a seemingly calamitous misfortune, since I was en route to the West and was due, after changing trains, to proceed immediately to Berlin and London for urgent engagements in America. But as things turned out, far from a calamity, loss of the passport proved to be a sheer stroke of luck, for I was forced to stay a month in the Soviet capital while the authorities struggled to establish my identity, and I had a rare chance to look the place over.

Those Moscow days in the fall of 1926 had turned my world upside down: the young Chinese being trained as revolutionaries; Radek's "Come back in twenty years . . . ;" "Roar, China!" and the livid faces of the Komsomol girls in the audience.

It took my Uncle Phil (New York Supreme Court Justice Philip J. McCook) a month to get Washington to contact Moscow's German Embassy[14] for my exit permit. By that time I had become considerably impressed by much of what I had seen. One thing tempered my interest.

It was a few days before I was to leave Russia, and I had been asked to supper at the austere flat of a Communist friend—a hero of the Civil War and a ten-year Party veteran. I found my

---

[13] See Chapter III for the story of my experience with Borodin in Canton in 1926.

[14] The U.S. recognized the U.S.S.R. only in 1933. Before then, Washington transacted essential business through the Embassy of the Weimar Republic in Moscow.

host in a mood of black despair, which the excellent meal, served by his wife, did nothing to dispel.

After supper he saw to it that we were alone and came quickly to the point.

"You're an American," he said. "Our two countries are so hostile we don't even recognize each other. But I have come to like and trust you, and I want to ask you something I cannot ask even my own closest colleagues.

"If you yourself were a Communist, and after many years in the Party you found there were other Party members you did not like, and, try as you might, you could not work with—what would you do? I have found in Communism the answer to every problem on this earth—*except that one.*"

His anguished eyes were fixed on mine. "This means life or death for me. What shall I do?"

At that moment I would have given a fortune to have had something to say. But the faces of two fellow Americans I detested—one, a man who had deeply wronged me, and another of whom I was fiercely jealous—came accusingly to mind, and I knew I could say nothing. I too had men I did not like and could not work with.

There followed what seemed an endless embarrassing silence.

Finally I must have mumbled some feeble excuse before thanking his wife for the meal and making for the door. We shook hands in silence and I looked up at him. His face was contorted in an agony of fear and foreboding, as he struggled to hold back the tears.

I never saw him again. Later I read in the Western press of the first great purges in the Soviet Union.

During the next few years back in America, a series of events unfolded for me new insights into human motives—especially my own—and into the questions posed in Moscow. I began to explore some of the basics of living that might bear on this central theme. I did not have far to seek.

The memory of the man I felt had wronged me began to haunt my days and nights. The truth was that I—a young American from free America—was as enslaved by hate as was my Communist friend in Moscow.

Clearly there was only one course to take, and I decided to take it.

So it was that one morning I found myself calling on an old professor of mine who, startled at the smile on my face, gruffly asked what I wanted.

"I just wanted to ask how you were," I replied, "and to tell you that for all this time I have resented and hated you. I want to say how terribly sorry I am, and to ask your forgiveness."

He stared incredulously. Then, slowly, his face took on the color of a ripe pomegranate. He lowered his eyes and stammered something about being glad that I'd finally seen how wrong I'd been! This last was, of course, not precisely according to the script, but strangely it bothered me not at all.

Years later on another continent, I received a letter written in a shaky hand, saying he had been desperately ill, and kept hoping he would recover in time to write me how much my apology had meant to him. We were friends till he died.

This and other incidents led in time to a freedom and effectiveness I had never known, and eventually took on ever-widening dimensions.

During the winter of 1937–38, with the Japanese advancing up the Yangtze, and the Chinese leadership, both Nationalist and Communist, concentrated temporarily at Hankow in a new popular front, the word spread that Bishop Roots, always widely beloved, had become profoundly stirred by the remotivation of his eldest son.

Chou En-lai, as usual, represented the Communists in the Hankow wartime coalition. The reports about my father intrigued him, for it so happened that he and Mao were, at that very time, increasingly preoccupied with the all-embracing problem of *how* to remold character and remotivate their new society.

This preoccupation first became known to my family during the spring of 1938 when Chou and Teng Ying-ch'ao were in and out of our Hankow home.[15] My sister Frances noted that after dinner the men would leave her to entertain Mme. Chou on the piano, while Chou, settled in the Bishop's study, would talk with my father far into the night.

Father was known for his scrupulousness about keeping confidences. So when my sister's curiosity got the better of her,

[15] See Chapters IV and VI.

and she finally asked him what they were finding to talk about, he replied, "I can tell you only one thing: our friend is fascinated by the idea of how to create a new type of man to live in his new society. So you can imagine we have plenty to discuss."

These far-ranging evening discussions apparently left a lasting mark on Chou En-lai, as they had on my father. During the postwar years (1949–70) when there was virtually no communication between Peking and Washington, Premier Chou, through U.N. Secretary-General Dag Hammarskjöld and other intermediaries, took particular pains to send messages to our family in America. Certainly there was no doubt about the genuine warmth with which he greeted me when, after years of applying for a visa, I finally arrived in Peking and was able to see him.

After the first interview (a three-hour midnight visit not long before the Nixon arrival) and a few hours' sleep, I accompanied the Pakistani Ambassador to the airport to welcome Prime Minister Bhutto. During the official greetings, Chou brought me over to meet the Pakistani Premier, and then drew me aside. For a moment we were alone on the tarmac in the midst of the celebrities and the crowd.

"Last night," he said in Chinese, laughing and gesticulating. "Hao! Ding hao! [Very good!]" He reiterated the warm invitation he had previously extended to my sister and her husband to visit China. Then he took my arm and, very quietly and with some emotion, said in his rarely used and halting English: "Your father—I loved him."

Throughout his career as Premier, Chou En-lai stood staunchly for the new ethic which motivated the building of their new society. Perhaps the model of his own personal life, described by one of my professional colleagues, not noted for enthusiastic views on Red China, as "a virtual idyll of monogamy among the much-marrying [old-time] Communist leaders," heightened this picture of him as a man of principle.[16]

In his last years, the sole insignia on Premier Chou En-lai's neatly tailored tunic was a small red badge reading in Chinese: "Serve the People." This was the main slogan of the so-called Great Proletarian Cultural Revolution of the mid- and late-sixties.

[16] Robert Elegant, *Mao's Great Revolution*, p. 322.

Wherever I traveled in China it stood out to remind citizens of their calling.

Certainly Chou and Mao, as always operating in tandem, were discovering that their experiences during the Long March had prepared them to understand in a unique way the theme of this chapter. As history unfolded in the succeeding years, they were to explore its further ramifications. "It is painful," writes Mao, speaking of his own adventures in remotivation and how he had remolded himself from an intellectual into a peasant. "As a student," he continued, "having acquired the habits of a student, I used to feel it undignified to do any manual labor. At that time it seemed that the intellectuals alone were clean while the peasants and workers were rather dirty. The Revolution brought me into the ranks of workers, peasants and soldiers. Gradually I became familiar with them and they with me. It was then that a fundamental change occurred in . . . me."[17]

Chou En-lai, in a 1964 interview with Edgar Snow, goes still further: "In our view," he said, "only when we dare to face up to difficulties can we overcome them, and only when we dare to admit our shortcomings and mistakes can we rectify them."[18]

How is it done? How have the Chinese gone about "remotivating men" to live in their new society? It should be helpful to examine some of the experiments of the early years of the Revolution. When the Communists first took over the government in 1949, Dr. Ralph Lapwood (now Professor of Seismology and Mathematics and Vice-Master of Emmanuel College, Cambridge University, in England) was Professor of Mathematics at Yenching—the present Peking University. His book, *Through the Chinese Revolution*, co-authored with his wife, Nancy, contains some of the earliest firsthand evidence to reach the West of the radically changed outlook and motivation among students, faculty and staff and the man in the street.[19]

Most valuable are some of the notes he made during the initial university meetings when self-criticism was the central theme. A department chairman would speak at length of the mistakes in his work, analyzing the reasons and setting the tone for the other teachers: "I now see many errors, mostly unconscious. These

[17] Han Suyin, *China in the Year 2001*, p. 149.
[18] Snow, *The Long Revolution*, p. 237.
[19] Ralph and Nancy Lapwood, *Through the Chinese Revolution*.

arose because I thought of my own advantage. Self-sufficient. Onlooker. Question of 'face.' Self-protecting individualism. Purely academic attitude . . . This desire to please everybody . . . Now I realize the need to change . . ."

Apparently his attitude, showing little evidence of inner struggle, still did not satisfy his colleagues. After several days of consideration, the department chairman made a second and much shorter report: "I realized I had not really hated the faults I confessed . . . Inadequate to call myself an individualist . . . more honest to speak of personal ambition—the desire to make and leave a name . . . Did not care enough for my colleagues . . . wasted budget funds . . . I want to beat down that selfish 'I' . . . uproot the old ways and make a new start . . . my only desire now to become identified with the people in building a new China."

Lapwood reports:

> This statement met immediate general welcome. After various expressions of approval and joy, the meeting closed with what sounded quaintly like a benediction. Colleagues and students looked forward to a new relationship. The department chairman himself felt a sense of relief from a great burden; he had become one of the group. He had emerged from the shame of admission of failure, and discovered that instead of losing the respect of all, he had gained a firmer place in their affection.[20]

Another Western scholar, Dr. William Sewell, former professor of chemistry at West China Union University in Chengtu, writes candidly of how the new China affected him, his students and colleagues:

> A few days after the change-over, at the end of 1949, our entire community—staff, students and workers—was called together. The leader of the Liberation Army, which had entered the city, told us that as soldiers they

[20] Ibid., p. 171. The candor of the Lapwoods' book makes it exceptionally valuable. Excesses are faithfully reported, but it also pictures an entire community striving to root out hypocrisy and sham.

knew nothing of educational affairs. It was our business to discover by discussion together how a university should best be organized to help the people of China. This we did; but more important we became in this informal manner members of small groups. . . . People all over the city and throughout China were forming groups according to their work, as rickshaw pullers, engineers, postal workers, school teachers and so on. . . . They were concerned with our daily work and life: making us better chemists, postal workers . . . teaching us to think of others before ourselves, to be better neighbors . . . We came inevitably to our own personal involvement . . . We remembered our responsibilities, we paid for bus rides even if no conductor was there, we did not cheat in examinations, we refused tips and commissions, did not defraud, we no longer sought advantages in bargaining, we thought of others before ourselves.[21]

Edgar Snow, with his long experience in China and unique access to her officialdom, gives us a vivid insight into the punitive aspects of the Cultural Revolution:

"You can have no idea how agonizing these self-criticism and group meetings can be," I was told by one American-educated intellectual who returned to China a decade ago and joined the Party. "Everybody in my bureau from the office boy or scrubwoman up can tell me how bourgeois I am, criticize my personal habits, my family life, my intellectual arrogance, the way I spend my leisure, even my silences. I have to sit and take it." He paused to grimace. "Some people prefer suicide rather than submit to it. It took me years to get used to it but now I believe it has been good for me. I needed it—how I needed it! I am a lot humbler than I was, I value people more. I am better able to help

[21] Robert Jungk, et al., *China and the West: Mankind Evolving*, pp. 51–52, 58.

others." And he, I repeat, was a Party member in good standing.[22]

Ho Li-liang, wife of the former Chief of China's Permanent Mission to the United Nations, now Foreign Minister in Peking, once said virtually the same thing when describing to me her time in one of the May 7 schools for ideological training. "It was awful!" she laughed. "It was as if you were in a gold-fish bowl. Everything was exposed. But it was very effective!"

There is the striking account by two Americans, Mr. and Mrs. Allyn Rickett, Fulbright scholars in China when the Communists came to power, and detained for four years by the authorities early in the regime. In a book on their experiences,[23] they record a notable case of remotivation in one of their young Chinese fellow prisoners.

This "completely inoffensive little fellow" would sit nervously in class, until finally one day he admitted to being a professional pickpocket. "From then on," they write, "every time any one of us noticed Li picking up things we would immediately pounce on him, but all our shouting, arguing and lecturing seemed to do little good." Finally the supervisor explained to them that Li had been trained that way as a child, and that such ingrained habits could not be changed overnight. "Simply reprimanding him won't do any good," he explained. "We've got to dig deep into the reasons why he does these things."

After trying to help Li, the other prisoners realized they were getting nowhere. "We still could not get him to think out why he had become a habitual criminal . . . after two days we gave up." Eventually Li was transferred to another cell and they did not see him for two years.

Meanwhile he had been caught stealing again and was put into handcuffs and ankle chains.

"With help from prisoners who had come to know him better, he had been forced to make a thoroughgoing self-criticism. . . . Layer after layer of his motivations had gradually come to light, until the heart of the matter had been reached."

It seems that as a child Li had been abandoned by his parents

[22] *Red China Today,* p. 390.
[23] Allyn and Adele Rickett, *Prisoners of Liberation.*

and picked up by a gang of thieves, used first as a beggar, then as a robber and later taught the art of a pickpocket. Whatever he got was turned over to the gang. He was virtually their slave, and when he displeased them he was beaten and starved. He had lived in a realm of fear for years, been imprisoned for months by Nationalist police and released only after paying a bribe and consenting to work as a stool pigeon.

"As his pathetic story had unfolded, Li had broken into tears . . . He realized that he had never looked upon stealing itself as something wrong. For him it was just a way of making a living. . . . Being a pickpocket was as much an art as that of a juggler, magician, or storyteller. His cellmates then reasoned with him that there was nothing that did not come about through someone's labor, and that stealing the fruits of another man's work was criminal."

Gradually they were able to break down his fear a little until he saw the wrongness of what he had been doing. At this point the authors continue the story:

> He developed a passionate hatred for the old society which had produced not only himself but countless others like him. The dream of a world in which there would be no fear or want became almost an obsession with him.
>
> The authorities then did what seemed a strange thing. This spineless pickpocket, the dregs of humanity, was made leader of a cell. For the first time in his life he was given some responsibility and a position of respect. In coming to a realization of his own background he found that he could help others and in so doing help himself. His fears gradually disappeared almost completely. . . .
>
> I hardly recognized Li the next time I saw him. . . . When he looked at you it was straight in the eye . . . not a shadow of his former cringing self. . . . He could now read and write . . . and was helping increase production in the prison sock factory. I had no doubt that he was well on his way toward building a new life and would soon be released.

One of the most startling transformations in all China took place in her greatest city, Shanghai. Having been to school there, I knew firsthand its unbelievable pre-Revolution degradation—like Calcutta today, only worse. Opium dens, brothels, gangsters in alliance with big business, the ultimate extremes of wealth and poverty—Shanghai had it all.

Undaunted, the Party took on the herculean job of persuading the people of this teeming waterfront metropolis to live by the principles of altruism and frugality. A discerning English school-teacher, employed in Shanghai during the Cultural Revolution, describes what happened:

> I realized that the Mao group's aims were as much moral as political. They were determined not only to oust the revisionists from the Party but also to galvanize Chinese society from top to bottom. In this sense, they were waging not class struggle but a veritable "moral war"—a war against the policies of compromise as well as against the men who had carried them out. This became clearer as the tactics of the movement took shape. Even before the Red Guards appeared, the Central Committee stated categorically that violence would not be tolerated. "Fight nonviolently" was the watchword, and there was hardly a student in China who did not know the adage, "You can change a person's skin by hitting him, but you can't change his soul that way."[24]

In spite of this, it is true that terror and violence occurred, particularly during the early phases of the Cultural Revolution, with many outbreaks of actual fighting. It should be remembered, however, that, for the most part, violence was deplored by those in authority.

Chou has sometimes related his and Mao's personal philosophy on the thorny subject of dealing with internal opposition to the regime. Unlike Stalin's Russia, in Communist China the death penalty for offenders, except during the earliest transitional years, seems to have been rare—for reasons which bear directly on the subject of this chapter:

[24] Neale Hunter, *Shanghai Journal: An Eyewitness Account of the Cultural Revolution*, p. 10.

1. If you kill a man in the opposition, you put him forever beyond the possibility of redemption and change.

2. If you kill a man, you automatically offend, grieve or, more likely, make enemies of all his family, relatives and a wide circle of friends.

3. Always remember that the opposition may *just possibly* be right.

Who are the "heroes" of the new society? "Not sportsmen, film stars, millionaires or politicians, but simple folk," writes Ralph Lapwood:

> The fisherman who organised co-operatives, and called other ships when he found shoals of fish instead of keeping the find to himself; the cotton-spinner who found a quicker way to tie broken threads; . . . the old farmer who found a better way of collecting grubs off the corn plants; the peasant who lost his feet in guerilla warfare, but carried on and organised his village Farmers' Union; these were the heroes . . . the humble and honest men whose conscientious work set the challenge and example.[25]

Heroes who have stood for moral values have always been especially revered in China; as in any culture, they reflect something of the character of a nation. Particularly since the Cultural Revolution, China places such examples in the forefront of every child's imagination, from the time they can comprehend the simplest stories. Typical is the tale of Norman Bethune, a Canadian surgeon, who today exemplifies for every Chinese the ideal of selfless service, utter devotion to others, warmheartedness, responsibility, integrity, constancy and purity of motive. Known by all school children is Mao's famous speech, "In Praise of Norman Bethune"—delivered a year after Bethune's tragic death from blood poisoning while operating at the North China front. In this vignette, Mao also spells out the qualities to be abhorred:

[25] Lapwood, *Through the Chinese Revolution*, p. 183.

indifference, apathy, buck-passing, self-centeredness, vulgarity, coldness and pride.[26]

One can hardly overestimate the near-worship of such heroic qualities in today's China, whether the hero is Bethune, or the woman factory worker who turned down a prize for over-fulfilling her quota. "I am already being paid for serving the people," she protested. "To give me something extra would simply be a misuse of public funds."[27]

My Harvard classmate Stanley Marcus, head of the famous Dallas firm of Neiman-Marcus, told me, with the amazement of a first-time visitor in the People's Republic, about his pedicab driver at the Canton Trade Fair who politely refused his proffered tip—and for basically the same reason.

President Julius Nyerere of Tanzania, returning from a visit to Peking, remarked how deeply stirred he had been "as a Christian" by what he called the "divine discontent" of China's leaders with their present achievements.[28] Black Africa's most respected Chief of State had not changed his views when I interviewed him in Dar-es-Salaam not long afterward. His two visits to China, he told me, had been highlights of his still youthful career. "Like us," he emphasized, "they are a poor country, but they offered us a thirty-year interest-free loan, and ten thousand skilled workers to build our Tanzam railroad, linking central Africa's copper mines to the Indian Ocean.

"I am a friend of America," he said. "I would have much preferred American aid, and I begged Washington and the World Bank to help us, before trying elsewhere. They were courteous but explained that such a deal would not be profitable. Under our poverty-stricken circumstances, China's offer was simply irresistible."

Does China's prodigious nationwide drive toward producing a new man result in a lasting change of motive?

[26] Deirdre and Neale Hunter's book *We the Chinese* points out the irony of this bluff, tempestuous foreigner's being made a model of virtue. My sister, who knew him well when he was assembling his medical supplies in our Hankow home in early 1938, agrees he was no saint but still was a single-minded, committed revolutionary. The Hunters also remind us that the Chinese are basically more interested in the kind of morality a man represents than in his personality. This could explain Chou En-lai's inflexible refusal to reveal anything remotely personal about his own life.

[27] *Time*, July 12, 1971.

[28] Joseph Lelyveld, New York *Times*, April 4, 1974.

The staying power of the new ethic was apparent to Dr. Lapwood when he revisited China some years later and met with many of his old friends. He comments: "They really do begin to assume that service is better than gain, and that if you have enough means for livelihood there is no point in having more. To enjoy wealth or take a job for extra money, when others suffer hardship, seems to them very immoral."[29]

Roger Garaudy, the French Marxist philosopher, remarks succinctly:

> What gives meaning, beauty and value to life is for the Marxist, as for the Christian, to give oneself without any limit to what the world through one's sacrifice can become.[30]

Returning to Shirley MacLaine: in her report from China, *You Can Get There from Here*, she concludes with a revealing commentary on our two societies:

> I suppose what shook me the most about China was that it completely altered my notions about human nature. I used to believe human nature was absolute; it had been a foregone conclusion to me that certain flaws and weaknesses were basic and permanent. Faced with the existence of evil, I would shrug and say, "Well, that's human nature! . . ."
>
> But I couldn't feel that way anymore. I had seen an entire nation, once degraded, corrupt, demoralized, and exploited, that was changing its very nature. . . .
>
> I realized that if what we call human nature can be changed, then absolutely *anything* is possible.[31] [her italics]

Their Chinese hosts must sometimes be puzzled by the simple enthusiasm of some Western visitors, who react as if they had never before seen individual or community demonstrations of un-

[29] From personal correspondence with the author.
[30] Robert Jungk, et al., *China and the West*, p. 64.
[31] MacLaine, op. cit., pp. 246–47.

selfish living, and first come alive in China to the universal truth
expressed by Lord Eustace Percy: "To expect a change in human
nature may be an act of faith, but to expect a change in human
society without it is an act of lunacy."

Yet China's historic genius for absorbing the best of the outside world into her own tradition and culture continues as she
entertains her increasing flood of visitors.

One of the most illuminating analyses of the objectives and
results of the Cultural Revolution and its role in remotivating society, was given me in a personal discussion with T'ang
Ming-ch'iao, China's Under Secretary-General at the United Nations and father of the capable young interpreter Nancy Tang,
who has translated for President Nixon and many world leaders:

> The basic mistake of the rulers of the Old China was
> being cut off from people. If we ourselves are ever so
> cut off, and cease to understand them, our society will
> perish, and deserve to.
>
> As long as you have institutions you'll have bureau-
> cracy. We must constantly fight against it. If it gets too
> bad, we'll just have to have another and deeper Cul-
> tural Revolution.
>
> Mao says: "Our children have been like green-house
> plants—no exposure to winds and storms. They should
> be like young pines—exposed to all weathers."
>
> You can put a man in jail, but not his ideas. Regimen-
> tation is wrong. We're not going to be so foolish.
>
> As far as ideas are concerned, you can only persuade
> and convince—not force or coerce. You remember Gali-
> leo. Ideas are very delicate, and must be handled with
> great delicacy and care.
>
> Brainwashing is not a bad phrase. We wash our
> faces. It's the same with the brain. You must clear up
> the accumulated dirt—the old ideas. You can only wash
> it through education, persuasion, caring—not with an
> iron brush!
>
> A man may be convinced today. Tomorrow he may
> not be. So you wait.

Mao said: "We must permit our people to make mistakes—also to correct their mistakes."

No one is born perfect. Everyone must learn through error, failure, defeat.

The history of the Chinese Revolution shows we made so very many mistakes. But don't get discouraged. You can always learn from them.

One pre-eminent result of any honest Westerner's experience of the new China is that it compels him to re-examine both the quality of life and the national philosophy of his own country.

Before leaving on my 1971–72 China trip, I phoned Scotty Reston of the New York *Times*, himself recently returned after an epochal interview with Chou En-lai and an equally famous appendix operation in a Peking hospital. "Now that you've been there," I said, "if you were going back again, what would you concentrate on? What would you regard as the most important single thing to do?"

Reston's reply was emphatic. "Out of a hundred extremely important things to see and do, only one really matters, and that's this 'remotivation bit.' It's never been tried before by any nation, certainly not from the top, or on anything approaching the present scale. But the Chinese are very determined. They seem to have put it across so far, and they may just have a fighting chance to keep it going."

He paused before hanging up. Then: "But even if they fail, it may still be one of the greatest steps forward in life styles in history."

The distinguished journalist-author Harrison Salisbury, former Associate Editor of the New York *Times*, makes some relevant comments in his *To Peking—and Beyond*.

Salisbury was having a last talk in Peking with a high government official. He was imparting to his attentive Chinese listener, who had been asking him about the "new tsars," something of his own extensive knowledge of the Soviet Union. The new rulers of Russia, he said, "had been overtaken by materialism. The young people chased Western fads like butterflies—the latest song, the latest dance, the latest style. Hippy clothing. Hippy haircuts. Drugs. They were aping the Western drug culture. It was hard to see what remnants of the Revolution were left."

But in China "there was something new," with the greatest change "the spirit of the people." Reflected Salisbury: "I think it is the miracle of the modern world."

His host demurred.

"No," Salisbury countered, gently overriding his Chinese friend's instinctive protest, "I don't think I am going too far. I think that it is a great achievement to put a man on the moon. But to put a man on the earth—that is even more."[32]

Chou En-lai, ever the political catalyst of his era, ever the human factor synthesizing the forces of left and right in the People's Republic to form the successive new dimensions of the new China, would have agreed with Salisbury's verdict. "Why," he once asked an American friend, "does your country spend such huge sums to explore the moon, when we haven't yet discovered how to live together here on earth?"

Today, with Chou and most of the country's founding fathers gathered to their ancestors, the challenge of a vast, unpredictable future dominates the councils of the Peking government and the deliberations of its leaders.

It dominates, too, thousands of gatherings in every province where Chinese of all ages and professions are struggling to achieve a new type of citizenry fit to pioneer ever new dimensions of living for the new society.

On the success or failure of this gigantic experiment in remotivating the oldest and most populous nation of all time depends the future of China's revolution itself, and its impact on our age.

[32] Harrison E. Salisbury, *To Peking—and Beyond: A Report on the New Asia*, p. 371.

EPILOGUE

Following Peking's ten-day period of official mourning, the ashes of the late Premier Chou En-lai, who had died on January 8, 1976, were scattered by plane, at his request, over the rivers, fields and mountains of China.

Self-abnegating to a degree rarely known among history's great, the man who for sixty years had devoted himself to China's revolution chose this means of dramatizing his belief that it was ever the cause, not the career, that mattered.

As during the lifetime he spent serving his people, so during this final illness, no one knew what it cost him.

No one in all these years had heralded "The Thoughts of Chou," or built marble and plaster busts of "The Great Leader's Friend." Until America's ping-pong team visited Peking, no one in the West knew the pattern of his living—that he worked all night, continued all day, his sleeping hours snatched almost as an afterthought.

Teng Ying-ch'ao, his devoted wife, knew, and long before had given up trying to change her husband's ways.

When the malignancy was first revealed to his doctors, no one among the millions he served—and especially among the young he loved—no one knew except that one day, a year and a half later, Premier Chou was reported receiving state visitors "in a hospital" while recuperating from "a heart ailment."

No one knew the pain that crept into that slight frame, then lessened, leaving him free to steer his government through three perilous years of change and upheaval, of diplomatic triumphs abroad and bitter factionalism at home. No one may ever know for certain whether he was being singled out as a veiled target for vilification, even when fresh pain was undermining his strength. And no one could measure the superhuman act of will it took—after over two years of fighting his illness—to organize in January of 1975 and keynote the long-postponed National People's Congress, called to stabilize China's political future.

When did the Premier know, for sure, that he had cancer?

We are now told that it was diagnosed as a terminal illness in 1972. Certainly, however, he gave no indication of knowing this when I saw him in January and February of that year, nor during his brilliant personal handling of the Nixon visit shortly afterward. But had the situation changed by October, when he entertained my sister and her husband at a private dinner?

On that occasion Premier Chou En-lai—known also for years in the Red Army as "General Chou"—took particular pains to explain that the following poem was written by the great Ts'ao Ts'ao, China's Prime Minister and General during the period of "The Three Kingdoms." He never revealed the reason for his sudden turning of the conversation that evening; but he did take the trouble to speak the lines for his guests, slowly, and with an amused smile as he approached the enigmatic ending.

THOUGH TORTOISE LIVES LONGER
(c. 220 a.d.)

Though it lives longer than most,
The tortoise, too, comes to an end.
Though it flies beyond the clouds,
The serpent at last will turn to dust.
Though he is confined to his stable,
Still the old horse has the will
    To gallop for a thousand li.
Approaching now his final years,
The aged hero has the wish
    To aim high at the last . . .
Heaven may not decide how long
The span of human life will be.
He who would indeed live longer,
Must guard his health—unquestioningly![1]

[1] Revised translation by Frances Roots Hadden.

APPENDIX

NEW YORK TIMES MAGAZINE, DECEMBER 26, 1926

Mysterious Borodin Sways South China

Soviet's Envoy Talks of Mission That Has Guided Cantonese to Victory

by JOHN McCOOK ROOTS

Michael Borodin, a Russian, formerly connected with the Moscow International and delegated three years ago by the Soviet Government to be the adviser of the Cantonese Government of Dr. Sun Yat-sen, has become the hero of the successful nationalist movement in South China. The greatest mass meeting ever held in Hankow welcomed the Russian when he visited that city recently. In the following article the writer tells of an interview with Borodin who, during his stay in Canton, has been very little known outside Russian and Chinese circles.

A Russian, speaking no Chinese and giving no orders, has in three years won a position of power in South China never before attained

by any white man, a sphere of influence stretching from Canton to the
Yangtze River. His name is Borodin—Michael Markovitch Borodin,
Communist, Bolshevist, atheist, apostle of Soviet philosophy and Soviet method. Foreigners in China have said his chief business was to
make the Chinese hate England and America. They called him a dictator. The Cantonese said his wise and friendly counsel had made
their Government what it was—the only effective political unit in the
country.

Sun Yat-sen met him in Shanghai in 1923, liked him and invited
him down to assist with the new social democratic experiment in Canton. The Soviet Government, seeing a chance of using his influence to
win the friendship and alliance of Canton, and through Canton,
China, gladly let him go. After Sun's death in 1925 he was retained as
general efficiency expert by the Nationalist Government.

Outside Canton he was blamed for everything that went wrong in
China. Foreigners spoke of him, wrote of him, laughed at him, swore
at him. He was lampooned and cartooned. But no one had ever seen
him. He remained a mystery.

All this I knew before I landed in Canton. Even here, where he had
lived for three years, most foreigners knew only that he was a recluse
to everyone except his Chinese and Russian coworkers, that he
loathed publicity and distrusted all journalists on principle. But I
made connections with a Y.M.C.A. secretary who was also a member
of the Kuomintang—the "People's Party," established by Sun Yat-sen—
and found myself one morning in a rickshaw en route to Borodin's
residence. He was very busy, but had promised to spare some time on
that, his easiest day.

The runner pulled up at the side of one of Canton's broad boulevards and dumped me out in front of an ugly, yellow structure. Two
Chinese sentries with rifles and shoddy gray uniforms warily examined my credentials, and I was escorted through the large, bare
hall, upstairs past another armed sentry in trim khaki with orange
braid, and into the spacious waiting room. On one side was a heroic
portrait of Sun Yat-sen; opposite and equally imposing, a likeness of
Lenin. Otherwise the walls were bare.

Beyond, the study door swung open and a deep voice spoke in Russian. In a moment I was shaking hands with the "dictator" of Canton.

A large, rugged, middle-aged man, with a shock of dark hair
thrown back from a high forehead, serious black eyes, a bushy mustache and a hearty handshake. The day was hot, even for semitropical
Canton, and Borodin wore only a thin, white suit with cotton jacket
that buttoned at the throat in military style. It was the plain type of
summer uniform that Sun Yat-sen used to wear, and which is so popular today among Chinese students all over the country.

The room was comfortably furnished. Over the desk was an en-graved likeness of Sun Yat-sen, and underneath, his last will scrawled in bold, black characters.

Borodin spoke excellent English, with only a slight accent, which was not surprising because he had studied no Chinese and depended on English entirely as a medium of conversation with the young group of foreign-educated officials in the Canton Government. For an hour he talked of the Kuomintang, the liberal political party that runs the Nationalist Government much as the Communist Party runs Rus-sia. He spoke of the need of its keeping close to the people, of the wretched condition of Chinese laborers and farmers, and how they were being unionized for the sake of protection against unscrupulous employers and lawless militarists; of the young Canton Nationalist Government, of the need for honesty and efficiency. He spoke of the Revolutionary Army which was to be the instrument of China's unification and was even then starting north toward Wuchang and the Yangtze River Valley; of his efforts to make it an army which, in con-trast to most Chinese forces, would understand government as well as war. It was most essential, he said, for the military not to encroach on the civil power, and he believed that this could be brought about only by educating the soldiers politically in the same way that the officers were already being trained by the Kuomintang at Whampoa Acad-emy, nine miles outside Canton.

Medieval China

I asked Borodin guardedly what he thought of foreign nations and their attitude toward China and her problems. His reply was delib-erate.

"China is still in the clutches of medievalism," he explained. "She remains so because of the selfishness of her own politicians, busi-nessmen and militarists, who are indirectly assisted in their work of bleeding the country by the treaty rights of the foreign powers. Eng-land, America and Japan, having large business interests in China, are interested above all in preventing a revolution. They do their best to preserve the status quo. But in doing so they unconsciously work against the progressive elements in China that are seeking to revolu-tionize her internal condition."

"Then, of course, you do your best to turn the Chinese against other foreign nations?"

"Not necessarily. The Chinese are perfectly capable of choosing their friends and recognizing their enemies. A year ago, for instance, when the British killed and wounded a hundred and fifty demon-strators near the foreign settlement on Shameen, there was no need to incite the people of Canton against their murderers. My problem is more to hold them in check and keep them from doing foolish things that might bring on a war with the West."

I was reminded of what a prominent Cantonese had told me about this same Shameen shooting affair of June 1925. Apparently in the mass meeting which was hurriedly called to consider reprisals for the massacre, the infuriated Chinese were unanimously in favor of attacking the island settlement and annihilating the hated foreigner. Borodin, so the story ran, sprang to his feet, the only cool head in all that angry mob—warned them of the British fleet at Hongkong which would surely come up the river and blow Canton to pieces, and finally persuaded them to be content with their original program of a strike and boycott directed against British goods and against the neighboring British island of Hongkong.

"And how does Russia differ from the other foreign nations?" Borodin was asked. "Why are you accepted here while we are not?"

"I will be frank with you," he answered, looking straight ahead and pulling on his cigar. "Russia has won her present position in China because she has proved to the Chinese that she sincerely means them well. Speaking generally, we have done two things that you have not done. We have given up our treaty rights; that proves our sincerity. We have given them a program of social, political and economic reform which proves the value of our help. You keep the treaties and you give no program. How can they believe you mean them well?"

"Surely you must expect some reward for what you give these people?"

"Our reward lies in the future. Of course, we do expect to get something out of it. And we say frankly to our Chinese friends: 'There are certain stages which China must go through—steps such as the establishment of local good government with honesty and efficiency in administration, such as the strengthening of the labor movement, such as the abolition of the unequal treaties, and such as national unification. Now we will work together with you for the achievement of these ends. Later on, after China has become a modern state, we will expect the same consideration for our economic and political principles that you accord to those of any other nation.'"

"But isn't it a trifle selfish to make them go your way and no other?"

"No one is making them do anything. These stages are necessary. If they were not, then you could call me selfish in working for them. But they are bound to come in any case, and we are the only ones who are offering any practical help in their solution."

"You know that people believe this is merely a propaganda center for Communism. What do you say to that?"

"I would ask them," he replied, rising and pacing up and down, hands behind him, "to look at the work of foreign Christian missions in China. Is not that propaganda? You have something that you consider the greatest thing in the world and you bend every effort to induce the Chinese to accept. In short, you propagate it." He stopped short and faced me. "I, too, have something which I consider to be the greatest thing in the world, something which, if China accepts, I believe will bring her the greatest happiness. And I will give my life to propagate it."

"But you are not achieving Communism here."

"Of course not, any more than we are in Russia," he said. "The Chinese are not ready for it. We know that, and we tell them so quite openly. To attempt Communism now would be like eating dessert before the soup. It is too early even to discuss the matter. When China becomes a modern state with free play for all her economic, social and political powers—then there will be plenty of time for her to decide for or against Communism."

"Do you think, then, that China will go on developing industrially along the lines followed by capitalist society in the West?"

"Most emphatically. We count on that."

"And the class war?"

"It is inevitable."

The next morning I hunted up an official of the Canton Government who, like all the leading men in the city, was also a member of the Kuomintang. The man happened to be on the Political Bureau, an organization adapted from the Politburo of Moscow and the real ruling force in Canton. Borodin had recently been appointed high adviser to the Kuomintang—the only foreigner except one ever asked to join—and he was a nonvoting member of this Political Bureau.

"Why do you allow it?" I asked. "How does this man get his power?"

My host told of Sun Yat-sen's implicit trust—how, shortly before his death, he had said in a speech: "Remember, Borodin's word is my word"—and of the effect this had had among people who had grown to regard Dr. Sun's every command as an inspired utterance.

"And then," continued my companion, "he is a Russian, and Soviet Russia has introduced a new kind of diplomacy into China. When you go down to Hongkong tomorrow you will have to go aboard the British steamer in a private launch. No native sampan will take you, for we have declared a boycott of English ships and English goods. With Russia it is different. Instead of treaties and gunboats and massacres of our people such as the Shameen affair, she is offering equal treatment, sympathy and friendly counsel. You may not accept many of Russia's ideas. Neither do we. You may not like some of the advice she is giving our Nationalist Government. But the fact remains that she has put herself on our level, that she is giving practical help in our efforts to build a good Government, and that consequently we feel we can accept things from her representatives. Russia has made herself indispensable.

"But the real reason for Borodin's influence," he went on, "is neither the endorsement of Sun Yat-sen nor the diplomacy of Soviet Russia.

"For three years now he has worked here in a trying climate and without rest. He has made our cause his cause. He never puts himself forward. In meetings of the Political Bureau he sits silent till he is asked for his opinion. His advice is sound.

"Three years have taught us not only to value him as a friend but to depend on him in every emergency. At first Moscow paid his salary. Now we do. He is worth it."

BIBLIOGRAPHY

This selected bibliography lists, in addition to works cited in the text, books and articles providing 1) historical and background materials and 2) comment and stimulus concerning problems raised in certain chapters, for example: the Western impact on China, the Sino-Soviet "Honeymoon" and "Split," and "Remotivating Society."

Alsop, Stewart. "Mystery Man of Peking." New York *Herald Tribune*, March 18, 1951.
———. "The Madness of Mao Tse-Tung." *Saturday Evening Post*, October 26, 1963.
Anderson, Jack. "Washington Merry-Go-Round," January 20, 1976.
Auden, W. H., and Isherwood, Christopher. *Journey to a War*. New York: Random House, 1939.
Barnett, A. Doak. *Communist China in Perspective*. New York: Praeger, 1966.
Baskin, Wade, ed. *Classics in Chinese Philosophy from Mo Tzu to Mao Tse-tung*. New York: Philosophical Library, 1972.
Beal, John Robinson. *Marshall in China*. New York: Doubleday, 1970.
Belden, Jack. *China Shakes the World*. New York: Harper, 1949. Reissue, Monthly Review Press, 1970.
Bertram, James. *North China Front*. London: Macmillan, 1939.
Bianco, Lucien. *Origins of the Chinese Revolution, 1915–1949*. Stanford, Calif.: Stanford University Press, and London: Oxford University Press, 1971.
Blankfort, Michael. *The Big Yankee—The Life of Carlson of the Raiders*. Boston: Little, Brown, 1947.

Bloodworth, Dennis. *The Chinese Looking Glass.* New York: Dell, 1966.

Butterfield, Fox. "Chou, 12 Months After His Death, Emerges As a Folk Hero to Chinese." New York *Times,* January 8, 1977.

Ch'en, Jerome. *Mao and the Chinese Revolution.* New York: Oxford University Press, 1972.

Chow, Ching-Wen. *The Years of Storm.* New York: Holt, Rinehart & Winston, 1960.

Clubb, O. Edmund. *Communism in China—As Reported from Hankow in 1932.* New York: Columbia University Press, 1968.

——. *Twentieth Century China.* New York and London: Columbia University Press, 1972.

Collis, Maurice. *Foreign Mud—The Opium Imbroglio at Canton in the 1830s & The Anglo-Chinese War.* London: Faber & Faber, and New York: Norton Library, 1968.

Congress of the United States, Joint Economic Committee. *An Economic Profile of Mainland China.* Washington: Government Printing Office, 1967.

——. *China: A Reassessment of the Economy.* Washington: Government Printing Office, 1975.

——. *Mainland China in the World Economy. Hearings Before the Joint Economic Committee.* Ninetieth Congress, First Session, April 5, 10, 11, 12, 1967. Washington: Government Printing Office, 1967, pp. 187–88.

Davies, John Paton. *Dragon by the Tail.* New York: Norton, 1972.

Day, John A.; Fost, Frederic F.; and Rose, Peter. *Dimensions of the Environmental Crisis.* New York: John Wiley & Sons, 1971.

Deutscher, Isaac. "The Moral Dilemmas of Lenin." *The Listener* (Journal of the British Broadcasting Corporation), February 8, 1959.

——. *The Ironies of History: Essays on Contemporary Communism.* London: Oxford University Press, 1966. Paperback: Ramparts.

Deutscher, Tamara. *Not by Politics Alone—The Other Lenin.* London: George Allen & Unwin, 1973.

Douglass, Bruce, and Terrill, Ross, eds. *China and Ourselves.* Boston: Beacon, 1970.

Durdin, Tillman; Reston, James; and Topping, Seymour. *The New York Times Report from China.* New York, Chicago: Quadrangle Books, 1971. Paperback: Avon Books, 1972.

Eckstein, Alexander. *Communist China's Economic Growth and Foreign Trade.* New York: Council on Foreign Relations, 1966.

Elegant, Robert. *Mao's Great Revolution.* New York: World, 1971.

Esherick, Joseph W., ed. *The World War II Dispatches of John S. Service.* New York: Random House Vintage, 1975.

Fairbank, John K. *Chinese-American Interactions: A Historical Summary.* New Brunswick, N.J.: Rutgers University Press, 1975.

——. *China Perceived.* New York: Random House Vintage, 1976.

——. *The United States and China.* Cambridge, Mass.: Harvard University Press, 1971. Also paperback.

Galbraith, John Kenneth. *A China Passage.* Boston: Houghton Mifflin, 1976.

Galston, Arthur W. with Savage, Jean S. *Daily Life in People's China.* New York: Crowell, 1973.

Garaudy, Roger. *The Alternative Future.* New York: Simon and Schuster, 1972.

—— (ed.). *China and the West.* Atlantic Highlands, N.J.: Humanities Press, 1970.

Gompertz, G. H. *China in Turmoil—Eye Witness, 1924–1948.* London: Dent, 1967.

Greene, Felix. "The Further Thoughts of Premier Chou." *Sunday Times* (London), April 30, 1972.

———. *The Wall Has Two Sides.* London: Reprint Society, 1963.

Gurley, John G. *Challengers to Capitalism—Marx, Lenin and Mao.* San Francisco: San Francisco Book Company, Inc. 1976.

———. *China's Economy and the Maoist Strategy.* New York and London: Monthly Review Press, 1976.

Han Suyin. *China in the Year 2001.* London: Penguin Books, 1970.

———. *The Morning Deluge: Mao Tse-tung and the Chinese Revolution 1893–1954.* Boston, Toronto: Little, Brown, 1972.

———. *Wind in the Tower: Mao Tse-tung and the Chinese Revolution 1949–1975.* Boston, Toronto: Little, Brown, 1976.

Hedin, Sven. *Chiang Kai-shek, Marshal of China.* New York: John Day, 1940.

Hinton, William. *Fanshen—A Documentary of Revolution in a Chinese Village.* New York: Vintage Books, 1966.

Hocking, William Ernest. *Human Nature and Its Remaking.* New Haven, Conn.: Yale University Press, 1929.

Hoffman, Paul. "Vatican Sees Christian Ideas in Maoism." *New York Times,* April 19, 1973.

Horn, Joshua S., M.D. *Away with All Pests: An English Surgeon in People's China, 1954–1969.* London and New York: Monthly Review Press, 1971.

Hsu Kai-yu. *The Chinese Literary Scene—A Writer's Visit to the People's Republic.* New York: Random House, 1975.

———. *Chou En-lai: China's Gray Eminence.* New York: Doubleday, 1968. Also paperback.

Hughes, Richard. "Peking's 'Indispensable' Front Man." *New York Times Magazine,* October 4, 1964.

Hunter, Deirdre, and Hunter, Neale. *We the Chinese: Voices from China.* New York: Praeger, 1971.

Hunter, Neale. *Shanghai Journal: An Eyewitness Account of the Cultural Revolution.* New York: Praeger, 1969. Also paperback.

Isaacs, Harold. *Scratches on Our Minds.* New York: John Day, 1958. Greenwood, 1973.

Jen Yu-wen. *The Taiping Revolutionary Movement.* New Haven, Conn.: Yale University Press, 1973.

Jungk, Robert; McMullin, Ernan; Needham, Joseph; Robinson, Joan; Schram, Stuart; Sewell, William; and Towers, Bernard. *China and The West: Mankind Evolving.* New York: Humanities Press, 1970.

Kessen, William, ed. *Childhood in China.* New Haven, Conn.: Yale University Press, 1975.

Kraft, Joseph. *The Chinese Difference.* New York: The Saturday Review Press, 1972.

Lapwood, Ralph, and Lapwood, Nancy. *Through the Chinese Revolution.* London: Spalding & Levy, 1954; reprint ed., London: Hyperion Press, 1973.

Larkin, Bruce D. *China and Africa, 1949–1970.* Berkeley and London: University of California Press, 1971.

Larson, Robert C. *Wansui—Insights on China Today.* Waco, Tex.: Word Books, 1974.

Latourette, Kenneth Scott. *A Short History of the Far East*. New York: Macmillan, 1957.

Lelyveld, Joseph. "China Seeks Acceptance in Third World." New York *Times*, April 4, 1974.

Li Tien-min. *Chou En-lai*. Taipeh: Institute of International Relations, 1970.

Lifton, Robert J. *Revolutionary Immortality: Mao Tse-tung and the Chinese Cultural Revolution*. New York: Random House, 1968.

Liu Ning. *The Autobiography of a Proletarian*. Chungking: 1941.

MacLaine, Shirley. *You Can Get There from Here*. New York: Norton, 1975.

Malraux, André. *Man's Fate (La Condition Humaine)*. New York: Random House, Modern Library, 1934.

Maxwell, Neville. *India's China War*. Garden City, N.Y.: Doubleday Anchor Books, 1972.

Mehnert, Klaus. *China Returns*. New York: Dutton, 1972.

Milton, David, and Milton, Nancy. *The Wind Will Not Subside: Years in Revolutionary China—1964–1969*. New York: Pantheon, 1976.

Montgomery, Field Marshal Viscount Bernard Law. "My Talks with Mao." *The Sunday Times* Magazine (London), June 12, 1960.

Morison, Samuel Eliot. *The Oxford History of the American People*. New York: Oxford University Press, 1965.

North, Robert. *Moscow and Chinese Communists*. Stanford, Calif.: Stanford University Press, 1953 and 1963.

O'Connor, Richard. *The Spirit Soldiers: A Historical Narrative of the Boxer Rebellion*. New York: Putnam, 1973.

Paloczi Horvath, Gyorgy. *Mao Tse-tung: Emperor of the Blue Ants*. London: Secker & Warburg, 1962.

Panikkar, K. M. *Asia and Western Dominance*. London: George Allen & Unwin, 1959; New York: Collier Books, 1969.

Payne, Robert. *Mao Tse-tung*. New York: Weybright and Talley, 1969.

Phillips, Warren, and Keatley, Robert. *China Behind the Mask*. Princeton, N.J.: Dow Jones Books, 1972, 1973.

Pye, Lucien W. *Mao Tse-tung, The Man in the Leader*. New York: Basic Books, 1976.

Quotations from Chairman Mao Tse-tung. Peking: Foreign Languages Press, 1972. Bantam (U.S. ed.), 1967.

Quotations from Premier Chou En-lai. New York: Thomas Y. Crowell, 1973.

Rice, Edward E. *Mao's Way*. Los Angeles: University of California, 1972.

Rickett, Allyn, and Rickett, Adele. *Prisoners of Liberation*. Garden City, N.Y.: Doubleday, 1973.

Robinson, Thomas W. *The Cultural Revolution*. Berkeley: University of California Press, 1971.

Ronning, Chester. *A Memoir of China in Revolution: From the Boxer Rebellion to the People's Republic*. New York: Pantheon, 1974.

Roots, John McCook. "Mysterious Borodin Sways South China." New York *Times* Magazine, December 26, 1926.

——. "The Canton Ideal." *Asia* (New York), April 1927.

Salisbury, Harrison E. *To Peking—and Beyond: A Report on the New Asia*. New York: Quadrangle Books, 1973. Also paperback, Putnam.

Scalapino, Robert A., ed. *Elites in the People's Republic of China*. Seattle: University of Washington, 1972.

Schram, Stuart R. *The Political Thought of Mao Tse-tung*. New York: Praeger, 1963.

Schurmann, Herbert Franz, comp. *The China Reader.* 4 Vols. New York: Random House, 1967–74.
    Vol. I: *Imperial China* . . . The Eighteenth and Nineteenth Centuries.
    Vol. II: *Republican China* . . . 1911–1949.
    Vol. III: *Communist China* . . . 1949 to the Present.
    Vol. IV: *People's China* . . . 1966–1972.
Schwartz, Benjamin I. *Chinese Communism and the Rise of Mao.* Cambridge, Mass.: Harvard University Press, 1951.
Service, John S. *Lost Chance in China.* New York: Random House, 1974.
Sheean, Vincent. *Personal History.* Garden City, N.Y.: Doubleday, 1937.
Shewmaker, Kenneth E. *Americans and Chinese Communists 1927–1945.* New York: Cornell University Press, 1971.
Smedley, Agnes. *Battle Hymn of China.* New York: Knopf, 1943.
——. *The Great Road: The Life and Times of Chu Teh.* New York: Monthly Review Press, 1956. Also paperback.
Snow, Edgar. *The Battle for Asia.* New York: Random House, 1941.
——. *Journey to the Beginning.* New York: Random House, 1958. Also paperback, Vintage, 1972.
——. *The Long Revolution.* New York: Random House, 1972. Also paperback, Vintage, 1973.
——. *Red China Today—The Other Side of the River.* New York: Random House, 1971. Also paperback, Vintage, 1971.
——. *Red Star Over China.* New York: Random House, 1938; rev. ed., 1968. Also paperback, rev. ed., Grove, 1968.
——. "A Conversation with Mao Tse-tung." *Life,* April 30, 1971.
——. *Journey to the Beginning.* New York: Random House, 1958.
——. "What China Wants from Nixon's Visit." *Life,* July 30, 1971.
Snow, Helen Foster (Nym Wales). *The Chinese Communists: Sketches and Autobiographies of the Old Guard.* Westport, Conn.: Greenwood, 1972.
——. *Inside Red China.* Garden City, N.Y.: Doubleday, 1939.
Snow, Lois Wheeler. *A Death with Dignity.* New York: Randon House, 1975.
Spanier, John W. *The Truman-MacArthur Controversy and the Korean War.* New York: Norton, 1965.
Spence, Jonathan. *To Change China: Western Advisers in China, 1620–1960.* Boston: Little, Brown, 1969.
Stein, Gunther. *The Challenge of Red China.* New York: Whittlesey House, 1945.
Stewart, Roderick. *Bethune.* Toronto, Canada: New Press, 1973.
Stoessinger, John G. *Henry Kissinger—The Anguish of Power.* New York: Norton, 1976.
Strong, Anna Louise. *China's Millions.* New York: Coward, McCann, 1928.
Stuart, John Leighton. *Fifty Years in China.* New York: Random House, 1954.
Sullivan, Michael. *The Arts of China.* Berkeley: University of California Press, 1973.
Sulzberger, C. L. *The Coldest War—Russia's Game in China.* New York and London: Harcourt Brace Jovanovich, 1974.
Sutton, Horace. "Scotty Reston of the *Times.*" *Saturday Review,* January 29, 1972.
Terrill, Ross. *800,000,000—The Real China.* Boston: Little, Brown, 1972.

——. *Flowers on an Iron Tree: Five Cities of China.* Boston: Little, Brown, 1975.

——. Memorial Address at Harvard University following the death of Chou En-lai. Cambridge, January 1976.

Thomson, James C., Jr. *While China Faced West: American Reformers in Nationalist China, 1928–1937.* Cambridge, Mass.: Harvard University Press, 1969.

Topping, Audrey. *Dawn Wakes in the East.* New York: Harper & Row, 1973.

Topping, Seymour. *Journey Between Two Chinas.* New York: Harper & Row, 1972.

Tuchman, Barbara. *Notes from China.* New York: Collier, 1972.

——. *Stilwell and the American Experience in China, 1911–1945.* New York: Macmillan, 1970–71. Also paperback, Bantam.

Van Slyke, Lyman P. *Enemies and Friends—The United Front in Chinese Communist History.* Stanford, Calif.: Stanford University Press, 1967.

Wales, Nym. (See Snow, Helen Foster.)

Walker, Richard L. *The Human Cost of Communism.* Washington: Internal Security Subcommittee on the Judiciary, United States Senate, 1971; Reprint Edition, Washington: ACU Education and Research Institute, 1977.

Wedemeyer, Albert C. *Wedemeyer Reports!* New York: Henry Holt, 1958.

White, Theodore H. *China: The Roots of Madness* (television script). New York: Norton, 1968.

White, Theodore H., and Jacoby, Annalee. *Thunder Out of China.* New York: William Sloane, 1946, 1961.

Wilson, Dick. *The Long March, 1935.* New York: Viking, 1971.

Wolf, Margery, and Witke, Roxane. *Women in Chinese Society.* Stanford, Calif.: Stanford University Press, 1975.

INDEX

Acheson, Dean, 121, 123
Afghanistan, 106
Africa, 78, 105, 109–10, 159, 166, 190 (see also specific countries); Afro-Asian conferences, 107, 109
Albania, 103, 106, 108, 110
Allen, Robert S., 126
Alsop, Joseph, 133–34
Alsop, Stewart, 126
America(ns). See United States of America
Anderson, Jack, 91, 159–60
Anyuan, 145–46, 149
Art(s) and creativity, 118–19, 141–42, 160
Arts of China, The (Sullivan), 119 n, 207
Asia, 24, 78, 108, 109–10, 111, 166 (see also specific countries, developments, individuals); Afro-Asian conferences, 107, 109
Asian Party, 24
Auden, W. H., 87, 138

Bandung, Indonesia, International Conference in (1955), 107
"Barefoot doctors," 118, 142
Barnett, A. Doak, viii, 203
Battle for Asia (Snow), 63 n, 66 n, 207
Beebe, Lucius, 125–26
Belden, Jack, xv, 203
Ben-Gurion, David, 106
Berlin, Germany, 21–22, 23, 25–26, 158; Chou En-lai in, 21–22, 23, 25–26, 158
Bethune, Norman, 87; Mao Tse-

tung's eulogy to, 87 n, 138, 189–90
Bhutto, Zulfikar Ali, 153, 182
Blair, June, viii
Blankfort, Michael, 89 n, 203
Bloch, Polly, viii
"Blue Ant" myth, 121, 122
Book of Songs, 162
Borodin, Mikhail M., 16 n, 28, 29, 30, 31–36, 42, 45, 46, 49–50, 77; described, 32–36, 198, 199; and revolutionary change, 33–34, 179, 197–202
Borodin, Norman, 35, 46
Boxer Rebellion, 9, 15
Brezhnev, Leonid, 2
British. See Great Britain
Brown, Pat, 130
Bucharest Communist Assembly (June 1960), 104
Budapest, Hungary, 110
Bukharin, N. I., 53
Bulgaria, 106
Burma, 102, 106, 107
Butterfield, Fox, xvi, 204

Cambodia, 5, 8, 102, 107, 111
Cameron, James, 166
Canada, 106, 128–29
Canton, 6, 7, 26, 27, 28, 30, 36, 39, 43, 44, 45, 46, 178
Capa, Robert, 87, 138
Carlson, Captain Evans, 89 n, 166–67, 173–75
"Carlson's Raiders," 173–74, 175
"Century of Humiliation" (colonialist China), 5 ff., 8, 131 ff. See